Advanced Brand Management

Every owner of a physical copy of this edition of

Advanced Brand Management

can download the eBook for free direct from us at Harriman House, in a DRM-free format that can be read on any eReader, tablet or smartphone.

Simply head to:

ebooks.harriman-house.com/ AdvancedBrand

to get your copy now.

Advanced Brand Management

Building and Activating a Powerful Brand Strategy

Third Edition

By Paul Temporal

Hh Harriman House

HARRIMAN HOUSE LTD
18 College Street
Petersfield
Hampshire
GU31 4AD
GREAT BRITAIN
Tel: +44 (0)1730 233870
Email: enquiries@harriman-house.com
Website: www.harriman-house.com

First published in 2002 by John Wiley & Sons (Asia) Pte Ltd.
This third edition published in 2019
Copyright © Paul Temporal

Hardback ISBN: 978-0-85719-589-0
eBook ISBN: 978-0-85719-590-6

British Library Cataloguing in Publication Data
A CIP catalogue record for this book can be obtained from the British Library.

Cover design by Christopher Parker.

About the author

Dr. Paul Temporal is a leading global expert on brand strategy and management. He has over 30 years of experience in consulting and training, and is a much sought after speaker. He has consulted for many governments and top brands across the world, and is well known for his practical and results-oriented approach. Paul is an Associate Fellow at Saïd Business School and at Green Templeton College in the University of Oxford, and a Visiting Professor at Peking University HSBC Business School, China.

Paul is a regular contributor to major international conferences and has published widely in mainstream global media. He has written more than sixteen bestselling books, including *Branding in Asia, Romancing the Customer, Asia's Star Brands, Islamic Branding and Marketing,* and *Branding for the Public Sector*. He can be contacted at www.paultemporal.com.

Acknowledgement

I am very grateful to Maria Temporal for her assistance in the editing and writing of cases in the book, especially with respect to digital content. As a 'millennial' consumer herself, working for a global luxury brand group, her sharp, perceptive insights and market knowledge were extremely valuable.

Contents

Preface   ix

Part 1: Introduction   1

Chapter 1: Branding in a Changing World   3

Chapter 2: The Changing Roles of Brand Management   15

Part 2: Branding and Consumers   33

Chapter 3: An Introduction to Branding and Brand Strategy   35

Part 3: Building a Powerful Brand Strategy   57

Chapter 4: Brand Architecture and Portfolio Management   59

Chapter 5: Brand Visions and Brand Personality   109

Chapter 6: Brand Positioning   135

Part 4: Activation and Management of Brand Strategy   177

Chapter 7: Brand Communications   181

Chapter 8: The Digital World   213

Chapter 9: "Long Live the Brand!" Employee Engagement
to Create a Brand Culture   233

Chapter 10: Brand Planning and Control   257

Chapter 11: Measuring Brand Success: Market Research
and Brand Valuation   279

Endnotes   296

Index   299

Preface

It has been eight years since the second edition of *Advanced Brand Management* was published, and many things have changed during that time which impact on the work of brand managers. While their role remains the same, brand managers now have to cope with a broader range of variables and pressures from the marketplace and consumers. The dynamic changes we have seen in world markets over the past decade have been especially challenging for brand managers. They include:

- the pursuit of speed, agility, and innovation are now seen as areas of strategic competitive advantage in a world characterized by a faster pace of change;

- the growth of the digital world and increased use of the Internet in building brands;

- greater emphasis on the projection of brand personality as a means of differentiation;

- the spread of branding in business-to-business markets and the public sector;

- the continued brand architecture trend away from product branding toward corporate branding;

- increased pressure from consumers on organizations to adopt better ethical branding and corporate social responsibility practices;

- the adoption of internal branding and employee engagement to enhance the customer experience and attract and retain talent; and

- an increased number of mergers, acquisitions, and alliances.

To illustrate these changes, I have made many adjustments to both the text and the case studies in this new book. All the chapters have been updated, and a completely new chapter is included on the growth of the digital world and the use of the Internet. There is an increased emphasis on brand strategy and an update to some cases, with entirely new cases being added as well.

Overall, the book has remained steadfast in its philosophy of, and approach to, brand management, but it now reflects the new challenges and opportunities facing practitioners in this highly exciting field.

As I complete this book the business world has changed again in a fairly positive way. Gone is the global recession, to be replaced with astonishing developments in the world of technology and innovation, bringing both opportunities and challenges. To survive in this fast-changing world it is vitally important that brand strategists apply their skills with even more vigor and discipline.

I hope you enjoy reading this book and take away some ideas to put into practice.

Paul Temporal
Oxford 2019

PART I

Introduction

CHAPTER I

Branding in a Changing World

B rands have never been more important than they are today. The accelerating rate of turbulent change, the volatility of economies and markets, the relentless progress of technologies and innovations, and increasing market fragmentation, have caused the destruction of many companies and their products that have failed to develop the lifeline of a strong brand. Though we are not very far into the 21st century, already markets are littered with failures, physical and virtual, that could have survived had strong branding been in place.

Seven world market trends

The significant elements of change encountered over the last three decades can be categorized into seven world market trends that affect today's businesses. These are:

1. The breakdown of market boundaries

2. Globalization and the development of global brands

3. Increasing market fragmentation

4. Product diversity and shorter life cycles

5. Greater customer sophistication

6. The digital world

7. Economic instability and market volatility

1. The breakdown of market boundaries

Traditionally, markets and sectors have been to some extent self-contained, but the advent of new technologies has allowed many companies to move into markets and sectors that were previously unknown and inaccessible. Industry crossovers are no longer unusual. For example, IT companies are now developing driverless cars.

Another contributory factor to the breakdown of market boundaries is deregulation, where international legislation has hurried this process along, for instance, with the ASEAN Free Trade Area.

A third cause for the erosion of market boundaries is the increase in the number of strategic alliances, which continue to prove attractive to companies, offering them global reach and access to new and distant markets.

2. Globalization and the development of global brands

Globalization is both a boardroom buzzword and a commercial reality as more companies seek to achieve a worldwide presence. One influential factor here has been the standardization of buying patterns, with people in most countries inclined toward buying similar products and services. Travel to any major city and you will see familiar fashion goods, fast-food outlets, motor vehicles, mobile phones, financial services, and so on. This makes it easier for firms to produce and market generic products and services that deliver volume sales at a lower cost base. There is no doubt that this phenomenon has been a catalyst in the development of global brand strategies.

3. Increasing market fragmentation

Having said there is a trend toward increasing standardization of buying patterns, it seems contradictory to now say that markets are becoming more fragmented. However, within broad markets, there is an increasing number of customer groups that identify themselves by their distinctive needs and wants. So it is true to say that although consumers generally tend to buy similar generic products and services, they are demanding that these be tailored to their specific requirements. Companies have reacted to this by shifting their stance from mass marketing to mass customization.

4. Product diversity and shorter life cycles

One of the reactions to greater competition fueled by the above factors is product development and innovation, which have been made easier by the speed of technological advances and their availability. This, coupled with the demand for more customized products, has resulted in product proliferation, so much so that customers are sometimes bewildered by the wide range of choices on offer. A consequent challenge is the increased difficulty to produce a product or service that is enduringly different. To use marketing jargon, unique selling propositions (USPs) are hard to find and sustain. While technological advances spur further innovation and become more freely available to everyone, leadership in product innovation is more difficult to achieve but easier to emulate and, therefore, short-lived.

The rate of technological change is staggering. In some categories, product life cycles have been shortened to a matter of weeks instead of years, as is the case with mobile technology. As a result, companies are caught in a trap. On the one hand, they cannot afford to lag behind in the race for new product development, and on the other, to keep ahead in the race, they have to invest heavily in technology research and development with its built-in obsolescence, and thus aim to gain mandatory rapid returns at the same time.

5. Greater customer sophistication

Nowadays, people are better educated, possess greater spending power (often fueled by credit), and have better lifestyles than before. They are also more demanding in their determination to secure value for money. This independence has manifested itself in a greater tendency by customers to exercise their right to choose, resulting in more fragility of customer loyalty and shifting from ordinary and weakly branded companies and products to powerful brands.

6. The digital world

The next trend is the advent of the digital age. We're very familiar with this term, but what are the elements associated with the digital age? First of all, we've got fast and instant global communication. I mentioned this earlier, but it is as well to stress this, because now anyone can communicate instantly with anyone else, on anything, in any place around the world, at any time with communications technology. We're also seeing the equalization of knowledge. The Internet is a source of unbelievable amounts of knowledge. Everyone is becoming very knowledgeable and can find out anything by using search engines, such as top global brand Google.

Doing business on the Internet is also on the increase. In some countries, up to 30–40% of transactions are now done online. But we also have this slight conundrum about bricks and clicks, bricks being the traditional models of shops, and clicks to do with online business. In some areas of business, the bricks are losing and the clicks are winning, but in other areas of business, the retail channels are very much alive, and people can look, touch and feel products before they then go back and perhaps buy them online. So, people still want to see things, sometimes before they make big online transactions. Companies are trying to deal with this massive change and need online as well as offline strategies.

The Internet provides new segments, opportunities and challenges. And the change rushes on. Now people are talking about the Internet of Things – interconnected networks of smart devices. Your house, heating, whether your fridge is full or not – you can find out and change things in a fraction of a second on your mobile phone. The Internet is thus changing how products in a huge number of categories are developed. As the world dives deeper into the digital age, companies have to adapt to new ways of doing business online and deal also with social media, where people can connect to anyone.

Sophisticated info-communications technologies drive these new marketing channels, and the trends, challenges and opportunities presented by the digital world are discussed in Chapter 8.

7. Economic instability and market volatility

No economy has been spared the destabilizing forces of recent times, and it is highly unlikely that companies will ever again experience the long periods of stability that they had known in the past. However, companies that appear to have been least affected by the chaos are those with powerful brand names.

These seven trends are continuing to roll forward, accelerating the pace of change and creating more turbulence in world markets. What can be predicted about the future are the following:

- Change will continue to accelerate
- Uncertainty will deepen
- Markets will become more dynamic and fragmented
- Customers will get more sophisticated and demanding
- Competition will get tougher
- Survival will become more difficult
- Companies will have to deal with issues that they did not have to confront before.

Given this somewhat frightening scenario, there are several questions that are increasingly finding space on boardroom agendas.

Eight strategic issues for the 21st century

Eight urgent, strategic questions face most companies these days, specifically, how can they:

1. Gain international and global recognition?

2. Reduce their dependence on contract manufacturing and other less desirable alliances?

3. Access and penetrate new markets?

4. Avoid their products and services being seen and bought as commodities?

5. Reduce their costs and increase their value?

6. Establish a presence in new and emerging industries?

7. Secure long-term profits and growth, and survive the hard times?

8. Break parity and stand out from the crowd?

The answer to these questions is the creation, development and management of international brands. The market power of brands is astonishing. Here are some ways in which strong brands can transform ordinary businesses into elite ones.

Strong branding represents one of the best defences against adverse economic and other market conditions. They differentiate companies and products from their competitors, are accepted and wanted around the world across all cultures, make access to new markets and industries easier, attract the best talent, provide returns on investment worth multiples of the value of the net assets of businesses through endless streams of profit, and – best of all – have no life cycle if they are looked after and managed well.

Powerful brands, when nurtured and managed properly, give companies longevity, and the potential for immortality. Coca-Cola is around 130 years old, and Tide washing powder is over 70 years old, but both are still leaders in their chosen markets, despite intensive competition. Powerful brands such as these would not have lasted so long without careful management, and it is the building and management of strong brands that this book is about.

The power and rewards of branding

It is well known that branding can bring with it an immense array of financial and other benefits. In brief, they are as follows:

1. *Riding out adverse conditions*: when recessionary times come, the stronger brands fare better than weaker brands. During the recession that started in 2008, Louis Vuitton and Armani sales and profitability were not damaged and at times increased.

2. *Transportability across cultures*: great brands are desired across the world and can cross continents and cultures. McDonald's is a good example. It has to slightly modify its product ingredients to suit local tastes but the franchise is demanded all over the world.

3. *Moving across industries*: brands like Virgin have several hundreds of businesses in diverse sectors and categories – all under one umbrella brand.

4. *Accessing new markets*: connected with point 3 above, strong brands can access many new markets. For example, Google has recently started to manufacture driverless vehicles.

5. *Moving from commodity to value status*: water is a commodity, but skillful branding has made it almost a luxury item! It really started in the modern era with Perrier. Great strategy, packaging, design, and celebrity endorsements resulted in Perrier sales in the US increasing from 2.5 million bottles to more than 75 million during 1975 to 1978. There are a huge number of water brands now, many sold at premium prices, not all of which are spring or natural water – some are just tap or drinking water. Indeed, the principles of branding that have proved so successful for wine producers are now being applied to water products. For a really interesting article on this see 'Water waste of money!' [1]

6. All these benefits that arise from building a brand impact on the bottom line. Brands generate competitive differentiation that allows premium pricing, together with higher sales volumes that provide economies of scale, coupled with greater stability of demand. The result is higher sustainable profits and increased asset value. Brands are intangible assets and, as you will see in the final chapter, can be valued in monetary terms. Indeed, brands can often be worth more than the net tangible assets of a business.

Good brand management helps make strong brands and great customer relationships, but it is surprising that many companies still pay less attention to managing their brands than to managing other aspects of their business. One reason for this might be that in many parts of the world, including Asia and the Middle East, strategic brand management is still fairly new to marketers. Branding itself is an ever-evolving concept, and the techniques associated with managing brands are constantly changing.

This book provides a guide to the various aspects of brand strategy and management, and includes examples of practice – both good and not-so-good – from around the world, in the hope that the reader will learn from the experiences of others. The book will provide you with answers to many of the main issues facing brand strategists and managers, such as:

- Should the brand vision replace the corporate vision?

- Should the brand determine business strategy, or vice versa?

- What returns on investment do brands bring?

- What is the role of emotion in building and managing brands?

- Why do companies look to personality to strengthen their brands?

- Should brands be proactive or reactive, strategic or tactical?

- How is it possible to gain a strong and sustainable brand position and differentiation in crowded markets?

- How are decisions made to reposition brands, revitalize them, or let them die?

- How far can a brand be stretched, and what are the pitfalls to avoid?

- What impact do new technologies have on brand management and consumer relationships?

- How is brand management different in the physical and virtual worlds?

- What options are available for organizing and structuring the brand management process?

- What role should the CEO play in brand building and management?

- What trends are taking place in brand communications?

- How can we create a brand culture so that everyone lives the brand?

- How can we measure the success of our brand(s)?

Just to give you a flavor of what is to come in the book, here is a light-hearted, but nevertheless accurate, view of just a few of the decisions and situations that face those whose job it is to manage a brand, as seen from the brand's perspective.

A day in the life of a brand

I'm a quite famous brand – well I like to think so. I'm available in most parts of the world and have pretty good market share and profitability in many markets. I've been around for quite a while (don't ask me my age), and hope that what they say about brands having no life cycles is true.

I have a brand manager (chief brand officer or BM as we call him) who is very senior in the company here. He reports to a brand management council that includes other brand managers in our product brand portfolio, plus corporate marketing, and various others who seem to be determined to influence my future in some way. People think strong brands have it easy, but that's not the case. Here's a typical day for me.

8 am: Agency news. The worldwide advertising agency has got the boot, and has to re-pitch against the competition next month. Well, they've not done too badly, but I never thought they understood my personality very well. I hope the top guys give the new agency a thorough briefing – I seem to remember the last one was a bit waffly and didn't focus on my strategy.

9 am: Panic in the camp. Europe had a quality problem in the German factory the day before yesterday and it hit the press. There were actually accusations that I was deceiving people! Why do the press always report the bad news? Discussions here (most of which I can't repeat) centered around what we *might* say. They are still talking – the phones are going berserk, and we still haven't replied to the public at all. This is going to get worse if Corporate Communications doesn't snap out of it. Haven't they heard of crisis management? And what about my image? People trust me; I stand for top quality! I feel a headache coming on, and I suspect other heads will roll.

10 am: Good news at last. I have been valued in dollar terms and have made it into the top 20 most valuable brands in the world. I've been telling top management that I'm a strategic asset, not just a brand, but did they believe me? I restrained myself from saying, "I told you so."

11 am: Request from Asia to change my personality to fit the local culture. My BM said, "No way." Good for him. He replied that we have to be consistent with my brand character, but we can emphasize the more appropriate attributes in campaigns, and can use market communications to localize me and make me more relevant.

12.30 pm: Lunch and indigestion. I was asked to co-brand with a drinks brand that appeals to an entirely different audience. Thanks, but no thanks. Despite promises of more sales, which has the sales force leaping up and down at the thought of year-end bonuses, my values just don't fit. I mean, really! Who wants to be seen arm-in-arm with a downmarket product? Image is everything.

2 pm: My BM was put on the spot by the chief executive officer (prompted by an outside consultant, I suspect), who has asked him what business I am in. To make it clear, he said, "Not the company business, the business of your *brand*." A great question and a predictable answer from the BM of, "Let me give that some serious thought." I wonder how long he's got to come up with the answer, and where this will lead us.

2.30 pm: The rack. This is pure torture. They are having discussions about how far they can "stretch" me – or "extend the brand," as my BM puts it. Much talk of which target audience, why, will it work, what about my current positioning, etc. I feel most uncomfortable – like a patient being discussed by a group of specialists, some of whom are of doubtful origin and qualifications.

4 pm: Message from London asking HQ to refresh me as I'm looking a bit old-fashioned. Thanks a lot, guys – and what about yourselves? Well, I don't mind some new design or packaging if my fans like it, but let's be sensible and not do anything that is out of character. Evolution is OK – revolution is out. My BM says he will take a look at this.

4.30 pm: Gloom all around. The markets have dropped further as politics rears its ugly head and uncertainty fears abound. People at the top want my talk time cut – "Reduce all A&P expenditure on all brands" came the imperative from on high. Argument ensues, with one camp saying, "Cutting down is good if we focus a lot more," and another saying, "If the competitors are going to be quiet, now is the time to spend more, create more market share, and be remembered as the brand that is always there for people." I kind of like that last argument, but I fear the cost-cutters will win. Courageously, the director of marketing supports my BM in asking that brand expenditure should remain and costs be slashed elsewhere.

6 pm: I was just about to call it a day when I heard that the proposed customer relationship management program for me has been given the go-ahead. Great! Now I can begin to get to know all my customers individually, and reward those who are high value and have been very loyal to me. I hope the team doesn't get too caught up in technology, and that they concentrate on how better relationships can really benefit my customers.

6.30 pm: Let's go out on a high note. I have to attend an event I've sponsored tonight, which will feature me on my YouTube site. This will be backed up by a worldwide digital campaign. It appears it is cheaper and more effective than previous advertising and promotion campaigns, although my BM says I have to have both an online and offline presence. Digital is the word these days and my strategy, including e-commerce, is looking good. See you tomorrow!

Brand strategy and management

Of course, not all matters of importance hit brand managers every day, like the above suggests, but these are typical important strategic issues that brand managers have to deal with over time. They also have to involve themselves in many other things as part of their work, but put very simply, brand management is a process that tries to take control over everything a brand does and says, and the way in which it is perceived. There is a need, therefore, to influence the perceptions of various target audiences to ensure that people see what you want them to see with respect to your brand. This means identifying clearly what your brand stands for, its personality, and how to position it so that it appears different from and better than competing brands. It involves integrated communications, and constant tracking of the brand and its competitors.

The overall aim of this process, naturally, is to increase the value of the brand over time, however that may be measured. Profitability will be one measure, market share another, volume of sales perhaps another, and the emotional associations of the brand with consumers yet another. These will be discussed as we go along. But one of the hardest parts of brand management is to achieve a balance between the short-term numbers demanded by top management to satisfy various stakeholders, and the long-term growth of the brand and sustainable profits. For example, price-cutting might buy short-term market share, but at what cost to the brand's long-term image? For listed companies there is the need to perform to stock market requirements on a quarterly basis in terms of sales and profitability while maintaining, or even increasing, investment in the brands that deliver the results. There can therefore be conflicts of interest between the needs of the business and those of the brands.

As you will now have begun to see, brand management is a difficult job. What makes it more difficult is the fact that many of the elements that influence a brand's success are often partially or totally outside the control of those responsible for its management, such as competitor moves, economic factors, and consumer trends. Proactivity and reactivity live side by side in the daily work of brand managers, and this is the very reason that makes brand management so exciting – brands live in ever-changing landscapes, full of opportunities and challenges.

There are also several dimensions of a more tactical nature that have to be given meticulous attention on a daily basis. Brand managers have to juggle constantly with many activities to ensure that they can affect the image of the brand in both the short and long term. The situation becomes more complex and difficult for those whose job it is to manage a corporate brand under which there may be several sub-brands and/or product brands, as consistency and autonomy of brands can conflict. All of these factors will be discussed in the book. Also discussed will be the culture of the company, whether the right brand culture has been put into place, and how to do this.

But it all starts with brand strategy. Every aspect of brand management should be driven by the strategy of the brand, whether corporate or product. Unfortunately, many companies don't have a clear brand strategy and end up with confused images and consumer perceptions of the brand. They concentrate on trying to control the outside elements without having clear guidelines upon which they can do this.

So, although there are many issues that I will address, it is appropriate to start the book with a look at the changing roles of brand management, brand strategy, and how the interaction between brands and businesses has changed in recent times.

CHAPTER 2

The Changing Roles
of Brand Management

There have been several developments over the last 30 years or so with respect to how businesses have changed their view of the customer, and how consumers have changed their views about businesses. These changes have led to the emergence of brand management as an increasingly important and highly complex activity. A short summary follows of how business relationships with consumers, whether business-to-business (B2B) or business-to-consumer (B2C) in nature, have evolved and how the role of brand management has changed as a result.

Business evolution and the consumer

The dreadful days of product focus

Some of you may remember the early days of mass production, when companies developed products that they thought the public needed and would want to buy, produced them, and then threw them into the market with the conviction that sales would result. The consumer often responded by buying the products because they were new and enhanced their quality of life. Consumer-durable and fast-moving goods – such as refrigerators, televisions, and cosmetics – had triggered the insatiable appetite of the consumer for branded products. However, there were as many failures as there were successes during this time. Marketers hadn't really understood what consumers wanted, because *they hadn't asked them*. This approach to marketing has now largely disappeared, although sometimes when I meet with companies I have my doubts. Some Japanese companies, for instance, still have a mind-set that says, "Let's develop a great product and then go out there and sell it to the consumer, who doesn't know what he or she wants."

The emergence of market orientation

Marketers soon learned that it was a wise move to understand a little more about what customers had in mind. Mass marketing was still predominant, but marketers began to realize that not all markets were homogenous. They discovered that within categories such as washing powders, different people expected different types of product performance; for instance, some people wanted a heavy-duty detergent, while others wanted a product suitable for use with delicate fabrics. So, during the 1970s we saw the introduction of market segmentation and the growth of market research as an industry. For the brand manager, this meant substantial growth of product categories and many opportunities for brand extensions.

The age of the big brands

The age of the big brands rapidly grew in the late 1970s and early 1980s, when powerful brands, led by a new breed of brand managers, began to dominate their chosen markets. There was a tremendous demand for aspirational brands during this time, with some, such as Nike, becoming global players. By this point, the whole world had become more brand-conscious. Research studies claim that children become brand-conscious from as young as four years of age. Even in the less-developed and underdeveloped countries, the big brands have a presence and are the focus of consumer attention. However, the fragmentation of markets referred to above has led brand management into the complex world of mass customization, and there has been a strong movement away from pure, generic products manufactured to suit mass markets. This has led to a proliferation of products available to consumers, with tremendous profits for those companies that understand these complex markets correctly.

The realization of brand value

It is now widely acknowledged that brands, if created, developed, and managed well, can achieve spectacular financial results. If we look at the market capitalization of well-branded companies versus relatively unbranded companies in both the United States and the United Kingdom (the S&P and FTSE markets, respectively), and many other markets around the world, we see that around 70% or more of market capitalization isn't represented by the net tangible asset value of the companies concerned. There is a huge gap between market capitalization and net tangible assets, and this unexplained value is represented by intangible assets, a significant part being the value of brands themselves. Other intangible items include patents, customer lists, licenses, know-how, and major contracts, but the value of the brand itself is increasingly becoming the biggest item. Brand names are often worth multiples of the value of the actual businesses they represent. As a result, brands are often bought and sold for considerable amounts of money, which represent not so much the tangible assets belonging to the company, but the expectation of the brands' premium prices applied to the level of sales projected into the foreseeable future.

A strong corporate brand name brings with it additional financial strength which can be measured and used in many ways. They include:

- *Mergers and acquisitions*: brand valuation plays a major part in these undertakings. Potential acquirers of branded goods companies, together with their investors and bankers, find comfort in the knowledge that the price being paid for a company can be substantiated by reference to the value of the specific intangible, as well as tangible, assets being acquired. For sellers, there are opportunities to add intangible brand asset value to the overall purchase price.

- *External investor relations*: for some major companies, building a portfolio of world-class brands is a central objective. Brand valuation can be used to provide hard numbers in what is often a soft power argument.

- *Internal communications*: brand valuation can help explain performance and be used as a means of motivating management. The use of internal royalty rates based on brand value can also make clear to a group of companies the value of the corporate assets they are being allowed to use.

- *Marketing budget allocation*: brand valuation can assist in portfolio marketing budget decisions, providing a more systematic basis for decision making, with greater allocation of funds given to high-performing brands.

- *Internal marketing management*: strategic use of brand valuation techniques allows senior management to compare the success of different brand strategies and the relative performance of particular marketing teams.

- *Balance sheet reporting*: in certain parts of the world, acquired brands are now carried as intangible assets and amortized. In some markets, placing the value of an acquired brand on the balance sheet is compulsory.

- *Licensing and franchising*: accurate brand valuation allows a realistic set of charges to be created for the licensing and franchising of brand names.

- *Securitized borrowing*: companies such as Disney and Levi Strauss have borrowed major sums against their brand names.

- *Litigation support*: brand valuations have been used in legal cases to defend the brand value, such as in the case of illicit use of a brand name or receivership.

- *Fair trading investigations*: brand valuation has been used to explain to non-marketing audiences the role of brands, and the importance their value has for the companies that spend so much to acquire and maintain them.

- *Tax planning*: more and more companies are actively planning the most effective domicile for their brand portfolios with branded royalty streams in mind.

- *New product and market development assessment*: new business strategies can be modeled using brand valuation techniques to make judgments on, for example, best brand, best market extension, and best consumer segment.

Brand value versus brand equity

Brand value and brand equity are often confused. When we talk about *brand value*, we mean the actual financial worth of the brand. The term *brand equity*, on the other hand, is often used in referring to the descriptive aspects of a brand – whether symbols, imagery, or consumer associations – and to reflect its strength in terms of consumer perceptions. It represents the more subjective and intangible views of the brand as held by consumers, and is somewhat misleading, as the word *equity* has a financial origin.

There are several dimensions of brand equity, as opposed to brand value. Some of these key aspects of brand performance or strength are:

- *Price premium* – the additional price that consumers will pay for the brand compared to other offers.

- *Satisfaction/loyalty* – levels of satisfaction with the brand that helps determine loyalty and prevent price sensitivity.

- *Perceived quality* – relative to other brands.

- *Leadership* – in terms of market leadership, connected to market share.

- *Perceived value* – a value-for-money concept linked not just to tangible items such as quality, but also to intangible factors.

- *Brand personality* – the attributes of the brand's character that differentiate it from others and add charisma.

- *Mental associations* – the most important one being trust.

- *Brand awareness and recognition* – key measures of brand strength concerned with how well the brand is known in the market.

- *Market share* – volume and, in some cases, perceived positioning.

- *Market price* – premiums enjoyed by the brand.

- *Distribution coverage* – including percentage share.

There is no absolute score for these dimensions, but this mix of attitudinal, behavioral, and market measures of brand equity should be the focus for good brand management practice. What is interesting with this list is that it contains a mixture of what I would see as some of the drivers of both brand value and brand equity. Calculating brand value is, of course, a very specialized area, and the key drivers of brand performance are not all contained in the above list; however, there is a substantial overlap. For those readers interested in establishing the financial value of brands, brand valuation methodology is outlined in detail in Chapter 11.

So, although there is a difference in terminology, it appears that there is a connection between brand value and brand equity, because many of the components of brand equity have been found to be the drivers of brand value. Companies wishing to achieve spectacular rates of return on investment should concentrate on building up the strength of their corporate brand name in their chosen markets. And the only way to do this is to concentrate on providing consumers with the best possible brand experience. This is where strong brand management is essential.

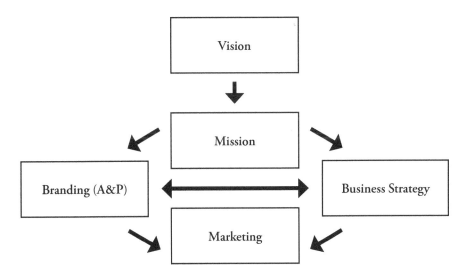

Figure 2.1: Brand link to corporate strategy in the 20th century

Brands driving business strategy

Branding has been so successful that companies are now replacing corporate visions and missions with brand visions and missions. Figure 2.1 shows what I believe to be the old, 20th-century business model. With this business strategy, companies developed corporate visions and missions that, while they looked impressive when mounted along the corridor walls, were largely ignored by anyone other than top management, who used them to drive the business forward. Branding merely provided support, usually in the form of advertising and promotion activities (A&P).

This business process has now changed. In the 21st century, the model being used by successful brands is to develop a vision and mission for the *brand*, and to let this drive the business strategy and all related activities, as shown in Figure 2.2. You will notice that brand strategy drives business strategy followed by activation through marketing and internal initiatives. This concentration on relationships is explained in further detail below, but a key point to note here is that world-class practice focuses on brands driving marketing and not the other way around.

Great focus on the brand-consumer relationship

Using this view of the consumer world – that is, focusing on how brands relate to consumers – the latest and most profitable strategies are those that strengthen the relationship of the brand with consumers, and then use this as the basis to drive the business forward and build brand value. Consumer insight plays a vital role here. Examples of how branding has been affected by this new way of thinking are given in Chapter 3.

Figure 2.2: Brand link to corporate strategy in the 21st century

Brands – fascists or friends?

Occasionally, global brands are criticized by writers who argue that they are too powerful and tend not to act in the public interest in their pursuit of profits. This argument is typified in the book *No Logo* by Naomi Klein, who suggests that branding is a somewhat anti-social activity. Taking an anti-globalization stance, Klein declares that brands have come to represent "a fascist state where we all salute the logo and have little opportunity for criticism because our newspapers, television stations, Internet servers, streets, and retail spaces are all controlled by multinational corporations." She goes on to say that the power and presence of advertising curtails choice, that brands are symbols of American power, and that they result in environmental damage, human rights abuses, and sweat-shop labor.

In its issue dated September 8–14, 2001, *The Economist* magazine led with an article arguing why brands are good for everyone. The article, entitled "Pro Logo®, The case for brands," argues that brands are becoming more vulnerable (and thus less powerful) and consumers more promiscuous (and thus more powerful). It further argues that brands enable consumers to express themselves and to enjoy the benefits of trust, self-expression, and new ways of enjoying their lives. Rather than promoting poor environmental and working conditions, brands are held captive by public opinion and are actively encouraged to help create a better world. The article makes the point, with some force, that, "far from being instruments of oppression, [brands] make firms accountable to consumers." To my mind, brand management is the conduit through which the psychological demands of consumers are delivered. If brand managers fail to satisfy these complex desires, then the brands they have responsibility for will cease to exist.

Brands that care

It is my belief that the great brands of the future will be brands that care. They will be able to balance profitability with social responsibility. They will balance brand spirit with human spirit. They will be less unilateral in their actions and more altruistic. They will behave not as businesses, but as living entities that care for what happens in the world and for the people who live in it. Above all, they will focus on relationship building and bringing people together.

All of the above add up to a distinct shift in the role and status of brand management in today's global commercial world.

The changing role of brand management

Over the last couple of decades, there have been some discernible changes in the role of brand management and the activities of brand managers. Principally, they consist of the following changes in emphasis.

Change from an industry to a market focus

One of the more obvious trends in business has been the move away from product-led to customer-led marketing. This change needs little explanation, but its impact on brand management in one sense has been to force managers to get closer to, and listen to, the customer. This has brought about many innovative initiatives in market research, customer service, and quality management, and has also meant that brand managers are increasingly getting involved in new product development.

Change from tactical thinking to strategic thinking

Another change has been the move of corporate strategic thinking away from looking purely at how to grow the business within a specific industry, toward a mindset that looks at expansion across many industries and in multiple markets. This has led brand management to take a much more strategic view, and to become a more holistic activity, looking at how to project consistent identities and create consistent images in a variety of different situations. Brand managers still, however, have to fight the day-to-day tactical battles associated with shifting markets and competitive attacks.

Change from local market focus and analysis to global market focus and analysis

The economies of scale required to achieve world-class brands and the breakdown of market boundaries have meant that more companies are adopting a global focus, and that brand management now has to achieve the right balance between global identities and local adaptations. This trend has also led to the emergence of many more strategic alliances involving co-branding, in order to reduce the cost of global reach. In some cases, companies are now requiring brand managers to tailor brand offerings specifically to local markets. For instance, all advertising and promotion for Nestlé's Milo must show local sports, facilities, talent, and so on.

Change from product management to category management

Vicious competition in many markets, especially in fast-moving consumer goods, has given rise to the management of categories as opposed to individual products, with the brand manager looking at a multi-product portfolio and a complex set of positioning alternatives. This has been spurred in part by the fact that consumers think in terms of categories, such as shampoos, skincare products, and so on. There has also been a shift in power – again, especially in fast-moving consumer goods – from the brand manager to the retailer and e-tailer, and so brand managers must cope with the reality that their brands have to fit in with what sellers would like to offer to consumers. Brand managers must constantly assess what value their brands are providing to retailers and consumers in their chosen categories. Constant monitoring of competitive intruders is mandatory, as they may quickly erode the value a brand represents. Brand managers now have to view individual brands within a mix of several brands that satisfy both the consumer's desire for choice and the seller's need for profitability and a target audience.

As a result of this competition, the creation of new categories has now become important as some of the power brands crowd existing categories with their product line extensions. Brand and line extensions are discussed in Chapter 4. Smart companies are even changing the nature of categories. A great example is the energy drink Red Bull. Although not the first of its kind, the brand has dramatically changed and grown the market category for this kind of beverage, making it the number one energy drink for young, active people.

Change from product branding to corporate branding

There has been a marked change in direction, by companies around the world, away from concentrating on product branding and toward focusing on the corporate brand. Even the master of product branding, Procter & Gamble (P&G), is now putting much more strategic effort into leveraging its corporate brand name, as is its arch-rival Unilever. There are many reasons for this. It is an expensive exercise for a company to create and build brands independently with little endorsement from the parent company. Product branding requires each brand to stand on its own and have its own investment, which in research and development (R&D) and A&P alone can be enormous. Without generous parental support, getting through the stages of brand awareness, trial, acceptance, and preference in the marketplace can be highly resource-consuming. This is one reason why Unilever has reduced the number of its brands from 1,600 to approaching 400, its declared target. Even within this reduced number the company puts more resource into its power brands (less than 20) that have revenues in excess of US$1 billion a year.

While product branding continues to play an important part in brand strategy, there has been a marked trend toward corporate and umbrella branding, with even the traditional diehard product brand organizations such as P&G bringing the corporate brand more into the spotlight. P&G has made leveraging the corporate brand a global strategy, and throughout the world we are now seeing its initials used in support of product brands. One reason for this is that, for decades, P&G has been losing out on building the dollar value of the parent brand itself. In 2000, the market capitalization of the company declined, but if we look at the stock market indices around the world over the last 20 years, it is plain to see that heavily branded companies consistently outperform unbranded companies in terms of market capitalization. With corporate branding, most frequently seen where the company adds its name to the product brands it launches, there is the added value of trust and the shared synergies of the other investments needed. But one of the main determinants of this trend is the fact that brands can be valued in financial terms. Since adopting a strategy of leveraging the corporate brand, P&G has seen large increases in market capitalization.

Change from branding consumer products to business-to-business (B2B) and commodity branding

There is a rising interest in branding many types of entity. The success of consumer product and corporate branding has led to an increase in B2B branding, and even the branding of commodities. Companies such as Accenture, IBM, BASF, and Hewlett-Packard (HP) have all carried out comprehensive branding initiatives. And in order to rise out of the commodity trap, basic commodity and trading entities have also begun to brand themselves, as the case study below illustrates.

Case Study 1: Thung Kula Farm

From commodity product to premium brand

Thung Kula Rong Hai – or Thung Kula for short – is an area approximately 500,000 acres in size covering five provinces in northeast Thailand. With no major rivers, the area is poorly irrigated and thus dry and barren. The Ministry of Agriculture and Cooperatives, in cooperation with other government agencies, has a mission to improve the quality of life of the 85,000 or so local farmers and their families. To this end, it has developed a five-year plan with the objective of increasing farming incomes through the promotion and export of the locally produced jasmine rice, which has a unique fragrance and taste, due to the high concentration of sodium and silica components in the soil. The project includes improving the area's irrigation systems and developing the infrastructure for farmers to produce high-quality rice to certified international standards such as GMP and ISO.

Farmers in the Thung Kula area have been encouraged to form themselves into six 'cooperatives', each with its own mill, to produce jasmine rice for sale. The Ministry of Agriculture and Cooperatives has encouraged the development of one co-managed brand of jasmine rice that the farmers in the area can 'own'. This system enables the farmers to bypass the middlemen, who would normally buy their rice very cheaply, process it themselves in their own mills, and then sell the final product at a premium price under their own brands. Equipped with modern rice mills, all certified to international standards of manufacturing, the local farmers have instead been enabled to create and sell their own brand.

The farmers started the branding process by focusing on the fundamentals. Consumer research was conducted in order to understand consumers' consumption habits and attitudes toward brands. Over 100 key members of the six cooperatives were educated about the branding process and instructed in the key elements that contribute to building a great brand. Forty managers in total from all the cooperatives then got together to craft the brand strategy, starting with what they wanted their brand to stand for emotionally in the minds of consumers, and extending through to the brand personality and brand positioning.

The cooperatives stipulated which rice seeds farmers were to use, available from certified nurseries in the area, and agreed on uniform milling standards (for instance, a standard length and color of the grain). A team of quality control inspectors was assigned to check the quality of every batch of production from each of the six mills. These and other measures resulted in a great-quality, standard product that delivered on the brand promise. In return, the cooperatives agreed to buy only from their cooperative members.

The rice was marketed under the brand name 'Thung Kula Farm'. The name evoked the heritage of the land, while also referring to the farmers' decision to join forces to create their own brand. Confident of the high quality and unique fragrance of the product, the farmers then positioned their brand head-on with premium-grade jasmine rice from other parts of the country, and with other big brand names produced by the middlemen, with the goal of exporting the brand in the future.

Understanding how consumers develop an emotional connection with brands, Thung Kula Farm has escaped the commodity trap and become a symbol of love and care. The farmers' own love for their product, as evidenced by the care they take in its production, is seen by consumers as extending to their love for their families, as evidenced by their selection of this particular brand of high-quality rice.

In the selection of packaging for their product, the farmers decided to move away from the traditional rice bag to the modern-day 5 kg package suitable for today's households. The gold and purple packaging design, colors not traditionally used for commodity rice products, reinforces the product's 'elegant' brand personality. The 'caring' personality of the brand was portrayed through special package design for ease of handling and to avoid the use of extra plastic bags (care for the earth). Every touchpoint of the Thung Kula Farm brand has been managed to ensure that customers have only great experiences with the brand.

This has been a good beginning for a brand co-managed by a group of farmers; and from a marketing point of view, the business has a unique competitive advantage. The bigger brands of packaged rice normally have to buy their raw produce from rice fields all over the country, which results in a product of variable quality. By contrast, the farmers of the Thung Kula area are able to bring to market a high-quality product, with a unique fragrance, whose consistency is second to none. And consistency in product quality is at the heart of success for any business and brand.

Despite these advantages, Thung Kula Farm faces quite a few challenges over the long term. One of the key challenges will be the farmers' ability to market and distribute their product. Traditionally, the middlemen to whom they sold their product performed these functions. In addition to sharpening their trading skills, they need to learn how to build business connections with modern trade channels.

Investment in the brand is another key challenge. In order to compete with big brand names in the market, Thung Kula Farm needs to invest in its brand, from creating awareness to enhancing loyalty and trust, particularly in the first few years following its launch. The responsible government agencies may need to provide some support in this area. Finally, the ultimate challenge will be the unity of the six cooperatives. They must work together as one team with one vision if they are to consistently manage customers' experiences with the brand. This will be a long-term journey, but the brand is likely to be successful, driven by loyalty and trust from happy customers.

Change from product responsibility to customer relationship responsibility

Another interesting development has been the move away from the management of product(s) to the management of customer relationships, signified by the fact that some companies are now giving brand managers responsibility for specific groups of customers, across an entire product range. In this respect, *brand* management is becoming *customer* management. Customer relationship management, as a discipline, is now regarded as a necessary part of the brand manager's skill repertoire. This topic is dealt with in detail in Chapter 8.

Change from managing the physical brand world to both physical and virtual brand worlds

The onset of Web 2.0 (the new digital Internet revolution) forced traditional brand companies to enhance their established Internet branding strategies. The virtual world raises additional problems for the brand manager, especially in terms of providing consumers with a consistent brand experience. The Internet world is complex and extremely volatile, but the rewards can be huge. The rules of branding in the virtual world are somewhat different from those that apply in the physical world; nevertheless, it is a 'must have'. It is true to say now that any brand manager or company with expectations of building a strong brand must create a viable and attractive online strategy.

In addition to the use of the Internet as a brand-building vector by traditional brands, we have recently witnessed the gradual demise of traditional advertising and other media, as the Internet has given consumers more power in the brand-building process. The growth of the digital world has hit traditional brand building with a tsunami-like force, and brands can now be built with enormous speed. Companies such as Google, YouTube, and Facebook have all developed into hugely powerful and valuable brands in just a short time, fulfilling the wish by today's consumers to be involved with brands that look after their needs while helping them to express themselves and build their own personal brands. The success of these brands endorses the fact that it is *consumers* who build brands; companies merely give them the opportunities to do so.

The impact of the digital world will be discussed at length in Chapter 8.

Change from managing brand performance to managing brand value and equity

Companies have now become much more concerned with the total value of their brands, not just with revenues and profitability. The valuation of brands is by no means an exact science, but the sale of brands for prices far in excess of their asset valuation has meant that brand building has become a business in its own right. For the brand manager, this means that several measures of performance have to be taken into account simultaneously, as brand equity measurement can include a whole host of variables, including brand awareness, brand loyalty, perceived quality, price, market share and cash-flow premiums, internationality, support, protection, and many others.

Brand valuation has come into play over the last two decades as a technique for justifying, and measuring returns on, brand investment. Brand management has now become the management of profitable strategic assets (brands) that can often be worth multiples of the net assets of the business, and so the performance of brand managers is now more closely evaluated on this basis.

Strong brands continue to give organizations spectacular advantages. In adverse times, they hold up better and in good times they rise above ordinary brands. They are more easily transportable across markets and industries and make it easier for companies to go international and global. They attract the best talent and help companies escape from the commodity trap gaining value status and differentiation. They allow for premium prices, increase sales volumes generating economies of scale and give stability of demand. All of these advantages impact on the bottom line in terms of higher sustainable profits and increased asset value.

One example of the astonishing value created by a brand is the historic market capitalization reached by Apple in February 2015 of over US$700 billion. Apple made history again in August 2018 with a market valuation of US$1 trillion. At the time, this was then equivalent to over three times the GDP of Malaysia! And all for a company that outsources all of its manufacturing, owns little in the way of tangible assets, and has only a few products, some of which are not superior in terms of features and attributes from some competitors. This extraordinary record demonstrates the financial firepower of branding.

Change from financial accountability to social responsibility

While those people responsible are very much judged on the financial performance of the brands under their charge, they also have to balance this with a commitment to social responsibility. Many companies are now tying their brands to the needs of communities, and helping to solve societal problems. Examples are HP, with its community programs, and General Electric (GE), with its environmental initiatives. Brand management isn't just about creating profit at all costs, as Naomi Klein would have us believe; it is about encouraging people to do better, and helping them to enjoy a better quality of life.

Neither is it about capitalizing on events that are problematic to other people. The terrible events of September 11, 2001 gave some companies the opportunity to make money out of the tragedy and human suffering. But other companies acted in a more socially responsible manner. As Professor Stephen A. Greyser said, "Some of the immediate donations of goods and services presumably were driven by a clear philanthropic motivation." Hallmark Cards Inc., which saw sales of greetings cards rise rapidly, was meticulous in its brand management by subjecting all cards to a special test so as not to offend. In fact, the company's first action was to search for cards among current offerings that might be offensive. Avoiding offense was more important than boosting card sales, and Hallmark withdrew nine cards from distribution. Its second action was to create cards that fitted the changing mood of the nation. Hallmark delivered new, patriotic cards in six weeks as opposed to the 12–15 months normally required for new product development. Dan Sifter, general manager of Hallmark's seasonal card unit, said, "It's a question of finding the right balance between what consumers want to say to each other – finding warmth – and striking the right patriotic note without being jingoistic."

American Greetings took a similar stance. Within 24 hours of the attacks on New York and Washington, it posted four patriotic electronic greetings on its website[2], which offers e-cards free of charge. Visitors to the site sent 350,000 of these greetings during the first week after the attacks.

Brand management is all about building relationships with consumers, not about taking advantage of those relationships. Companies such as Enron that behave in an unsatisfactory way are likely to proceed to bankruptcy or to face legal action, or both. An abundance of such cases revealing poor accountability, transparency, and corporate governance in the last few years has led to an increase in corporate social responsibility (CSR) activity; in fact, CSR is now an important part of brand management. A good CSR strategy has become a necessity for brands wishing to build and maintain trust and loyalty with communities and the general public.

Indeed, people all over the world have forced brands to give back to communities if they wish to keep their trust and support. Again, the top brands lead the way. The Unilever corporate vision as at February 2017 is "to grow our business, while decoupling our environmental footprint from our growth and increasing our positive social impact." The rationale given for this is:

> "We continue to believe that business must make a positive contribution to addressing the challenges the world faces and that this is the only way a business will succeed. In 2009, we launched The Compass – our strategy for sustainable growth, setting out our determination to build a sustainable business for the long term. The Unilever Sustainable Living Plan, launched in 2010, laid the blueprint for achieving this strategy. We continue to work towards the ambitious targets we have set ourselves for halving our environmental impact, improving the health and wellbeing of 1 billion people, and enhancing the livelihoods of millions."[3]

All in all, the above changes mean that brand management is a much more dynamic and complex function than it has ever been. The challenge now for many companies is to develop the right blend of skills and experience in their managers, whose focus must be clearly on the consumer, the source of brand equity and value.

So, who owns and builds brands?

The movement toward a focus on the relationship between the brand and consumers has forced managers to answer the question of who actually owns and builds brands. Until recently, many companies believed that it is *they* who build brands. The correct answer to this question, now acknowledged by leading brand companies, is that it is the *consumer* who owns and builds brands. The enlightened companies have remembered that brands exist only in the minds of consumers, and without the psychological commitment from consumers, they are merely companies, products, and services, and will remain so.

This undisputed fact is the rationale for replacing corporate visions with brand visions, and for allowing the brand to lead business strategy. The fact that it is consumers who own and build brands doesn't mean that brand management has nothing to do with the brand-building process. On the contrary, brand management is the catalyst that helps consumers to recognize and build relationships with brands.

Brands are relationships, and brand managers have to nurture the relationships between brands and consumers. This means, of course, that brand managers have to understand the consumer even better than before, and gain real insight into how consumers' minds work. This only comes from outside-in thinking, as opposed to inside-out thinking. In other words, while business goals are highly important, managers should not presume that they know what consumers really want and what emotional drivers motivate them to choose one brand over another.

In the next chapter we will look closely at how brands must be strategically designed and grown with due consideration to both the business and customers, and how brands, as relationships, can be built. This chapter will also give an overview of the main steps required of managers who seek to create a strong and sustainable brand strategy.

PART 2

Branding and Consumers

CHAPTER 3

An Introduction to Branding and Brand Strategy

This chapter looks at how brand strategy and management are intrinsically linked to business strategy and how building a powerful brand relies strongly on developing an emotional connection with consumers. It highlights the need to get close to customers, really understand what they want, and build close relationships with them. The chapter concludes with an overview of the four main steps necessary to build a strong brand and these are then considered in depth over the subsequent three chapters.

Before the detail of what goes into building a strong brand is explained, it is appropriate that we are clear on what can be branded, what a brand actually is and what it is not, and dispel some of the myths about branding.

What can be branded?

It's a given now that anything can be branded. So nations and places and destinations, for example, can be branded – places like Hong Kong have a brand management unit to look after them. You can brand corporations – like Microsoft – and products (huge global products like KitKat have great brands and strategies). You can brand events: London 2012 was considered a well-branded Olympic games, bringing in massive wealth to the British economy, post-Olympics. You can brand places like Disneyland – everyone knows about Disney. You can even brand ingredients – things you can't see, and are in other products, such as Lycra. You can brand endorsements. ISO started off as a quality standard, and is now a global brand. And finally, you can brand individuals. I've worked with CEOs to build their personal leadership brands, how they can become better than everyone else. And of course celebrities –

being branded and presented to the marketplace. People like David Beckham, his group of brands, his family, have been carefully looked at in terms of brand strategy and brand management in order to get the Beckham brand group where it is today.

Having established that anything can be branded, I would like to mention some myths about branding that are commonly held around the world.

Some myths about branding

Myth 1: Quality is a differentiator

Well, it's not really true for products anymore as many products nowadays are of very high quality, even though they may be 'Made in China'. For all countries, all businesses, quality is a must-have for survival in today's business world whereby it used to be a nice-to-have. In the service sector though, there is still room in some categories for differentiation on service quality. But even these opportunities are now beginning to close. Quality, then, is the price you must pay to get into the game. If you slip up on quality, your brand will suffer, your image will suffer, you will lose revenue, profits, and if listed, market capitalisation. So the fact remains that you cannot develop a powerful brand without world-class quality.

If you look at some of the companies recently that have slipped up on quality – Toyota, VW – you can see the immense hits they've taken to share price and profits and revenues. So you must have at least as good a quality as your competitors, because if not the prognosis is bad. Bluntly put, you will not survive.

Myth 2: There are too many products to choose from

Well, this is largely true. Product and service proliferation comes from vastly increased competition, and it brings vast amount of choice – sometimes very confusing for the consumer. So many products and services, which to choose? But if you really think about it, it's too much of the same kind of thing. There is no difference between a lot of the products and services, and consumers are quick to spot a lack of authenticity. And what they're really looking for is authentic products and services, with high perceived value. It's what they think about the products and services that really counts. So we've got to get out of the commodity trap, and make sure we build a brand that people view as adding value to their lives.

Myth 3: We understand the consumer

I get lots of companies telling me this, but sometimes I think, in actual fact, they don't. They don't understand the consumer, and many companies still tend to think from the inside out. They make products and try and find consumers that will buy it. So there is a lack of consumer insight in many businesses today. Sometimes companies don't really look hard at why people buy certain things, and what they really want and need. We should be finding products and services for consumers and not the other way around. So instead of inside-out thinking, we need to have outside-in thinking. Companies have got to talk to customers, and really understand what makes them tick.

Myth 4: Brand awareness is the key to marketing success

Well, it is important, and if people aren't aware of your brand, then it's highly unlikely that they'll buy it. But there are other things to think about. What about consumer consideration? What do they think about our brand? What about preference? Do they prefer our brand to others? What about trust? Do they trust the products and services that we are providing? All of these questions are very important. If there is no consumer trust, you'll never have a strong brand. What about referral and repeat purchase? Will they come back again and buy your products and services, having experienced them already? Will they refer you and become your brand advocates, talk to friends, and sell your products and services for you? What we really need to do is to create value in order to earn customers' lifetime loyalty, and we'll talk about this later in Chapter 5. But one thing is certain, you have to make sure that you give customers a great experience, and then they'll keep coming back for more.

Myth 5: We dictate prices

This is what some companies say to me, but it's wrong. Actually customers dictate prices and they will buy or not, depending on what they really feel the value is in what they're going to purchase. So their propensity to pay rests on more than just price, and more than just quality. It's when they feel they have value for money. It's not just the price-quality relationship. It includes other aspects of value, the intangible aspects, such as what do people think about your brand? What do people feel about your brand? These intangible feelings, if positive, are what really create value and give you the ability to deliver products at premium prices. A strong brand creates the intangible positive emotional connections in peoples' minds, that enables premium price, and financial intangible asset value.

Myth 6: Marketing drives branding

This is what most academics say – actually academics are light years behind the practical world. In the real world it's the other way around. Branding drives marketing. It also drives business vision and direction for many of the world's companies. Having worked with great brands over three decades I know that brand drives marketing, and there will be a fundamental change you have to make in your business if you're working the other way around. So marketing is really the execution or implementation of a brand strategy.

This is the new brand-business paradigm shift: businesses do not drive brands anymore – brands drive businesses. I've worked with some of the top brands around the world and I know this to be true. With a powerful brand you can take your business anywhere, into any industry, sector or any part of the world. You can use your brand to drive your business and increase your effectiveness, profitability and market share. Fantastic! Brands deliver for consumers and brand owners, but what actually is a brand?

What is a brand?

There are many misconceptions about what a brand is and I have discussed some of the myths surrounding branding earlier in this chapter. I would like to clarify my views on this before I propose a simple but powerful definition for use based on over 30 years of experience working with some of the world's top brands.

I think it is useful to start by saying what a brand is not. Firstly, some people, including many CEOs I have talked with, see a brand as a name, a logo, and/ or a slogan. These are useful elements of a brand but do not make up a brand. Names are naturally required but a name without an identity is not very useful. Logos are useful, because they bring to people's minds various associations to do with the brand, business, products etc. Nike's swoosh sign is very famous, as is the Apple logo, but again they do not really make up the totality of a brand; they are clever communications devices that stimulate mental associations. I know several companies that change logos completely and at great expense in the hope that this will positively affect the fortunes of the business, all to no avail as the customer experience doesn't change. And slogans are often used on a fairly long-term basis to communicate one or more key messages or calls to action about the brand – 'Because you're worth it' from L'Oreal and 'Just do it' from Nike, for example.

A second main area of misconception is that brands are seen as the product of advertising, promotion and public relations. Again, this is not quite accurate as although these activities do help communicate with consumers, that is all they do – communicate tactically. And they all depend on what the strategy of the brand is. Without a clear strategy to guide messaging, it is likely to be inconsistent and possibly damaging to brand image. Nor are they likely to produce business results. I have recently been in discussions with a company in China that spent over US$8 million on advertising and promotion in its last financial year only to see no upward movement in sales at all. The CEO was not happy at all and told me that the money was "wasted" and he has since stopped all advertising and promotion until a brand strategy has been built. In the absence of a brand strategy, communications were muddled and had not projected any sense of differentiation for the brand from its competitors. Communications activities are thus tactical and not strategic.

Brand management begins with brand strategy

When first joining Nissan, incoming chief operating officer Carlos Ghosn once said, "One of the biggest surprises is that Nissan didn't care about its brand. There is nobody really responsible for the strategy of the brand" (quoted in *Business Week*, October 1999). To my mind, this is one of the most common mistakes made by companies that want to have a strong brand, but that don't make the grade: *they don't have a brand strategy.* Without a brand strategy, brand management becomes very difficult, if not impossible. Strategy gives focus and direction to brand management, and provides the platform that enables brand managers to gain consistency in all their brand-related activities.

But we all know that strategy starts with the business. And for too long, companies have refined the art of inside-out thinking – designing and developing products they believe the market wants. The truth is that the most brilliant strategies come from deep consumer insight – really getting inside the minds of the consumers that you hope will build your brand (that is, outside-in thinking). It is this continual search for outside-in thinking that can lead to unusual but real insights into how people perceive things, and what 'hot buttons' will switch them on to your brand.

If we use consumer insight, the business of the brand might be different from the business of the organization; so, before we consider the key elements of brands, let's think about the *business of brands*. It's quite easy – all you have to do is ask yourself one important question: "What business is my brand in?" Consider the following examples.

What business is your brand in?

Charles Revson, of Revlon Cosmetics, when asked what business Revlon was in, famously replied, "We are not in the business of selling cosmetics; we are in the business of selling hope." He clearly saw that to think of his business as just cosmetics would lead to non-differentiation. By saying this, he was expressing the business of the brand. Cosmetics manufacturing/selling is clearly what the business *does*, but the brand also *gives hope* to those who want to be more attractive and beautiful, perhaps like the Revlon Girl of the Year. This real consumer insight led to a great positioning and, ultimately, global success.

Whiskey (whisky if you are Scottish) is another such 'commodity', but when Johnny Walker Black Label was researched by watching consumers drink it, the brand changed its business strategy. Videos of people drinking with others on different occasions led to a paradigm shift in thinking. After an 18-month boardroom 'discussion', it was decided that the company was in the business not of manufacturing and selling high-quality liquor, but of marketing fashion accessories. The consumer insight was seeing people 'wear' their drinks as they would a watch, bracelet, or other fashion accessory.

Similarly, chef Simon Rimmer pointed out on television (*BBC Breakfast*, 14 November, 2016) that people buying takeaway coffees wear their preferred brands such as Costa, Starbucks, and Café Nero as fashion accessories. We can also take the view that Nike isn't in the business of marketing sports shoes and accessories; the brand says it wants to help athletes and ordinary people get the best out of themselves. Nike stands for winning, an attribute strongly supported by endeavor, courage and empowerment.

Red Bull is another brand that has built its business on a simple product, and has inspired people with its 'gives you wings' message. It has moved from manufacturing its main drink to developing high octane sports such Formula One, the Red Bull Air Race, freestyle motocross, Red Bull Cliff Diving and so on. It not only promotes some of these events, it owns them and organizes them and has a successful media division. Red Bull has over 45 million followers on Facebook and the Red Bulletin sells 4.5 million or more copies monthly. The Red Bull Media House is a profitable business in its own right. So, in essence, the business and the brand are indistinguishable and the brand is the business. Red Bull has cleverly targeted a niche market and has a huge understanding of what makes this segment tick. It is not about energy drinks, it's about thrills, entertainment, vicarious living and performance under extreme conditions. In 2016 over 6 billion cans of Red Bull were sold in 171 countries.

I was once engaged in discussions with a CEO who also had a paradigm shift in thinking. His company made products that "make things shine", such as car polish, shoe-care products, and so on. After attending a brand strategy program he decided that his brand was in the "feelings" business, because the end result of using his brands is that consumers feel good about themselves and their image, whether it be through what they wear or what they drive. This paradigm shift in thinking has impacted greatly on the company and taken it into previously unsought and undiscovered areas.

The role of consumer insight

The examples referred to above indicate that brands are now driving business strategy, but *only* when they reach deeply into the psychological world of consumer insight. The really 'hot buttons' that consumer insights unveil are emotional, not rational, and lead to excellent brand performance.

It is the brand strategist or manager's responsibility to work to discover these insights, which are sometimes far from obvious. However, as it is an inescapable fact that consumers really create brand power, brand owners must discover the underlying motives that exist in their minds that will trigger favorable attitudes and compulsive desires toward their brands.

Living with the consumer

In the never-ending search for consumer insights that may give a paradigm shift in thinking for brands and businesses, some companies are now hiring research crews to live for a few days with 'prototype' consumers, in order to learn how they think and behave in their everyday lives. (Bedroom and bathroom scenes are usually, but not always, excluded!) Traditional research – both quantitative and qualitative – has the drawback of relying on what consumers *say*, which is sometimes different from what they actually *do* in real life. What brand management has to do is find out how to press the 'hot buttons' that 'turn on' consumers, and this means gaining a full understanding of what motivates them in real-life situations.

Companies trying to create consumer brands are waking up to the fact that the place to start understanding consumer behavior is in the home – where people's real lives are lived in the context of wide-ranging emotions, the sometimes-conflicting demands of different relationships, and relaxed, rather than ideal, personal standards – as opposed to the office or a research room. For example, when Procter & Gamble filmed housewives going about their daily routines, the company noticed that mothers were usually multitasking. One mother was seen feeding her baby while preparing a meal and snatching glances at the television. In natural scenarios such as this, companies can see what programs and advertisements attract homemakers, and what products they use or could use. A bank in the United States has undertaken similar research to discover the process by which families at various stages of their life cycles discuss and make major financial decisions. Unilever has sent staff out into rural villages in underdeveloped areas to live with the villagers and learn more about their way of life, in order to help with brand relationships and product development (see Case Study 2).

Case Study 2: Unilever Malaysia

Romancing the consumer

One of Unilever's "Path to Growth" strategic agendas implemented over five years from 1999–2004 was "reconnecting with the consumer", with the aim of:

- focusing everyone in the company on the consumer;

- turning knowledge gained about the consumer into creative insight; and

- anticipating and responding to consumer change.

According to Unilever, the only way to achieve this is by:

- deepening its knowledge of consumers' habits and attitudes;

- having a culture of "getting close" to the consumer; and

- having the skills to tap insights into the consumer and to turn them into business opportunities.

Unilever used this strategic thrust as a global initiative, but this case shows how it has been done in this operating company in Malaysia.

Preparations for its "Romancing the Consumer" program involved the following:

- Managers of Unilever Malaysia visited 50 homes and held face-to-face interviews bi-monthly to gain consumer insights.

- Twenty staff brought 120 consumers to the factory quarterly for face-to-face understanding dialogue.

- All staff were given cross-category training so that not only could inter-brand communications be enhanced, but also staff could answer questions about any brands asked of them by consumers.

- A specific project – Project Rambo – was devised. The whole company was closed for one day, and every employee – old and young, from the tea lady to the chairman – went out to do merchandising of products in shops to ensure that the visibility of Unilever products at retail customers' premises was first class, and to get retail feedback.

Project Rambo saw high energy and a high commitment by Unilever Malaysia's entire workforce to work with trade partners to enhance product displays to better attract shoppers' attention. The experience even inspired Unilever's employees to tidy up merchandising in stores where they usually shop!

The Rural Marketing Program was another initiative aligned with reconnecting with the consumer, but primarily with those in the rural market. The idea of this program when it was conceived was to raise the awareness of Unilever products in the rural areas of the country by having rural-relevant activities, and at the same time putting products on sale. The program was also aimed at providing Unilever Malaysia with the opportunity to engage rural consumers with Unilever brands and people. The first event was a tremendous success, and similar events followed over subsequent years in different parts of the country.

Additional activities included marketing staff staying in villagers' homes for two days to gain a detailed insight into the usage and buying patterns of household, personal care, and food products. All such events were planned well in advance and started with a meeting with the head of the village and his committee. The team was briefed on the objectives of the event and the type of activities to be organized. These often included traditional games to enable participation by all age groups. The local villagers took charge of these activities, and Unilever staff organized prizes and appearances by special guests. Each of the events attracted between 3,000 and 6,500 people.

The company's "Romancing the Consumer" program proved successful in developing a culture of gaining consumer insights and using them to drive its business.

Moen Inc., a maker of plumbing equipment, actually videotaped American women in the shower (naturally, with their permission), and discovered that they tended to hold on to the shower unit heating control with one hand while shaving their legs with the other. This safety risk hadn't previously been apparent, and this led Moen to redesign its shower unit and prevent accidental burns.

Research of this kind underlines that brand managers must do their homework country by country, as cultural nuances determine consumer behavior. For instance, in the United States and in Mediterranean countries the kitchen is the central part of a family's home life, where they congregate and talk about their day; whereas in China, say, the kitchen is usually a small area designated just for cooking, and the family gather in the hall or living room to spend time together.

Intel employs anthropologists and ethnographers – people who study human behavior and culture – to gain insights into what consumers really want, and why they like to buy. The insights gained from studying 'the minutiae of daily life' help in making technology much more friendly and fun for consumers. Again, this involves making visits to people's homes, and accompanying them on shopping trips and other excursions away from the home. Intel, like many other companies, has come to see that creating products, and then trying to persuade consumers to buy them, isn't enough; if companies really want to understand what makes consumers tick, they must look closely at their behaviors.

For instance, the design of products such as the Sound Morpher and the QX3 Computer Microscope for children took into account the behavior of eight-to 14-year-olds, who tend to be a bit rough with the things they use and are very hands-on. The QX3, for example, although functioning when connected to a personal computer, was designed to be detachable from its stand so that children could share the experience with their friends. The Intel Play QX3 Computer Microscope has been further developed as the result of a creative partnership between computer chip giant and innovative toy designer Mattel as an electronic video toy designed to capture market share in science education using optics, digital imaging, and the latest computer technology.[4]

From a cultural perspective, Intel found that in Asia people are less individualistic and tend to share a lot more than people in the West do. So the company has moved into developing devices that will facilitate the sharing of technology. As Intel penetrates healthcare and other markets with its products, it is employing more scientists, doctors, and healthcare workers in order to understand more about real customer needs.

Consumer insight is the gateway to understanding people's rational and emotional behaviors, and there is no doubt that brand strategies that are built on emotion and the realism of everyday life have a better chance of success than those that are not.

Insight, innovation and category development – Athleisure

One enormous benefit of getting close to customers and identifying latent needs is that this can lead not only to profitable innovation but the initiation and growth of new categories. Athleisure is a prime example and one of the biggest trends in the fashion and retail world. Athleisure is athletic apparel that can be worn in both athletic and non-athletic situations. The latent need discovered was that consumers in general are becoming more interested in fitness, look at sport as part of their lifestyle, and want functional but comfortable clothing they can wear even in professional settings. For women, the largest target segment, one insight is that they want to show that they work out both in and outside of the gym.

Brands that have quickly entered this new category and established first or early mover status are Nike, Reebok and Lululemon. The latter has a more focused product strategy. For example, in changing from selling pants by sizes to segments such as "hugged, naked, relaxed, tight and held in", each serve a different purpose in the customer's life. Antonia Iamartino, design director of future concepts for the company said, "What it gives to our guest is ultimately choice and the ability to choose a way that they want to feel in a given activity."

As Lululemon is a small player compared to the sports giants such as Nike, Adidas and Reebok, it has to adopt a more niche strategy. Nike is building a much wider portfolio of athleisure products aimed at women, including comfortable fashionable and sporty clothes and footwear, geared up to different climatic seasons. Using its tremendous technological knowledge, it is combining polyester, spandex and other materials through innovative production techniques to create many apparel items that generate both form and function. Few know about the technologies involved but one example is Nike's 'AeroReact' that detects when the wearer is about to start sweating and loosens itself just before that happens. Remarkable. Nike uses digital communications as well as traditional methods and has 70 million women connected to its online community. Research agencies projected huge sales increases for 2017 and beyond in this category, possibly up by 40% to US$7 billion in 2017.

Reebok (now a subsidiary of Adidas), lost in the sports brand wilderness for so long, is trying to transform itself into a fitness training brand in order to regain some differentiation and positioning. According to Corinna Werkle, head of design and apparel excellence, "Athleisure is one of the big stories … Performance gear becomes part of your day to day. Even if somebody is not a high-performing athlete, the look fits into their casual wardrobe." And Nike women's training vice president of global design, Julie Igarashi said, although the brand is making apparel for sponsored athletes it's also designing for the non-professional athlete who is increasingly interested in wearing what their idols are wearing. Athleisure is one large category within the sports apparel industry. As it continues to grow we will see different segments within this category appear as the trend toward mass customization and individualization expands.[5]

Market segmentation

An essential technique for successful consumer insight is market segmentation. Consumers all over the world, while gravitating toward globally similar products, increasingly want them to be tailored to suit their various preferences and tastes. More and more importance is now attached to the understanding of different customers that exist in a particular market, allowing for a customer-driven as opposed to a product-driven approach.

Segmentation is the process whereby markets are analyzed into groups of customers who have similar needs and wants in common. This is fundamentally important because these similarities make it easier to predict buying behavior.

A good way of gaining consumer insight and identifying a new market segment is to study cultural characteristics. Nestlé's power brand KitKat drew on its knowledge of the Japanese consumer and through KitKat Japan introduced 300 exotic products. These were KitKat bars with flavors such as green tea (loved by the Japanese), yam, wasabi, passion fruit, melon and sake rice wine. By appealing to the tastes and cultural characteristics of the Japanese consumer a whole new market was created and the category extended. A master stroke by Nestlé was to recognize name relevance, as 'Kitto Katzu' means 'sure win' or 'you will surely win' in Japanese. For a full article on this huge innovation and the many unique promotional ways (such as postal KitKat bars for young people taking examinations) KitKat used to win over consumers, see www.telegraph.co.uk/food-and-drink/features/how-the-kitkat-became-a-phenomenon-in-japan.

Benefits of market segmentation

Helps select target markets

Within large groups of consumers, segmentation studies can help a business select the more attractive parts of the market. For example, a category may be enjoying an annual growth rate of 5%, but one segment within that category could be growing at 8% while another is growing at only 3%. Also, some segments may be more profitable than others, in terms of their propensity to pay or ease of serving them. Companies can also choose the segments that most closely resemble their brand identity or personality, or indeed help them shape or build their brand identity and personality to match that of the segment profile.

Gives companies focus

This is the laser-missile as opposed to the blanket-bomb approach. When the target market is narrowed down it becomes easier to penetrate with specific objectives and plans, and easier to tailor product offerings.

Helps smaller companies find niche markets

Segmentation helps smaller companies locate niche markets within a category. Once found, niche markets are easier to defend against powerful competitors and larger rivals cannot be all things to all people and satisfy the needs and wants of everyone. Segmentation helps small businesses to find the gaps worth exploiting. If a company can serve a niche market well, it has a greater chance of establishing and maintaining brand loyalty.

Facilitates efficient and effective brand positioning

Segmentation facilitates more efficient and effective brand positioning. By understanding a segment well, information such as lifestyle data can increase the effectiveness and lower the cost of advertising and promotions, thus avoiding wastage of resources. This also means the right messages get to the right people via the right medium.

Helps marketing to be tailored to specific groups

For brand development purposes, market segmentation allows companies to offer their brands to more than one customer group, depending on their needs and wants. This understanding of various segments in a category can provide the rationale for line and brand extensions, and sustainable, profitable growth.

Segmentation methods

There are many ways in which market segmentation can be accomplished, some of which require relatively simple research processes while others require more complex methodologies. The more commonly used approaches include demographic, geographic, geodemographic, corporate, socio-cultural, price-sensitivity, benefits, user-behavior, family life cycle and psychographic segmentation.

Psychographics is the most interesting and possibly the most exciting segmentation technique. It covers many factors including activities, interests, opinions, attitudes, values and lifestyles. Psychographics helps in the understanding why people behave the way they do and, therefore, in understanding the markets, which are made up of people. The advantages are:

- It can reveal new markets, whereas other methods such as demographics deal with existing markets.

- As it uncovers consumer thinking and motivations that govern behavioral dynamics it can explain why various markets do exist.

- It explains consumer behavior, including perceptions, needs, wants, motivations, preferences, brand awareness, trust and loyalty.

- It greatly assists in the creation of accurate positioning strategies, leading to focused and effective communications.

- It can facilitate brand personality creation and development.

- It can help position new brands and re-position old ones.

- It can reveal strategic positioning opportunities and the development of strategic competitive advantages.

- It can discover better ways for brand distribution.

The BMW case below shows how psychographic segmentation was used alongside other data in Asian markets.

Case Study 3: BMW in Asia: Psychographic segmentation and brand personality

The Asian car market is crowded with many brands, of which only a few can be regarded as global power brands. One such brand is undoubtedly BMW. We have discussed the fact that the value of a brand is built largely through the relationships and associations people have with them. Consumers can become highly attached to brands and use these as extensions of their own personalities.

One important technique in brand building then, is to understand the personality of the brand's target audience – their self-esteem, hopes and aspirations, motivations and behavior – and then build a personality for the brand that matches that of the targeted brand segment. This was a successful approach used by BMW penetrating the market and competing with Mercedes Benz, a brand that had high market share, used for self-expression and projection of status and prestige. Mercedes Benz was the car to buy when you had 'made it'. BMW looked at its three major ranges of products – the 3, 5 and 7 series cars – and gathered psychographic and other data on brand users.

The least expensive range was the BMW 3 series, and summary research said that drivers of this model were characterized as:

- Young professionals
- High-earnings potential
- Active lifestyles
- Independent thinkers, not influenced by peer pressure
- Desired a brand that reflects their own performance

In creating the brand personality of the 3 series based on buyer characteristics, BMW defined it as:

- Youthful
- Dynamic
- Fun
- Sporty

The second market segment, at which the 5 series was aimed, was found to have the following characteristics:

- Over 30 years old
- Middle managers and above
- People who relish challenges
- Opinion formers among their peers
- People looking for a brand that delivers on performance and driving experience, together with the design features of a luxury car

The brand personality focused on the attributes of:

- Innovative
- Professional
- Individualistic

The BMW 7 series segment buyer was seen as:

- Senior manager or equivalent
- Someone who had been successful in their chosen profession
- Independent
- Looking for a car brand that symbolizes their success, but not one commonly driven by their peers; a sophisticated luxury car that has technological superiority and is a pleasure to drive.

The brand personality focused appropriately on a person who values:

- Superiority
- Exclusivity
- Autonomy

As an example of what happened consequently, having established the data and the brand personalities, BMW then carried out more research into the driving population and discovered a large group of drivers who shared the same characteristics as drivers of the 3 series but who were driving Japanese cars. They did not buy BMW as monthly payment costs were too high, so an innovative finance scheme that increased payments over time was brought in that did not devalue the brand through a down market promotion. At the same time a creative proposition was communicated to this segment of' 'Don't Dream, Drive'. The whole value proposition was very successful in attracting new customers without compromising the aspirational nature of the BMW brand. In the Singapore market alone, more cars were sold in the three-week promotional period than the previous three-quarters of annual sales.

More recently, Hugo Boss has realigned its portfolio to make things clearer for the customer, based on psychographics, now using two brands – Hugo and Boss – on the group website. This is explained as follows:

"With its BOSS brand, the Company is reaching out to status-oriented, rationally-minded customers who wish to dress in a classic yet modern and high-quality style. The BOSS customer has exacting standards when it comes to quality and fit, and attaches great importance to an advantageous value-for-money proposition. The shopping experience must also meet the highest standards, particularly with regard to personal services. BOSS offers this customer confident businesswear and refined casualwear collections in the upper premium segment, characterized by the highest quality, sharp cuts and clear designs. BOSS invests in the value proposition of its products, particularly in the entry-level price range. The BOSS brand values are, Masculinity/Femininity, Sexiness, Success, Style and Precision".

"In contrast to BOSS, HUGO is targeted at customers who are significantly more fashion-conscious and who consider their style of dress to be an important element in expressing their personality. The HUGO customer is open-minded, individual and spontaneous, and likes to shop, frequently doing so via online and mobile channels. HUGO offers this broad and generally younger customer base fashionable business and casualwear collections that are distinguished by their progressive designs and clear fashion statement. HUGO will remain anchored in the premium segment of the market. With its focus on contemporary fashion, the brand now stands apart from BOSS more clearly in terms of its fashion statement and pricing. The brand values for HUGO are, Globally engaged, Always curious and Authentically expressive".[6]

More discussion of how brand personalities are built and why they are so important will be covered in Chapter 5.

The central message then, is that when building strong brands companies must use outside-in and not inside-out thinking. As a final example, I was once commissioned to help a Japanese-owned company to develop its Asia-Pacific business by strengthening its existing and future brand portfolio. Early on in the discovery phase when I sought to understand the business and its brands I found that the structure of the organization was wrongly set up for consumer understanding and relationship-building. Branding and marketing functions reported to new product development, which meant that new products were designed and developed without proper data on consumer insight. New products were, in fact, given to branding and marketing to 'sell'. The outcome of this was that many new products failed as they were not in line with the real needs and wants of consumers. It took two years of discussion with the head office in Japan to change the structure so that new product development reported to branding and marketing, the people who were close to the customer and understood what products they really desired. That turning point positively impacted on the revenues and profits of the company.

In Chapter 7 you will read about how Procter & Gamble uses its consumer insights and understanding in different markets to localize its communications for global brands such as Pampers and Always, and successfully appeals to the cultural norms that drive people's innermost emotions and aspirations. Meanwhile, in the following section, you will see how powerful the world of emotion can be in building and managing strong brands.

Building a brand strategy – four key steps

There are four key steps involved in creating a brand strategy – brand architecture, brand vision, brand personality, and brand positioning. These will be introduced briefly later in this chapter and then discussed in detail in subsequent chapters.

Alignment of corporate and brand strategy

Before we move on to look at the key steps in the building of an emotionally-driven brand strategy it is worthwhile to emphasize that many businesses I come into contact with focus hard on building the corporate strategy but neglect to build a brand strategy to complement it. Figure 3.1 illustrates the importance of parallel efforts, but it is usually the left-hand pillar that receives most of the attention. It is traditionally accepted that businesses must create corporate visions and missions, linked to strategic and financial objectives with some corporate values thrown in. This is the 'hard' side of how businesses work focusing on numbers and goals, and there is nothing wrong with this approach.

However, that does not necessarily mean that a strong brand will result as this requires the development of 'soft power'. Building up the right-hand pillar means that any brand strategy has to be built with relevance to both the business and its customers. Brand visions are different to corporate visions and brand personality is different to a set of corporate values, while brand positioning links customer needs and wants with strategic competitive advantages that combine a mixture of rational and emotional benefits.

While many businesses neglect the brand side, the really great companies are those that do both, like BASF, that says, "We rely on a strong brand in order to expand our position as the world's leading chemical company. Our brand is derived from our strategy and our corporate purpose … as well as our strategic principles and values." I will occasionally quote this business-to-business company as it is a wonderful example of the determination to not just build a brand strategy but manage it well.[7]

The two pillars of corporate and brand strategy are underpinned by the brand architecture, more of which will be said in the next chapter.

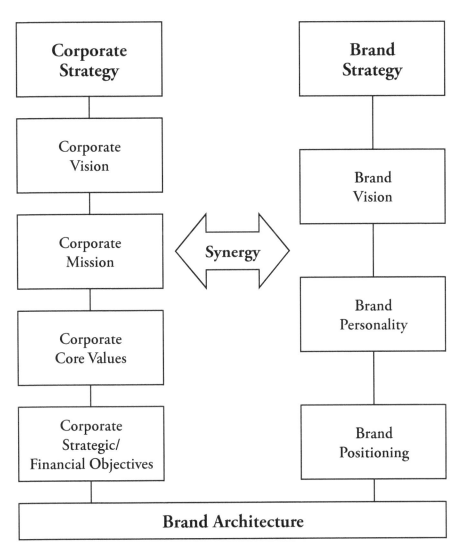

Figure 3.1: Alignment of corporate strategy and brand strategy

Overview of the four key steps in building a brand strategy

Having established the crucial importance of consumer insight and emotion in brand building we now turn to the four key steps that are necessary to build a powerful brand. In Figure 3.2 below we see the four steps in diagrammatic form.

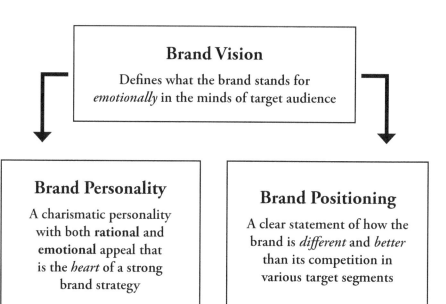

Figure 3.2: Building a powerful brand strategy – four key steps

In Chapter 4, we will examine the options available to businesses in clarifying exactly what kind of brand they are trying to build. Decisions of this nature come under the heading of brand architecture. Should an organization build a corporate brand, a product brand, or some combination of the two? This chapter will also discuss the implications of architecture choices for future growth, including line and brand extensions. It should be noted that brand architecture decisions should really be taken before the vison, personality and positioning items are built, as otherwise it is difficult to know what exactly the focus for the brand-building process is. In other words, we have to know exactly what kind of brand we are building.

In Chapter 5 we will look at the next two steps involved in the process by studying the concept of brand vision and brand personality. These steps involve identifying the emotional drive for the brand and humanizing it to assist in communicating with and attracting customers, in addition to driving employee behavior. In Chapter 6 we will review the final part of the strategy-building process, which is brand positioning. Brand positioning essentially asks why your brand is different and better than competitive brands for different stakeholders or customer groups, bearing in mind their needs and wants and the relevant rational and emotional benefits they will receive.

Summary

For brand managers in the 21st century, there are many complex tasks to undertake, but achieving brand trust, loyalty and lifetime relationships with consumers are the true goals, because only when these are achieved will the brand last and grow in value.

Brands are at their most powerful when they are linked to business aims and lead business direction, and when they bind themselves to consumers through the generation of strong emotional associations and relationships.

The power of emotion has been present since life began – it is the great motivator and the prime driver of the human spirit. Although rational attributes may attract, the natural power of emotions sells. Simply put, strong and sustainable brands cannot be built without the use of emotional strategies.

Understanding the consumer is absolutely critical in order for strong brand building to take place. Outside-in and not inside-out thinking has to prevail, and market research can help greatly in achieving pinpoint accuracy and in building the emotional associations with consumers.

Before I move on to take an in-depth look at how brand strategies are built in Chapter 5, we have to deal firstly with questions associated with what we want to brand. This is covered in the next chapter, on the subject of brand architecture.

PART 3

Building a Powerful Brand Strategy

CHAPTER 4

Brand Architecture and Portfolio Management

The his chapter is split into two sections. The first section looks at the concept of brand architecture: what it means, what options are open to organizations, and the advantages and disadvantages of these options. Section two looks at some decisions that sometimes need to be made in managing the brand portfolio, including extending brands, deleting brands, and revitalizing brands. I have decided to include these all in one chapter as they are all connected to the same issue – what we are trying to brand and what decisions do we have to make regarding the brands we have to manage.

Section one: brand architecture

Brand architecture is an extremely complex subject, where few rules apply, but no book on brand strategy and management would be complete without discussion of it. This chapter summarizes the basic choices and arguments for different types of brand architecture.

Brand architecture is a little like an organizational chart for brands; a family tree showing who relates to whom and how. It is concerned with how sub-brands fit in with master brands, and whether or not they should at all. The challenge for organizations grappling with decisions in this space is that there are no fixed rules and a variety of options, but fundamentally the main decision is to answer the question, does your organization want to be a 'branded house' or a 'house of brands'?

A 'branded house' is where the organization decides that it wants to focus on the master brand – the name of the organization – and give less focus to the sub-brands or product brands that lie within its control. Typical of brands that fall into this category are BMW, Virgin, Microsoft, IBM and others. A 'house of brands' is the reverse of this, where the focus falls on the sub-brands or product brands and the master brand gets much less of the spotlight. History tells us that corporations such as Procter & Gamble and Unilever are examples of those companies that have successfully built a house of brands, with product brands such as Pampers, Dove, Sunsilk, Axe and many others generating revenues of US$1 billion or more.

While these are polar opposites of each other, there are an increasing number of ways in which master brands and sub-brands or product brands can be linked together. We can look at the different levels of brand architecture in the following way.

Levels of brand architecture

The main levels of brand architecture can be identified as:

- true corporate branding;
- corporate branding with product descriptors;
- corporate and product shared branding;
- endorsed branding;
- product branding; and
- line branding.

Each level represents different degrees of differentiation and link to origin. I will briefly explain the differences between them and discuss the main advantages and disadvantages of each.

True corporate branding

Corporate branding tends to be the dominant form of brand architecture, with or without links to products. The companies who I tend to describe as the 'true' corporate branders are those that believe at all costs that they must project the name of the corporate master brand and link products to it as appropriate. This is because they say that at the end of the day the true value of the brand lies in the branded business. Examples of these are Virgin, BMW and others mentioned under the 'branded house' explanation above.

Advantages

- When the company adds its name to a product brand there is added value of trust and shared synergies. New products are easier to introduce into existing markets.

- Companies achieve economies of scale across communications platforms.

- Every product linked to the corporate brand contributes to overall corporate brand awareness, equity and value.

- Entering new markets becomes easier with new products as the parent brand is well known, accepted and trusted.

- Multiple line or brand extensions are possible.

Disadvantages

- A poor corporate brand image may well hinder new product introductions.

- Extending the corporate brand into too many categories may weaken brand image.

- Extensions via new products and brands may not be accepted by the consumer.

Corporate branding with product descriptors

This is where one single master brand name, the company name, covers all products. This level or type of architecture is often the route taken by companies that believe the master (corporate) brand is all-important. The products don't have names, but tend to have other descriptors, either functional (HP Color Laser Jet printers) or alpha-numeric (Mercedes AMG-C 63 S).

Advantages

- The corporate master brand adds power to the product brands, demonstrating heritage and encouraging trust.

- There are huge savings in advertising and promotion as opposed to launching new products without a master brand attached.

- There are economies of scale across all product communications platforms.

- Every product contributes to overall brand awareness, image, equity, and value of the master brand.

- It becomes easier to enter new markets.

- Multiple extensions are possible, but only with good new products.

- Horizontal extensions are easier than vertical ones.

Disadvantages

- A poor corporate brand image hinders new brand introductions and existing brand success.

- An unsuccessful new product will reflect badly on the corporate brand image.

- Extensions are easier, but are not always accepted by the public.

- The more categories the brand goes into, the weaker the overall image may become.

Corporate and product shared branding

This strategy is another highly favored corporate-linked approach where the products, or sub-brands, are named (for instance, Virgin Atlantic and Microsoft Windows). The product and parent brand share the spotlight, but the corporate brand name is usually shown in front of the product brand. In this way, there is full leverage of both brands.

Advantages

- It provides a tight and consistent branding system.

- Parental support adds trust and confidence.

- The product can ride on parental core values and image.

- Less expensive to launch than the above brand strategies.

- Products add to parental brand value.

Disadvantages

- Restrained by the core brand of the parent, and what it is known for.

- Allows for less freedom than the endorsement strategy (see below).

- Failure can damage reputation across the major corporate activity and devalue the corporate brand.

Endorsed branding

Here the difference from shared branding is the fact that the parent brand takes only an endorsement role – for instance, Band Aid (where the parent company name Johnson & Johnson appears only in a lower corner of the packaging).

Advantages

- More freedom to extend into many categories.

- Parent acts as a guarantee of quality and legitimacy.

- Products add to parental value.

- Failure doesn't transfer across many categories.

- Least expensive way of giving branding support.

Disadvantages

- Bad corporate reputation and performance can affect the product brand.

The above options represent a continuum from which a company can choose its architecture. However, there is a trend nowadays to favor the corporate end of the spectrum.

Product branding

This is where a brand name and exclusive position are allocated to one product. Companies adopting this approach give complete autonomy to every brand, and each brand stands or falls on its own merits. There is no apparent connection between the brand and other brands. For instance, Procter & Gamble has used this approach extensively with products such as Ariel and Dash in the household detergent market. However, it should be noted that this is now changing as nearly all major corporations are linking their names to product brands, however powerful the product brands might be in their own right. This trend is further explained below.

Advantages

- They can occupy precise positions and be aimed at precise target audiences.

- As a result, multiple brands from one or two companies can populate and monopolize a whole category.

- They allow for risk, as failure doesn't damage the parent.

- Retail shelf space may be easier to get, as the brand stands on its own.

- One brand name per product helps customers perceive difference.

Disadvantages

- They are costly, as each requires its own advertising and promotion (A&P) budget.

- They need individual brand management, which is again costly.

- There is little room for extension, which is only achieved by product renewal and innovation. (For instance, Tide has had over 70 changes to product, design, and other aspects of the brand.)

Line branding

Line brands usually start with one basic product under one name, but often this is extended to offer complementary products under the same name, as is the case with Vidal Sassoon shampoos, rinses, hair salons, and so on. Dove not only has soap, but now also has facial wipes, body washes, anti-aging cleansers, deodorants, and more. The original brand name, applied to all complementary products, thus assumes the role of a master brand although it may not be the company. An alternative name I have heard given to this option is product range branding.

Advantages

- The brand can be extended to some extent. However, this extent is dependent on whether consumers give the brand permission to move into other categories. With related categories this is less of an issue.

- Complementary extensions can reinforce and strengthen the brand image.

- Some marketing costs can be shared across products.

Disadvantages

- Lines are limited to the discrete positioning and core idea.

- Extensions into unrelated categories, away from the central brand proposition or idea, are difficult.

The trend toward corporate branding

There is a definite trend toward the company being involved in the branding process, whether through shared and endorsement branding, or other means. Even the masters of product branding, Procter & Gamble, now has a worldwide strategy to leverage the corporate brand name by attaching it to some of its product brands as a source reference.

To sum up, there are several reasons for the company brand name to appear in one form or another:

- For every product, you get a double message underlining the product and the company.

- The core values of the company wrap around the product, resulting in consumer confidence.

- There is less confusion for consumers, as they know the source of the product.

- There are more possibilities for brand extensions.

- There are many synergies and cost savings in A&P.

- The financial value of the company brand is enhanced, corporate brands being strategic business assets in their own right.

- Corporate branding increases overall image power and reputation.

- And as the late Akio Morita, founder of Sony, said, "I have always believed that the company name is the life of an enterprise. It carries responsibility and guarantees the quality of the product."

Portfolio management and sub-brands

As discussed above, the decision as to whether to have different brands requiring different branding strategies varies by company, and there are no hard-and-fast rules about what to do. One point to note is that not all line or brand extensions will be successful or profitable and, although these are tempting moves to make, they can be a drain on resources. Some brand managers actually calculate the value of extension brands and track that value, putting more resource behind those brands that are increasing in value (the valuation of brands is a topic that is covered in detail in the last chapter of this book).

The main reason for holding many brands is that no one brand can cover every market, or even every sector of a single market. Some companies attempt to do this by using saturation strategies, such as Seiko with its global range of over 2,000 watches under the Seiko, Lorus, and Pulsar brands. Others, such as Mars, hold only a few 'power' brands such as Snickers and Twix that are advertised strongly and produced efficiently in volume.

Some companies adopt corporate and product brand strategies. For example, Cadbury uses the corporate brand for chocolate bars and product branding for sweets. Google is a corporate master brand but a sub-brand of Alphabet. Google uses corporate branding with product descriptors (e.g. Google Maps), and endorsed branding (Gmail by Google), but also allows stand-alone brands such as YouTube, which it owns. When it acquired YouTube it decided not to attach the Google name to it in any form, probably because YouTube is itself a very strong brand and it did not want to disturb its brand equity or consumer base, and possibly for reasons of data privacy, although this latter point is merely speculation.

Perhaps one of the most successful companies to adopt mainly a shared-brand approach is Nestlé. Nestlé is a giant among brands. It has 328,000 employees in 418 factories making 2,000 brands in 86 countries, and produces some spectacular product brands that it links to its corporate brand. A Nestlé Walnut Whip is consumed every two seconds, and 1.9 billion Milkybar Buttons are sold each year. KitKat is a powerful brand in its own right but wears the parental endorsement right next to its name. Enough 'two finger' KitKat bars are sold every year to circle the world 1.5 times, and the corporate brand name gets leveraged with every sale!

By contrast, Toyota, a brand that is well established in most price sectors of the car market, found that the parental image wouldn't transfer to the luxury car segment and so it had to create a stand-alone brand, Lexus. This was a good move that is in danger of backfiring, so to speak, as the Lexus brand moves down into lower price ranges and opens up the dual possibilities of cannibalization of Toyota brands and a dilution of the Lexus brand. For many years now, Lexus has no longer occupied top position in the luxury car segment in the US despite increases in sales year on year. In 2015 BMW claimed top position.

What must be clearly established, whatever is contained in the multi-brand portfolio, is that there is no overlap between brand territories, as this can result in consumer confusion and sub-optimization (cannibalization) of sales. Finally, it isn't unusual to find a company with many brands promoting some to the detriment of others. It is vital that annual brand audits are undertaken, and financial valuations of each brand carried out if possible, to determine which brands are doing well and which are flagging, and why. Shell values each of its brands every year, and then uses this information to decide how to allocate market resources to the various brands.

Sub-brands are often confused with product brands, and tend to be used in industries dealing with fashion, trend-related categories, and fast-moving consumer goods, where different positions are required for different offerings and a single brand cannot cover them all. Versace presents itself under the main brand for its mature customer base, with Versus for the younger segment. Armani does the same with Emporio Armani. Sub-brands don't tend to be used when the main corporate brand can cover all products or services, as is the case with heavy machinery, consumer durables, and computers.

Case Study 4 illustrates how a fast-growing brand in a niche market paid attention to building corporate brand value through a consistent naming architecture across its product and sub-brand portfolio.

Case study 4: Raffles International

Master branding endorsement

In 1996, there was one hotel in the Raffles Group – the famous Raffles Hotel in Singapore. In 2001 there were 38 hotels under Raffles management. The Raffles International brand started in 1989, built around a famous product associated with top-quality service. The word "International" was introduced to add vision to the brand, and now the brand name stands for the promise of product and service excellence. Since then, Raffles has acquired other famous brand names, such as Brown's Hotel in London and Hotel Vier Jahreszeiten in Germany. Many other property acquisitions followed, including the Swissôtel chain.

But despite this rapid niche area growth, there was always a conscious effort to build consistent and meaningful brand architecture. The focus of the business of the Raffles brand is lifestyle, not property. The Raffles International master brand developed a two-tier strategy: the Raffles-branded hotels and resorts targeted affluent leisure and business travelers; while the Swissôtel and Merchant Court hotels aimed to give quality and comfort to the modern business traveler. The challenge for Raffles management was how to keep the brand equity of all the famous brand names in the portfolio, and yet build up the equity of the Raffles International master brand. The link was accomplished by keeping the "Raffles International" name in tag lines on all hotel corporate identity and communications materials.

For example, for the prestigious brand hotel Brown's, the endorsement was "Brown's Hotel, a Raffles International Hotel", while for the Swissôtel and Merchant Court hotels each name was signed off with the tag line, "Managed by Raffles International". On September 30, 2005, Raffles International announced a change in its ownership from Raffles Holdings Limited to Colony Capital, LLC. This change followed the successful completion of the sale by Raffles Holdings of its hotel business to Colony Capital, LLC for an enterprise value of S$1.72 billion. The successful Raffles branding brought huge financial rewards.

Linking visual identity with architecture

Top brands are good at linking their brand architecture well with the brand's visual identity. A case in point is Intel, which uses a shared branding approach. Intel is the corporate master brand, and there are three branded platforms, with all products fitting into one of these platforms. With every product, the parent name "Intel" precedes the product name, and the logo is consistently used on packaging along with the corporate colors.

The issue of concern is not with Intel's visual architecture – it looks very good, and is very consistent with respect to how the shared branding approach is applied. The issue is that, although neatly lined up, consumers have difficulty in understanding the differences between products. For instance, according to Intel's website, the Core family at present (although this is constantly changing) includes: Core Solo, Core 2 Solo, Core Duo, Core 2 Duo, Core 2 Quod, Core 2 Extreme, Core i7, and Core i Extreme Edition. Pentium was supposed to have been phased out but still appears occasionally in the line-up. From a brand management standpoint, there is a lack of clear explanation in the product promotional material.

While consumers are trying to get to grips with what all these product brand names mean to them, Intel has just announced that it will again be changing its branding line-up. Centrino won't remain as a 'platform', where it stood for technologies that included a microprocessor, a separate product category called a chip set, and chips that manage wireless networking. It will remain only as representing wireless networking technology. The brand name 'Core' will be the flagship brand. But brand extensions such as Core 2 Duo will also go. Instead, three performance grades are branded as i3, i5, and i7. Pentium and Celeron will remain. Now, how about that for simplicity?

These changes are supposed to help us, the consumer. Intel spokesperson, Bill Calder, is quoted in the *Wall Street Journal* of June 18, 2009 as saying, "The ... fact is, we have a complex structure with too many platform brands, product names, and we've made things confusing for consumers and IT buyers in the process." Right! Since this time Intel has continued to change brand names and spread confusion.

Co-branding opportunities

Co-branding, sometimes called cross-platform marketing, is increasingly popular as firms look for new ways to reach their target audiences. Credit cards are good examples of co-branding, linking up with all sorts of businesses. The main reason for co-branding is to reach more of the consumers you want who are currently customers of someone else. Another reason is that co-branding enables marketing costs to be shared – an important consideration when a major campaign can cost in excess of US$100 million. An example here is Formula One teaming up with SingTel to promote its inaugural night race in Singapore. In this instance, Formula One was able to leverage SingTel's marketing efforts in respect of its various services to promote its race in Singapore. In a similar vein, SingTel was able to garner massive exposure through co-branded marketing events and programs with Formula One. Of course, the third major factor in considering co-branding as a business opportunity is to give more benefits to your own customer base and so enhance brand loyalty.

Another significant co-branding exercise was the huge commitment by Coca-Cola to the Harry Potter movie, *Harry Potter and the Philosopher's Stone* (*Sorcerer's Stone* in the United States). Coca-Cola poured US$150 million into the movie, in return for which it received exclusive global marketing partner status. This allowed the beverage company to do what it had wanted to do for a long time, which was to reach out to its young target audience without alienating parents. What is more, it gave Coca-Cola better and faster brand communications coverage than traditional advertising. For the moviemaker Warner Brothers, there was a huge funding boost that took care of its advertising budget worries.

Coca-Cola is currently sponsoring the hugely successful television show *American Idol*, whose judges are all seen by the show's millions of viewers drinking from large cups of the famous drink.

One of the stories I remember from the past is about a sports management company that had tried for years, without success, to tempt Rolex into sponsoring Wimbledon. Eventually one year the head of Rolex was persuaded to visit Wimbledon on finals day, looked at the whole occasion, saw the crowd, the precision and performance of the players, the strawberries, the champagne, the film and music stars, and royalty attending, turned to the sports management company representatives and said, "This event is a Rolex," and since that time Rolex has endorsed and sponsored Wimbledon. The representation and values of the two luxury brands coincided, and were a good fit both functionally and emotionally.

When considering a co-branding opportunity, it is important to evaluate it carefully before making a commitment, as certain things must be in place for success to be achieved. Unless your customers are going to receive (and will be *aware* that they will receive) real benefits from the exercise, don't bother. Second, ensure that the target audiences of the partners have similar types of demographic and psychographic profiles. Third, ensure that the partners have brand values similar to those of your brand; otherwise, there will be significant strategy problems and working together will be problematic. Finally, make sure that the brand partner you have chosen doesn't eclipse your own brand name. If you get it right, co-branding is a good way of extending the reach of your brand portfolio without product extensions and new product launches.

Hybrid branding

Hybrid brands are brands born out of the intercourse between two or more companies or brands. The rationale is similar to that of co-branding where companies combine their experience in the hope of creating a winning brand that they might not be able to create on their own. It is a little like a merger, but where a newly formed brand is the focus. An example is Virgin joining up with Singapore Telecom's mobile company, Sing Tel Mobile, to form Virgin Mobile for the Asian market. Sing Tel had a good knowledge of Asia but not a really acceptable regional brand name, while Virgin had the brand name but little knowledge of mobile telephony and Asian markets. Potentially, it was an ideal marriage, which in 2001 was consummated by a grand launch, profiled and reinforced by somewhat fun, cheeky, and very different marketing activities in line with Virgin's brand values. Sadly, it wasn't a successful marriage and the brand was withdrawn from the market.

Another example, discussed in Case Study 5, is that of Sony and Ericsson. Barely in existence now, this hybrid brand was spectacularly unsuccessful, due, in my opinion, to poor brand management.

Case study 5: Sony and Ericsson

In September 2001, Sony Corporation and Telefon AB L.M. Ericsson launched a 50:50-owned new mobile telephone brand and logo called Sony Ericsson Mobile Communications. For Ericsson, one sensed at the time an air of desperation, as the brand's market share had dropped consistently over the previous few years to under 10% – left, like Motorola, in the wake of the Nokia revolution. Ericsson was literally banking on this new venture to pull it out of the financial problems it faced – namely, debt, a lack of profitability, and little consumer confidence in its brand, given a flagging market scenario.

For Sony, whose ambitions reached (as they still do) well beyond consumer electronics into infotainment, the proposition was expected to be a boost to its existing business in a market where it lacked expertise and needed to grow its relatively small market share in mobile telecommunications.

The 'big idea' was that Sony Ericsson would provide the technology capability and Sony the market understanding. The new president of Sony Ericsson, Katsumi Ihara, claimed the new hybrid brand made perfect sense. "We are still complementary. Ericsson is strong in wireless, and we are a little weak in that respect. But we know the consumer."

The author's opinion of this 'wedding' was, and still is, that there are several obstacles to overcome before both suitors would gel, namely:

1. the 'logo = brand' mentality;

2. spending on product versus spending on brand;

3. the volatile market;

4. the fickle consumer;

5. the incumbent giant; and

6. what's the big difference?

Let's have a quick look at each of these.

1. *Logo = brand*: Sony Ericsson created a new logo that looked like a green throat lozenge, and was to be seen moving in an animated phone screen as well as appearing on ads. On handset screens the logo would react "with emotion," according to company spokesman Mats Georgson. "It will behave like it's alive," he said. "It can morph and jump around – it's liquid identity or 'another me.' We want something that can constantly evolve and surprise you." To me, this is a creative idea overruling strategy. Logos are only valuable as memory recall devices and are usually constantly applied. This sounded like a gimmick that could backfire. Too much attention and money was given to the logo production. Logos aren't brands and aren't prime differentiators.

2. *Spending on product versus spending on brand:* Asian companies are famous for not investing in brands, which is one of the prime reasons why there are few global brands coming from that region. Japanese companies are typical of this and don't manage their brands as effectively as they might. Hence, we saw Sony Ericsson president Katsumi Ihara saying a big investment in this new brand wasn't required because the name on the logo speaks for itself. "It doesn't make sense to spend a lot of money," he said. "People will already know what it is. Instead of spending a lot of money on the brand, it makes more business sense to

spend on the product." This is dangerous thinking, as new brands aren't successful without strong promotional support.

3. *The volatile market:* with the launch of a new brand you have only one chance to get it right, and this brand was launched in a volatile market, which remains volatile and highly competitive. The mobile phone market experienced a slowdown due to the global economic crisis that set in during the fourth quarter of 2008. IDC (a global technology consulting firm) has reported that the global market for mobile phones has since experienced a decline of 12.8% in shipment volume. With strong competition, Sony Ericsson was in fourth position in the global rankings. With Nokia, Samsung, and LG leading the pack with their attractive brand appeal coupled with innovative technology and features, Sony Ericsson has to contend both with the competition and the global economic crisis.

4. *The fickle consumer:* consumers of mobile phones were already product and brand savvy. Sony Ericsson had to do a lot of persuading to get customers to switch from brands with which they were already familiar – and, to some extent, happy. With minimum brand spend this was unlikely to be achieved unless the product itself was spectacularly different. It was and still is unlikely that this will ever be the case, as Sony Ericsson is still a follower in new product development and innovation. Moreover, consumers are now more knowledgeable about corporate affairs, and neither of the two partners had been pushing out great results; just the opposite, in fact. Consumers are risk adverse.

5. *The incumbent giant:* Nokia ruled the market with a share in excess of 39.1% as at the end of 2008. Sony Ericsson's share of 8.4% never really made an impact on its own. Neither Ericsson nor Sony had created the emotional associations that consumers love, and which breed brand loyalty, and I saw nothing to suggest that things were going to be different with the new venture. Indeed, brand spend isn't a high priority, as we have seen above, and this is how emotional associations are largely created. Neither Ericsson nor Sony is an expert at branding, unlike their giant rival. (The reason Nokia lost out was it took its eye of the technology ball – brand-wise it was good.)

6. *What's the big difference?:* mobile phones are commodities, being more or less the same in terms of size, weight, battery life, features, and so on. Nokia was far ahead of the rest of the market at this time because of its superior branding and design. Only strong brands can command a differentiated offering that appeals emotionally to their followers. This has been illustrated by Apple, which, although it had no track record in

producing mobile phones, was able immediately to carve out a segment of the mobile phone market with its iPhone because of its massive emotional brand appeal among Apple brand loyalists. The question for Sony Ericsson that it failed to answer was: Given the absence of powerful branding, why is Sony Ericsson different and better than its competitors? Logo differentiation did not answer this question and was not a sufficient reason for success.

Merger and acquisition issues

Naming and consumer confusion

Mergers and acquisitions (M&As) can sometimes create problems for brands. For instance, if the names of the brands aren't retained, or if the names are joined, as was the case with ExxonMobil and DaimlerChrysler, then there is the issue of how to explain this to consumers. ExxonMobil explained its name change to consumers soon after the merger of the two companies in 1999. An advertisement that it ran in the press read:

> "We're as brand loyal as you are.

> Loyalty is a two-way street. So along the street, road or motorway we aren't about to confuse our customers. Yes, we've merged. But our brands Esso, Mobil and Exxon will still be there. What will change is the company behind them. ExxonMobil is a new name for technology, efficiency and service. Helping our old names treat you better than ever."

The ad, which included a website address, showed the two company logos, with the sign of ExxonMobil. Here was a company that cared about its customers and their emotional associations with their brands. It took the trouble to reassure them, and at the same time promise them a better experience.

By contrast, DaimlerChrysler, which was also formed in 1999 following a merger, took two years to explain its position to consumers. In the *Asian Wall Street Journal* of October 9, 2001 and in *Fortune* magazine of October 15, the company produced what I consider an appallingly uncreative advertisement, the copy for which showed on the left-hand page a telephone operator saying: "Good morning. Welcome to Mercedes-Benz-Jeep®-Dodgesmart-FreightlinerSterlingSetra. How can I help you?" This was followed by a headline on the right-hand page: "Just call us DaimlerChrysler." This, in turn, was followed by:

"We don't really need to introduce our brands anymore. They have all made history through their own achievements, and their names are known the world over. Of course, the fact that they all work under one roof means we will always have a wealth of experience and innovative ideas to draw on. Something that will help us stay miles ahead of the competition in the future. Find out more at www.daimlerchrysler.com."

The sign-off was the name "DaimlerChrysler" with the tag line, "Answers For Questions To Come."

I am tempted to say, "Words fail me." Now, I don't know what the DaimlerChrysler brand personality is, or even whether it has one, but any company that advertises will create a personality in consumers' minds, whether by default or not. This ad sends out awful messages about the DaimlerChrysler personality from the tone and manner of the copy. And I have no clue as to what the tag line meant. When agencies present brand managers with advertising copy, it should be checked against the brand personality to determine whether it is 'on strategy' or not. And above all, it should not be arrogant.

The following case illustrates the opposing views of whether to include acquired brands into existing architecture or to leave them as they were before the merger or acquisition.

Case study 6: Carrefour SA (France) versus Ahold NV (Holland)

Mergers and acquisitions – branded house versus house of brands

They sound like two football teams, but Carrefour and Ahold are, in fact, two of the largest supermarket chains globally. Interestingly, they have traveled down different branding routes in terms of naming strategy/architecture in the course of their rapid development over the last few years.

Carrefour is trying to build a global brand by acquiring other chains and changing their names to its own. For instance, in 2007, it bought Artima (in Romania) and Atacadao (in Brazil) for €55 million and €1.5 billion, respectively. In France, the French retailer has decided to rebrand all the Champion stores to the Carrefour banner. This is following similar projects in Spain, Argentina, Poland, Brazil, and Turkey. The initiative forms part of Carrefour's multi-format, single-brand strategy.

Ahold has done the opposite. Rather than converting its newly acquired stores to the Ahold format, which holds little resonance with customers outside Europe, the company has kept the local names and management in place – for instance, Giant, Stop & Shop, Peapod and Martin's in the US, Albert Hejin, Etos, and Gall & Gall in the Netherlands, Albert and Hypernova in the Czech Republic and Slovakia, and ICA in Sweden and Norway. Ahold's CEO, John Rishton, said, "At Ahold, our global strategic focus continues to be the transformation of all our banners into powerful consumer brands."

Ahold is a taskmaster at retail management, and is concerned with improving performance behind the scenes. The changes are at the back end, where ordering and shipping benefit from Ahold's global network, helping to lower costs.

Carrefour says it caters to local preferences by tailoring its food products to local tastes in 95% of cases. For instance, in China, most of the products sold in Carrefour stores are procured from China, and the store managers are empowered to run the stores according to the local requirements. "Our stores offer local products that local people want," explains a spokesperson for Carrefour. "In China, we are Chinese. In Malaysia, we are Malaysian." Food analysts say that food retailing doesn't behave like other categories, as most shopping for groceries is done close to home. If this is true, they say a trusted single brand will be difficult to realize. Mmmm – food for thought! [8]

Finally, I would like to take time to look at the companies who buy brands that are either very successful or on the way to success, and try to increase their value. They can be seen as predators in a cynical sense but they are extremely good at spotting brand potential and adding value. I call them the brand collectors, and the best examples are from the world of luxury goods.

The brand collectors

The fascination with luxury brands

The ultimate pleasure for any brand manager must be having charge of a luxury brand, with all its concomitant global glamor, prestige, and fame. This isn't to say, however, that competition isn't fierce, but it is surprising that ordinary products such as pens (sorry, writing instruments) can be priced on the same level as rock stars' and football players' salaries. Or should this observation be reversed? Of course, it's back-to-basics branding techniques and the management of perceptions, but the returns are huge. One would think that, in times such as the current global economic downturn, luxury brands would experience poor results, but this doesn't appear to be the case, as will be illustrated below.

'Watch' this space: opportunities to cross-brand

Typical of luxury goods categories that seem to have an endless range is watches (sorry, timepieces). Everyone appears to be extending their brands into the timepiece category. Calvin Klein has moved into wristwatches that tie in with the overall Calvin Klein clothes look. Emporio Armani has done the same thing, and Versace has a whole collection of different watch brands. There is an endless stream of others, including DKNY, Adidas, Bally, Benetton, Carven, Chanel, Christian Lacroix, Hugo Boss, Lacoste, Karl Lagerfeld, Lanvin, Nina Ricci, Pierre Cardin, Timberland, Yves Saint-Laurent, and more. The market has exploded, and the market for these fashion accessories is still growing quickly. Fashion-branded watches come in all shapes, sizes, and prices, but there is little doubt that consumers love them, because they love their brands.

If you aren't into fashion but prefer technology, don't despair. Breitling, Seiko, Nike, Casio, and other manufacturers are producing hi-tech timepieces, in some cases capable of downloading sophisticated files from the Internet and linking with mobile phones and tablet or laptop computers. There are watches that monitor heart rates, store electricity, receive emails, measure speed and distance for athletes, send out distress signals and have many other functions. Many companies are finding that extending their brands via this method keeps the sales tills ringing and brand awareness high. The total global market for watches is worth over US$100 billion in 2017.

If you don't want a watch, but want to show your affinity with, and express yourself and impress your friends through your favorite luxury brand, you need not worry. After all, you can buy a Chanel tennis racket, Gucci candles, Prada keyrings, an LV umbrella or teddy bear, or even a Versace dog bowl! Are these add-ons really profitable? Will they dilute the real brand? Only time will tell, but luxury brands are always tempted to extend into accessories, however odd the fit may seem. This leads us on to look further at the world of luxury.

The dream sellers

Let's move on to look at luxury products owned by brand collectors. The very smart companies are those that have a business strategy of creating and buying luxury brands. These are the brands that cause hearts to flutter, create insatiable desire, and sell more as the price rises. They are the stuff of dreams. They are truly emotional brands and are held by few companies. The two biggest holding companies of these luxury brands are LVMH Group and Richemont. Both of these groups give their brands relative autonomy in brand management, because most of them are power brands in their own right. The corporate branding face is rarely seen, and the brands stand alone. Both of the companies have been referred to earlier in this chapter as a 'house of brands', as opposed to a 'branded house'.

Richemont (Compagnie Financière Richemont AG) is a "Swiss luxury goods group with a view to the long-term development of successful international brands," according to its website. In addition to its luxury goods business, Richemont holds investments in the tobacco, financial services, wine and spirits, and gold and diamond mining industries. Being Swiss, it is predictably very low key in talking about its own identity. It leaves the talking to its brands, which include Vacheron Constantin, Purdey, Baume & Mercier, Jaeger-LeCoultre, Lange & Söhne, Cartier, Officine Panerai, IWC, Piaget, Lancel, Alfred Dunhill, Van Cleef & Arpels, Montblanc, Montegrappa, Chloe, Alaia, Shanghai Tang, and Roger Dubuis.

In the year to March 31, 2018, Richemont racked up sales of €10.9 billion, but it is well behind its more high-profile competitor, whose profile and ways of managing luxury brands are described in Case Study 7.

Case study 7: Möet Hennessy Louis Vuitton Group (LVMH)

The house of luxury brands

The LVMH group comprises 70 exceptional Houses that create high quality products. It is the only group present in all five major sectors of the luxury market: Wines and Spirits, Fashion and Leather Goods, Perfumes and Cosmetics, Watches and Jewellery and Selective Retailing. LVMH currently employs 134,000 people across the world and reported sales of €42.6 billion in 2017 and has a retail network of more than 3,860 stores in France and around the world. It's brand portfolio boasts around 50% of the world's most powerful brand names across various categories, as shown below. One of these brands, Christian Dior, is itself one of the indirect holders of LVMH. The brand portfolio includes:

- *Wines and Spirits*: Ardbeg, Belvedere, Bodega Numanthia, Cape Mentelle, Chandon, Chandon Argentina, Chandon Australia, Chandon California, Chandon China, Chandon do Brasil, Château Cheval Blanc, Château d'Yquem, Cheval des Andes, Cloudy Bay, Dom Pérignon, Glenmorangie, Hennessy, Krug, Mercier, Moët & Chandon, Newton Vineyard, Ruinart, Terrazas de los Andes, Veuve Clicquot, Wenjun.

- *Fashion and Leather Goods*: Berluti, Céline, Christian Dior, Donna Karan, Edun, Emilio Pucci, Fendi, Givenchy, Kenzo, Loewe, Loro Piana, Louis Vuitton, Marc Jacobs, Nicholas Kirkwood, Thomas Pink.

- *Perfumes and Cosmetics*: Acqua di Parma, Benefit Cosmetics, Fresh, Givenchy Parfums, Guerlain, Kenzo Parfums, Make Up For Ever, Parfums Christian Dior, Perfumes Loewe.

- *Watches and Jewellery*: Bvlgari, Chaumet, De Beers Diamond Jewellers, Fred, Hublot, TAG Heuer, Zenith.

- *Selective Retailing*: DFS, La Grande Epicerie de Paris, Le Bon Marché Rive Gauche, Sephora, Starboard Cruise Services.

- *Other*: Cheval Blanc, Connaissance des Arts, Cova, Investir, Jardin d'Acclimatation, La Samaritaine, Les Echos, Nowness, Radio Classique, Royal Van Lent.

As published on the website, "LVMH has successfully preserved a family spirit that places priority on long-term vision. The Group's vocation is to ensure the development of each of its Houses while respecting their identities and their autonomy, providing the resources needed to create, produce and market their products and services through carefully selected channels." Clearly spelt out is also the spirit of the company.

The LVMH spirit

"The LVMH group brings together truly exceptional Houses. Each of them creates products that embody unique savoir-faire, a carefully preserved heritage and a dynamic engagement with modernity. These creations make our Houses ambassadors of a distinctively refined art de vivre."

The LVMH vision

In LVMH's case, at least, we know that this isn't merely random buying of brands. Chairman Bernard Arnault says, "LVMH's vision is to represent around the world the most refined qualities of Western 'Art de Vivre'. LVMH must continue to be synonymous with both elegance and creativity. Our products, and the cultural values they embody, blend tradition and innovation, and kindle dream and fantasy."

The LVMH values

There are three priorities that reflect the fundamental values shared by all group stakeholders, as published by LVMH Group on its website. These are:

Be creative and innovative

Creativity and innovation are part of our DNA. Over the years, they have ensured our Houses' success and established their legitimacy. This combination of creativity and innovation is the foundation of our Houses and figures at the heart of the delicate balance required to continually renew our offer while resolutely looking to the future, always respecting our unique heritage.

Deliver excellence

At LVMH, we never compromise on quality. Because we embody the world of craftsmanship in its most noble and accomplished form, we pay meticulous attention to detail and to perfection. From products to service, we cultivate our difference through this constant quest for excellence.

Cultivate an entrepreneurial spirit

LVMH has an agile and decentralized organization that encourages efficiency and responsiveness. It stimulates individual initiative by entrusting each person with significant responsibilities. Our entrepreneurial spirit encourages both risk-taking and perseverance. It requires pragmatic thinking and an ability to motivate teams, leading them to achieve ambitious objectives.

The Group encourages this spirit, this thirst for progress, among all its associates. As an expression of what a real brand champion thinks and feels, I think we need look no further than the above statement. But let's have a closer look at how LVMH manages its brands.

In an interview in the *Harvard Business Review* of October 2001, Arnault describes the characteristics of what he calls "start brands": They are:

* timeless;

* modern;

* fast-growing; and

* highly-profitable.

And there are fewer than ten of these star brands in the luxury market. The reason for the paucity of numbers is that it is extremely difficult to balance all four of these characteristics at once. For instance, fast growth and high profitability have some tension between them, as do timelessness and modernity.

Timelessness takes years to develop, but Arnault says that the perception of this characteristic can be greeted by fanatical, uncompromising quality. Innovation drives modernity, which is harder to achieve as "you must know the past and invent the future at the same time." Much of his design team's time is spent on this, as star brands have to be current, fashionable, edgy, sexy and modern – fulfilling a fantasy. Constant brand reinvention is a key. Growth is a function of consumer desire, and depends to some extent on advertising to create that desire, but Arnault won't let his marketing people near advertising; it remains with his design teams, who, in his opinion, can better project the desired image.

Product quality and training of staff feature highly at the 'front end' of the star brand-building process, according to Arnault. For example, each model of Louis Vuitton suitcase is "put in a torture machine, where it is opened and closed five times per minute for three weeks. And that is not all – it is thrown, shaken, and crushed." That is how Arnault's company makes an heirloom. "A single purse can have up to 1,000 manufacturing tasks, and nearly every task is done by hand. People who work in the factories are trained for many months before they are even allowed to touch a product." Planning and discipline are paramount in the production process. The biggest mistake any company can make is to delegate advertising to the marketing department. For example, the advertising for the Dior brand personality (very sexy, modern, very feminine, and energetic) is often created by the Dior design team and John Galliano himself. Profitability for each brand comes later, of course, after all the innovation, advertising, and other expensive processes have been pumped in.

As for brand management, Arnault says many brands have the star potential, but are poorly managed. Brand management with luxury goods takes time, because all four elements have to be aligned, and that you cannot hurry. The up-side is that once you get there and manage the brand well, the returns are spectacular.[9]

Section one summary

Brand architecture is possibly the most difficult area of brand management, in that there are simply no rules, and endless opportunities to try out many variations. Some variations work, while similar ones don't. Corporate branding in one form or another is the trend, but sometimes product branding is necessary. Careful thought must be given to all decisions in this area, and specialist advice may be necessary.

Getting brand architecture right isn't easy. The next section of this chapter looks at some more tough decisions brand managers need to make, regardless of how well their brands are doing.

Section two: Three great dilemmas: Brand stretch, brand revitalization and brand deletion

In Section One of this chapter we looked at the options available to companies in determining the architecture they can use to build their brand portfolios. In this section, we will discuss some of the decisions that face brand managers in adding to or trimming those portfolios.

Brand managers will face three great dilemmas at some stage in their careers, and all are concerned with the life of the brand. While brands, if well managed, may live forever, there are situations that occur through both success and neglect that test the skill of a good brand manager. The three great dilemmas are: (1) whether to stretch a brand name into other areas – either inside or outside its existing category – when it is doing well; (2) what to do when a brand has been neglected and needs revitalizing, and whether this can be achieved; and (3) whether to kill or delete a brand if the future holds no prospects. None of these decisions is easy, and I will examine cases of each type of decision in this section.

One great temptation: stretching the brand

One critical question that all brand managers have to face at some stage is whether or not they should stretch or extend their brand, to which the answer is: it all depends. At its most basic level, extending or stretching a brand involves producing variants of the same brand in the same category. At another level, there is the issue of stretching a brand so that it breaks into other categories, but still sits in the same industry. Finally, there is the question of whether or not a brand can be stretched so far that it can move into totally different industries. The temptation is great to stretch a successful brand, and there are no rules to guide the brand manager here; at the end of the day, the *consumer* will decide, as it is consumers who own and build the brands. The limiting factor really is the brand promise and personality, and whether or not the consumer makes an emotional connection.

There are, of course, some brand extensions that just wouldn't work, and it is possible to look at various examples, and to make some judgments as to when brand extensions are possible. However, first I will clarify some of the basic reasons for brand extensions, as well as some terminology.

Reasons for brand extensions

There are three basic reasons for extending brands.

1. Natural causes

One of the main reasons for brand extensions is what I call 'natural causes'. This is where a brand may produce a product that is very close to its original offering, but which satisfies the desires of a different, or even the same, audience without significantly cannibalizing existing sales. These extensions are a 'natural' development as brand managers uncover and exploit more of the needs and wants of the consumers that exist in their category. Such was the case with the famous After Eight Mints. The Classic Dark Assortment has been complemented by the White Mint Assortment, while other extensions added by the brand include After Eight Straws, After Eight Orange, and Mint Ice Cream Bar. These kinds of brand extensions not only make sense, but are almost mandatory if companies are to grow and keep competitors at bay in the category.

2. Market growth reductions

Companies may try to widen their brand portfolio if their existing market(s) show signs of slower growth. For example, Intel – the world's number one semiconductor manufacturer – has countered the slowdown in the growth of its processor unit due to decreasing sales of personal computers, by building devices that connect to, and increase the value of computers and tablets, especially those that have Intel microprocessors installed. Intel has also made a strategic decision to produce other consumer devices such as healthcare measurement devices, and educational products. The extensions are close enough to existing businesses to avoid consumer doubts, although in the entertainment category Intel will have a tough time competing with products made by the consumer electronic giants such as Samsung, Sony, Philips, and others. Perhaps of more importance in the longer term is Intel's entry into healthcare, where its technology is expected to be used by doctors for remote patient health monitoring and other medical uses through new devices. Innovation is vital as market challenges and opportunities appear.

3. Confidence in the invincibility of the brand

While the above reasons are often based on solid market research and a strong degree of common sense, some brands are extended merely on the premise that, because the brand has been successful in one or more categories/markets, it will automatically be a star in others. This thinking may prove to be right in some cases, but very wrong in others. The Virgin Group has suffered from over-confidence in a few areas, such as with its Virgin Vodka, Virgin Cola, Virgin Cosmetics and some of its other forays into different industry categories. Thus, while there may be opportunities for stretching a brand, there may also be minefields that can affect a brand's ability to be stretched. Before we look at more examples, I would like to distinguish between what are often referred to as brand extensions and line extensions.

Brand and line extensions – possibilities and difficulties

Brand extensions involve the use of an existing brand name to move into a new product or service category, while *line extensions* of a brand use the existing name to offer a new product or service in the same category. Virgin Atlantic is an example of the former, and the Mercedes A-class is an example of the latter.

Examples of where it is possible for one brand, company, or product to line extend include cars, banks, and drinks. Cars can be 'flexed' via features such as engine capacity, coupé versions, and so on. Banks can be positioned broadly but be promoted differently to retail, corporate, small and medium-sized enterprises, entrepreneurs, public sector institutions, and so on. Drinks such as Schweppes' soft drinks are flexed via different products such as mixers, mineral waters, and fruit and health drinks, with many flavors to appeal to adults and young people, but all of these remain true to the company's basic positioning of quality soft drinks, and all remain basically in the same category.

Brand extension can also be achieved in taking the brand into another category or industry. For instance, Ford Motor Company once started a Jaguar Bank (unsuccessfully), and Virgin has moved into telecommunications and finance, among many other categories. The key to extensions of any kind is that the brand must stay true to its original identity. Only in this way will consumers accept the change.

While a company or product can have only one true, strong position, it can be tweaked, adjusted, and flexed to emphasize particular strengths or values that attract different customer groups, as long as it isn't stretched too far. The amount of stretch available is contingent upon knowledge of various market segments. So, multi-positioning can also be seen as line or brand extending, but there are limits to this possibility that mustn't be overstepped.

Harley-Davidson has been successful in marketing its apparel range because it fits well with both the needs and desires of the target audience, and the true personality and positioning of the brand. Associations of freedom, patriotism, heritage, and a macho attitude attract Harley buyers, and the accessories and clothing add value to the consumer experience. They are appropriate to the brand personality and positioning. But even power brands have their limits.

For example, Johnson & Johnson's baby shampoo could transfer from babies to children without much problem, but when tried with adults it didn't really make the cut. And the Nike product brand extension from footwear to sports apparel was successful, but the step from sports apparel to casual wear wasn't, as the casual wear segments didn't strongly associate with the true Nike position of athleticism, and it appeared that older people didn't feel like *just doing it* anymore.

Nevertheless, Nike has now found a great growth segment in the form of 'Athleisure' for those that want to combine sporting and fashion attire. Nike seems to have also got it right by introducing a line of heart monitors for athletes wanting to check their heart rate and other health and fitness monitoring features. Nike has also introduced watches and other products that allow athletes to capture various training data which can later be uploaded and shared with coaches and training companions over the Internet. These new training performance products still fit the brand personality of Nike, in terms of passion, commitment, winning, and getting the best out of oneself. The point, therefore, is that as long as the extension stays true to the brand personality and therefore matches consumer expectations, it is more likely to be successful.

Another way to analyze the issue of extensions is to look at the nature of the brand in terms of consumer associations, and whether the marketing strategy is to move the brand up or down with respect to associations of price, quality, and, ultimately, value. This is essentially looking at whether a brand can be considered as functional or symbolic in nature.

Symbolic and functional extensions – the fit with the consumer mindset

We must remember that brands exist only in the minds of people, and that they can be segregated into two basic types: functional and symbolic brands. This perceptual typology has implications for brand stretch.

For instance, Rolex is a symbolic brand, as it represents more than just a watch to buyers and occupies a position that is associated with high price, quality, status, and prestige. At the other end of the perceptual spectrum, Casio has a position linked to just functionality – it is low in price, with enough quality in terms of reliability and durability to do the job it is supposed to (and as good as high-end watches), but with little association of status or other intangible benefits. However, it has tried to rectify its rather down-market image with some hi-tech improvements.

In line extending a prestige brand such as Rolex, the only possibility is downwards. However, a step-down positioning via a product bearing the same name but with lower quality and price will almost certainly damage the original brand image and alienate its existing customer base, even though it might attract a newer clientele who aspire to own that brand. Rolex considered this matter carefully and created a separate brand, Tudor, for the middle market, with no Rolex endorsement. The brand communications are cleverly designed to create an air of familiarity as, to an extent, are aspects of product design.

For brands already positioned at the high end of a market, the distancing mustn't be so great as to eliminate all the positive associations of the strong, core, prestige brand name. Communications strategies must focus on relating the new product to the favorable aspects of the core brand. A good example of this is Hotel Chocolat, the luxury chain that sells 'hedonistic chocolate'. Sales rose 12% to £91.1 million in the year to June 26, 2016, with pre-tax profits rising from £2.9 million to £8.2 million. As well as line extending its portfolio through product innovation, for instance, with the first 'hardcore' 100% chocolate egg with no sugar, it has decided to make a play for a beauty products category, which only represents at present 1% of sales. The idea is to sell cocoa-based cosmetics including body butter and perfume, and given that the new business will be a joint venture with the former head of Lush, it has a good chance of making a great brand extension, fitting closely with the core brand's luxury offering.

Although there is a lot of room for positioning new brand extensions with a prestige parent brand, and the rewards can be substantial, great care must be taken to predict whether there will be any dilution or damage to the core brand image. This is the risk, no doubt calculated, that Mercedes and BMW have taken with their A-class and 1 series, respectively. The further down the quality/ price continuum the extension occurs, the greater the possibility of damage to image, and neither the A-class nor the 1 series got off to a great start, or really lived up to expectations.

Functional brands aren't normally positioned as high-quality items, and so there is often little room to extend downwards, and any new product introductions will have associations closer to the original brand than would be the case with symbolic brands. The result is that extensions are likely to inflict less damage on the brand image. The downside here is that, because there is less distance between the brands in terms of quality perceptions, cannibalization of sales for both products may occur through customer confusion. Another challenge in trying to extend a functional brand upwards in terms of quality by adding status and value to it, is that consumer perceptions tend to be locked on to the existing brand image and are likely to be very difficult to shift.

The only way that a functional product can really be branded in the symbolic bracket is by distancing the original brand from the extensions through careful positioning. This may well involve the creation of a new brand name, in the same manner described for symbolic brands considered above. For example, Casio had to create new brand names to break away from an image that wouldn't be acceptable to different market segments; hence the introduction of G-Shock and Baby-G. The functionally oriented Toyota brand also had to leave its name totally out of the picture in order to position a new product in the status and prestige category (Lexus). This strategy successfully created a luxury brand without the more down-market associations of its other products. The future of Lexus as a luxury car brand is somewhat questionable, however, as the brand appears to be extending downwards into lower engine capacities and smaller cars. Discipline is therefore necessary in brand management but on occasions guardians of the brand fail to resist temptation.

The bottom line for brand extensions, then, is that you cannot step away from your basic position or proposition as long as the brand name remains the same, because consumers judge perceptually whether or not there is a good 'fit' between the brand itself and the extension of the brand. Although the discussion above has concentrated on the most common elements of quality and price, this judgment also takes into account other elements of importance, such as usage occasions. It is for this reason that some companies are forced to step away from the main brand name and create a product that stands alone. Coca-Cola has done this in the past with Fruitopia and other beverages. Others play down the brand name of the company to give the product minimum association with the parent. Launching new products in such ways helps to position them with highly individual profiles while retaining subtle usage of brand equity from the parent, as with Dockers (Levi Strauss) and Lexus (Toyota), neither of which would have been as successful if positioned as another product line of the same major brand.

Temptation from desperation

If times are not too good and things are not going your way, there is always a temptation to try and stretch the brand to its limit.

Corporate versus product brand elasticity

As explained in the first section of this chapter, in general, we can conclude that corporate brands are more capable of surviving being stretched or extended than are product brands. Let's take the example of a successful product brand, such as Head and Shoulders shampoo. It has its line extended to provide a range of shampoos under the brand name 'Head and Shoulders' for different types of hair and different consumer benefits. However, it wouldn't survive a move into, for example, clothing. I certainly wouldn't be inclined to buy a Head and Shoulders suit or shirt!

Corporate brand names, on the other hand, are more easily stretched because the brand proposition isn't so closely focused and related to a single type of product. They can be successful because they can attach the perceived value of the brand name outside their categories – for instance, Sony has successfully transferred its brand name beyond consumer electronics to entertainment. The perceived value of quality has enabled this to happen in the minds of consumers. The Virgin Group has developed many brand extensions, but it hasn't stepped away from its basic brand proposition. Another great example of this is Caterpillar (see Case Study 8 below), which has successfully entered vastly different categories. There is more scope for brand management in corporate extensions, and the current trend is away from product branding to corporate and shared or endorsed branding.

Case study 8: Caterpillar Inc.

An example of successful brand extension

One of the most unlikely, but seemingly successful, examples of stretching a brand into a vastly different industry is that of Caterpillar Inc. The 'construction' company has moved into the fashion business. Seen for over 100 years as a supplier of heavy machinery used in construction activities, it has found a new way of building awareness and recognition (not to mention profits) by penetrating the notoriously difficult fashion industry; in the process, it has been accepted by consumers across multi-segments.

This has, of course, been no accident; rather, it was a carefully planned move by the Caterpillar global brand management group. The aim was to boost brand sales among those consumers who also operate Caterpillar machinery products, and to promote the brand to people who wouldn't normally come into contact with Caterpillar.

Caterpillar products have sold well in Europe, competing with specialist global brands and attracting youth with its edgy attitude. Cat apparel has a worldwide licensee brand in London, and a global licensee for Cat footwear based in the US, but it has its own stores in mind. The first of these was a 5,000-square-foot store in Illinois, near the company's headquarters; this was followed by several more in cities such as London and New York. It also has a growing online business.

The product range itself is astonishing – everything from casuals to luxury goods. For example, you can buy Cat jeans (with five pockets and a yellow patch on the back), limited edition jeans, sunglasses, sandals, and baby clothes. In many countries there are Cat hats, boots, bags, trainers, baby shoes, watches, and sweatshirts. At the major stores, upmarket products such as leather bomber jackets and timepieces are available. Cat crosses all boundaries, from the irreverent to the traditional, from the young to the over-sixties (and in some quoted cases, the over-nineties!).

Caterpillar brand personality

The secret to the success of Caterpillar's brand extension appears to be the consistent application of the brand 'personality', which could be seen as:

- hardworking;
- tough;
- resilient;
- determined;
- bold;
- rugged;
- independent; and
- a good friend when you get to know it.

This personality has been extended into both the product and the shopping experience. For instance, the boots and shoes look tough. The metal band on the Cat watch (introduced at over US$200!) looks like a bulldozer's tread lines. The flagship store's interior is decorated in the bold Caterpillar yellow color and features a replica of a Cat-sponsored racing car. Part of the floor is made of wooden blocks similar to those on the factory floor, and when visitors approach a display, reverse beeping sounds are activated.

The latest innovation for Caterpillar accessories is the Cat S60, the world's first smartphone with integrated thermal imaging capability. It too fits the brand personality attributes perfectly. Bullitt Group partnered with the brand to develop a new range of rugged smart and feature phones designed to challenge expectations of what a phone can and should do. Today, Cat® phones are distributed globally to over 70 countries, redefining the impact of workplace technology.

With 2017 sales revenues of US$45.5 billion, Caterpillar has proven that well-planned brand extensions reinforce and are consistent with the original brand proposition, so that consumers' emotional associations are in tune with the brand personality of the proposed brand extensions. Consistency is critical and Caterpillar's brand management has stuck to the rules; by doing so, it has added considerably to the total brand value.[10]

Increasing elasticity via product innovations

We have seen above how successful corporate branding can be with respect to increasing elasticity and brand stretch but it is not as easy with products, especially when perceptions are very entrenched and consumers aren't ready to accept the innovation. For instance, detergent manufacturers trying to market laundry-soap tablets to people who are used to powders and liquids found market acceptance difficult. The problem appeared to be the nature of the innovation – the product attribute/benefit of the tablet itself, with the attribute being the tablet's compact size and the consumer benefit the fact that consumers no longer have to scoop, measure, or pour. The innovation was aimed at younger working people and small households that essentially don't like doing laundry, and who want to minimize the time taken to do it. However, people seemed to want the option of being able to vary the amount of the ingredient to suit the relative dirtiness of the clothes being washed. The challenge for the brand managers was to convince consumers of the benefits of convenience and time saving, and has been compared to the problem encountered by the proponents of the teabag in the 1950s. Teabags eventually took off, as we all know, but not without considerable investment in educating the consumer. If perceptions are deeply entrenched, companies must be prepared for lengthy and costly advertising and promotion campaigns.

In the detergent case, it might be that research had asked only one of the two vital questions necessary to establish consumer acceptance – "Do you like it?" but hadn't asked the other – "Would you buy it?" This was the same issue that caused Coca-Cola massive embarrassment when the company tried to introduce New Coke. Taste testing carried out with over 100,000 people reassured the company that consumers preferred the new drink, but they just didn't buy it, because their perception of the old Coke as being "the real thing" was so deeply entrenched. Anything else must be a substitute. When you play around with brands, you are playing around with people's emotions, and brand managers need to understand what these are.

The Caterpillar case above shows how a major corporate brand can extend into categories most would think impossible. The case study below shows how Wrigley has in past years extended its brand into different categories via product innovation.

Case study 9: Wrigley

Gum does stretch!

Wrigley has been a leader in the chewing gum category since the 1890s and is famous for brands such as Juicy Fruit, Doublemint, and Winterfresh. Extensions have progressed into the sugarless market, where sales have accelerated as consumers have become increasingly health-conscious. New brands introduced into the US market include Extra Polar Ice, Everest (packaged in a tin box), and Eclipse, the company's first pellet gum. One of its more recent brands is a sugarless chewing gum called '5', which was first available in Rain, Cobalt, and Flare flavors, followed in 2008 and 2009 by additional flavor line extensions named Elixir, Solstace, and Zing. The packaging reflects the flavor color names and looks like a sophisticated cigarette pack design. '5' is aimed at the youth market, but some commentators have remarked that the packaging is more appropriate to an older audience and may not be seen by young people as being relevant to them.

To fuel corporate growth, the company has successfully targeted overseas markets. It currently maintains over 20 factories in various countries, and sells its products in more than 180 countries, including the US, Serbia, Mexico, Australia, UK, Canada, Spain, New Zealand, Philippines, France, Kenya, Taiwan, China, India, Poland, the Federation of Bosnia and Herzegovina, and Russia. More than 60% of Wrigley's sales now come from outside its home country, the US. Deutsche Bank Alex. Brown analysts have said of Wrigley, which can now be considered a global brand, "Not many companies can have 50% of the world market, no debt, very high returns, and that kind of brand awareness."

In 2004, Wrigley purchased the Life Savers and Altoids businesses from Kraft Foods for US$1.48 billion. On January 23, 2007, it signed a purchase agreement to acquire an 80% initial interest in A. Korkunov for US$300 million, with the remaining 20% to be acquired over time. On April 28, 2008, it was announced that Berkshire Hathaway and Mars, Incorporated would acquire Wrigley for approximately US$23 billion, and Mars is now listed as the owner of the Wrigley Group.

But Wrigley has no room for complacency, as competing brands have powerful owners including Cadbury, Kraft Foods, Mondelez and others. As of 2013, Wrigley had around a third of the global market share of the gum market and despite fierce competition has been maintaining its forefront position with innovative product development, such as its patented Viagra chewing gum. The new category of energy gum is another emerging area where most of the top players like Wrigley, Navson, and Kerry gum have already started production. Whether its healthcare, pharmaceutical and other innovative products will find favor and trust with consumers is another matter. Much will depend on whether Wrigley can manage consumer perceptions well enough to transfer the trust and loyalty it now enjoys into categories where it isn't known to have operated before, and where it will be fighting against already trusted brand names.

Wrigley seems determined to win, however, and its costly marketing campaigns have used tennis icons Venus and Serena Williams, entertainer Chris Brown, and other celebrities to endorse the brand. Although using celebrities can be highly effective, it can also be problematic. Chris Brown's arrest in early 2009 on a charge of assaulting singer Rihanna prompted Wrigley to suspend its Doublemint gum campaign that used Brown as a spokesman. "Wrigley is concerned by the serious allegations made against Chris Brown," Wrigley spokeswoman Jennifer Luth said in a CNN report of February 9, 2009. Nevertheless, the Wrigley brand name was sufficiently strong, and overcame this setback.

With the pack following closely behind, it remains to see if this global brand will keep its number one position.[11]

From the above examples we can see that there are both advantages and disadvantages of brand and line extensions.

Advantages

- Extending the brand is less costly than creating a new one.
- The consumer receives a better choice.
- There is less risk for consumers if the brand is trusted.
- There can be some synergy, and therefore savings in marketing costs.
- They help brand revitalization.
- If successful, they can add power to the main brand image.
- They can keep other competitors from entering the category, and increase coverage.
- They can pave the way for more extensions and foster innovation.

Disadvantages

- If the parent brand has a negative image, it is unlikely that an extension will be successful.

- If not clearly positioned, they can confuse consumers and cannibalize sales of existing brands.

- If not successful, they can damage the master brand image.

- Retailers might not appreciate them.

- All brands have their boundaries, and stepping outside these can dilute brand power.

Whatever the pros and cons, it is possible for a brand to be stretched way beyond its own category as long as it doesn't step outside its basic character and consumers can relate to it.

What happens when things go wrong with brands? Can they be brought back to their former glory or are they destined for the scrapheap?

The great gamble: brand revitalization/ repositioning

Another great dilemma facing brand managers is when a brand is seen to be going downhill, either through neglect, or because consumers no longer are strongly associated with it, or because competition has eroded the brand position. The decision that needs to be taken is whether or not to revitalize the brand, and if so, how. This process is often referred to as brand repositioning, and what is needed is to convince the target audience to change their perceptions about the brand in a more favorable way with regard to the competition.

Sometimes, brands that have lost their shine and market appeal are allowed to continue without substantial repositioning, or even where repositioning has failed, while others undergo tremendous changes aimed at making a low-key brand into a global player (see Case Study 10 below).

Case study 10: Tab Diet Soda

The customer lifeline

One famous brand story is what happened to Tab Diet Soda when it was on its last legs. Tab saw its market share shrink to less than 1%, and yet it was spared the axe by Coca-Cola. The brand, once so successful, now resides at the bottom of the category heap. It was launched in 1963, and immediately became the drink of the 'free' generation, the "Beautiful Drink for Beautiful People". But in 1982 Diet Coke was introduced to add more power to the Coke brand, and Tab began to go downhill. Basically, its demise has been due to cannibalization of sales by Diet Coke and a simultaneous competitive attack from Diet Pepsi and other such carbonated drinks. The company made several attempts to revitalize Tab in the 1980s and 1990s, through various product changes (for example, reducing the content of the carcinogen saccharin and increasing the amount of aspartame; adding calcium; and making a clear alternative), and even by repositioning Tab as the drink with "sass". However, all these efforts have failed to revive the brand.

The big question is, why should a company that is renowned for managing successful brands hang on to one that is certainly underperforming and may even be almost dead? The answer appears to be the fear of adverse customer reaction and publicity. Possibly at the back of Coca-Cola's mind is the terrible mistake the company made in attempting to replace Coke with New Coke in 1985. Customers around the world clamored for the old Coke, which had been positioned so strongly as "the real thing," and New Coke had to be withdrawn.

In this respect, regular Tab drinkers (although relatively few in number) have been very vocal about their brand, so much so that they have been described as "Taboholics". Those who still drink it are very loyal, and have gone to extreme lengths to prove this. Even though few distributors now stock Tab, some customers have reportedly driven far out of their way to find a store that sells it, and have complained vigorously to the Coca-Cola headquarters about the availability problem.

Herein lies another part of the answer to the question as to why the brand isn't deleted. The Coca-Cola distribution system allows the bottlers some autonomy in production, and if they cannot make a profit from a brand they will tend not to produce it. With many bottlers now choosing not to produce the brand, the few that do are meeting the market needs, and Coca-Cola itself isn't out of pocket. It stopped putting marketing resources behind Tab some years ago, but is content to receive a small profit from a select market.

But back to the consumer. What did Coca-Cola say about the Tab situation? Douglas Daft, former chairman and chief executive, said it shows the company cares: "We want to make sure that those who want Tab get Tab." Coca-Cola has remained steadfast in its commitment to the brand, and Tab can now be purchased online – for example, via the Dr Soda website. So, it would appear that some companies, under certain conditions, will continue to support dying brands if the consumers shout loudly enough. Tab lives on.

One of my favorite brands that underwent a true transformation and revitalization is Mazda under the leadership of Mark Fields who went on to become CEO at Ford. He generously gave me both time and information to show how an ailing brand became great again.

Case study 11: Mazda

The revitalization of a brand

This case study should be an inspiration to all brand management practitioners. It isn't only about revitalization of a brand; it's about how leading-edge practitioners take a holistic view of brand strategy, from consumer insight, through personality and product, to internal and external communication. Although leadership has changed in the company since this case was written, the same philosophy of brand management has continued.

I have always liked the Mazda brand. I have always thought its motor vehicles had style and 'class'; it's one of those brands that I somehow feel an affinity with. But Mazda, founded in 1920, is also a brand that makes one think, "It has so much potential. Why hasn't it ever become a world-famous brand?" (This question can be asked of many brands that originate from Japan, where brand management isn't a national strength, and therein lies the answer to the question.) Mazda has always kept a fairly low profile, with little advertising or promotion, and despite obvious talent in its design capability the brand had nearly faded into oblivion by the time it was acquired in 1996. (Ford Motor Company's initial investment in Mazda of 25% was made in 1986, with an increased investment to 33% in 1996.)

Since that time, the revitalization of the brand has become a significant focus for business attention, and Mazda has now achieved global brand status. However, it is important to point out that the Mazda repositioning and branding is very much Japanese, not Western; the heritage and future would have been blighted by an attempt to impose Western brand values on an Asian brand. It is an example of how Japanese brands are now starting to recognize the importance of brand management, whereas previously they had concentrated primarily on operational efficiency and quality. This case study illustrates how a brand can be totally reconstructed in every way, and how important the role of brand management is in saving a business and then building it up again. The case also demonstrates clearly the many skills a brand manager must have in order to successfully take on this type of huge responsibility, the importance of including all company employees in the brand vision, and how the brand really does drive the business.

The key to business success is the brand

From the very beginning of the business transformation, branding was always at the top of the agenda. Mark Fields, former senior managing director in charge of global marketing, sales, and customer service (and later president and CEO), said to Mazda employees in 1999:

> "For Mazda to take a giant leap forward in terms of business profitability, we have set the following goals:
>
> - establishing our brand management strategy;
>
> - successful launch of new products, and further strengthening of our existing products;
>
> - maintaining our sales momentum worldwide; and
>
> - bolstering our domestic dealer network."

Fields also commented:

> "To promote improvement of our market share and build our brand image, Mazda must completely understand and satisfy the needs and wants of our target audiences ... And we must continue to offer higher value and deeper satisfaction ... The key to this is brand strategy ... Through our brand strategy, we are aiming at building a brand that differentiates us from our competitors, one that enhances customer satisfaction, improves value – and in the end provides us enduring profitable growth ... As we go forward, all of our activity will be keyed to our brand."

The importance of brand strategy

Fields was clear about the importance of brand strategy and what it means to Mazda:

> "First, the brand strategy is about a relationship with the customer. By enhancing our customer insight we can understand their true needs and wants. Based on this, we should establish an emotional connection with them. It is through this and other touchpoints that we present our brand. Customers who come into contact and grow to love our brand become our assets, and their importance is in no way different from other assets such as profitability and our employees.

> "Secondly, it is a business growth strategy with a consistent management system. Why? Because branding requires two aspects: communication and products. Both must work in conjunction, and that makes it a management system. Since employees, products, sales, service, and the company itself all come in close contact with customers, everything must be coordinated on the basis of brand strategy.

> "Finally, brand strategy is a means to generate profitability. A brand with a strong emotional connection with customers can employ pull marketing, henceforth creating an efficient and highly profitable business environment."

Fields further commented:

> "The will and commitment of top management is, above all, most important. Brand strategy is not a simple matter of image strategy. Therefore, the senior management should take full responsibility and not let PR, marketing, advertising, and other communication groups act separately. The management must lead the entire organization to start brand building and create change.

> "The next most important thing is the cooperation and commitment of management. They must understand and share the management's direction, and promote coordination and cooperation among different functional groups in the organization, to develop products and services that clearly articulate our brand.

> "Finally, senior management must lead the organization to generate awareness and passion for what the brand stands for."

Push versus pull in brand direction

Mazda has taken steps to ensure that its brand image and company profitability aren't damaged by efforts to buy market share through discounting and rebates – the typical 'push' approach that many brand managers get tempted into pursuing as a result of competitor strategies. Instead, it has focused on the 'pull' approach, which involves giving customers what they really want and engaging them emotionally in the brand-customer relationship. This approach means that the custodians of the brand must understand which particular group of consumers they want to focus on, and then attempt to satisfy their needs, wants, and desires, and to add true value and other motivations.

At the heart of every brand is the consumer

It is a fundamental premise of branding that brands only exist in people's minds; that companies don't own brands – consumers do; and that it is consumers, not companies, who build brands. Mazda's philosophy is similar. It is therefore of critical importance that brand managers have a thorough understanding of the consumers they hope to attract and retain, and this means gaining consumer insight through research. For Mazda, this means understanding the deep-seated needs of the target consumer, and not just the generic needs that most people have. For example, Mazda uncovered the following deep-seated needs of its prototype target audience:

- Aspires to lead a life that is full of new stimuli and excitement while respecting his personal sense of style.

- Aspires to sustain the sensitivity of a child – moved and excited by the simplest things in life.

- Hates to be constricted by rules and norms, and allows his sensibility and emotions to lead him in pursuing whatever he wants to do.

- Desires to retain his personal uniqueness that invites attention and is respected by others.

- Aspires to enhance his presence as a highly competent person possessing a unique personality and opinions.

- Wants to impress and persuade people around him by expressing his unique values and views.

- By setting high goals for himself, aspires to challenge new possibilities by not adhering to current norms.

The Mazda brand DNA

Mazda takes a life-science approach, which is illustrated by the use of the term 'DNA', the very building block of human life. The core of the Mazda brand strategy is the Mazda brand DNA, the essence of the brand, which has two sides: personality and product. The personality side of the Mazda brand can be summarized by the following three characteristics: stylish, insightful, and spirited. This is the driving force behind the Mazda brand's personality and the foundation of the brand DNA; however, in order to understand the Mazda brand DNA, one must understand that key product attributes are included in it as well. These key product attributes are: distinctive design, exceptional functionality, and responsive handling and performance.

Brand personality

Mazda's brand personality attributes are defined as follows:

- *Stylish*: Every Mazda product should be a self-assured invitation to attention. With this, we acknowledge that Mazda customers are self-confident and truly distinctive individuals.

- *Insightful*: We imply that Mazda has a 'street-smart' understanding of its customers' needs and values, and it always takes a creative approach to meeting those needs.

- *Spirited*: We establish that the Mazda brand embodies an enthusiastic and expressive love of life, just like Mazda customers. Together, the Mazda brand personality creates a deep emotional connection with Mazda customers by reflecting how our customers feel about themselves and about life.

Product attributes

Product is an important part of the equation for the Mazda brand, and the elements are defined as follows:

- *Distinctive design*: The aim for all products is that Mazda products boast distinctive design inside and out; that is to say, they are athletic, youthful, solid, and substantial, both on the interior and exterior.

- *Exceptional functionality*: Mazda requires that its products possess exceptional functionality; this means the most intelligent use of space and functional efficiency with a high-quality fit and finish.

- *Responsive handling and performance*: This attribute is a Mazda legacy and creates a sensory driving experience that translates into significant and noticeable driving satisfaction.

It is the product/ownership experience that expresses brand connection.

While high-level product attributes help in understanding what Mazda wants all its products to represent, they are not specific enough to help planners, designers, and engineers. The company has therefore developed additional tools, the first of which is called *product philosophy*.

The product philosophy is comprised of quality innovation and design policy, as Mark Fields explains:

"Our Product Philosophy clearly states our priorities. We wish to be a Leader in these six areas: Design, Craftsmanship, Quality, Stability and Handling, Braking, and Package Innovation. While taking environmental friendliness and safety fully into consideration, our product development aims to take leadership in those six areas.

"This hardware exercise is a clear and consistent extension of how the brand DNA is executed within our new products.

"The 'Design Policy' uses Mazda's design theme of 'Contrast in Harmony', a guide to unique and best-in-class design. The new design theme 'Contrast in Harmony' aims at creation of Mazda's future products with designs that balance functions and styling harmoniously with each other. 'Harmony' refers to the underlying balance and proportion such as details, materials, color combination, configurations, space construction, function, and appearance in our products ... the very foundation of good design.

"To further the design direction among products, Mazda has developed the Family Face. The Family Face is a combination of the brand symbol and a five-point grille, and will be applied to all future models to make it a visual expression of Mazda's identity and distinctiveness. For example, some vehicles that are already in showrooms, like the Premacy and the MPV, as well as future concepts, both show Mazda's face – the distinctive five-point grille with Mazda's winged M brand symbol. The body language shows distinctive 'Contrast in Harmony' with a clear contrast of sharp and soft. So the Mazda brand strategy is not merely an image strategy; it is a central business strategy that includes product development. New products that embody all the aspects of the brand strategy will be introduced successively into the market."

The emotional connection

The key element in Mazda's brand strategy is building the 'emotional connection' with consumers. The key success factors for brand management are: 'Global Perspective', 'Listening to the Voice of the Customer', and 'Creating an Emotional Connection'. Here are a few examples of the initiatives that have been undertaken to make this happen.

In the area of product marketing, Mazda organized the 1st Shohin Ibento, or 1st Product Day, in September 1999 with their key domestic and foreign dealers and distributors from North America, Europe, Australia, Asia, and the Middle East, providing them with the opportunity to view and drive current and future products. Managers in various markets shared success and 'best practices' regarding new product events and product-focused strategies with the global team. This is a good example of sharing ideas/viewpoints and listening to the customer.

Mazda also ensures global consistency in its brand and marketing strategies through quarterly brand summit meetings with key Mazda marketing personnel from Japan, the United States, and Europe. Fields says:

> "These meetings drive home a common understanding of the brand and how it is steadily executed in the marketplace. Clear internal communication is vitally important in developing a consistent brand identity worldwide. A single brand message is required to support the brand globally. Our major market managers participate in this activity, providing input from a local perspective.

> "In order to establish a lasting emotional connection with the target customers, we need to deepen our understanding of their values. We need a deep understanding of the latent needs that exist in every human being. Only after we grasp this can we establish a strong emotional connection with our target customers. We call this 'Deep-Seated Needs' at Mazda. This is what we use to identify our target customer. And it is with this target customer that we aspire to create an emotional connection and encourage a love and passion for our brand."

Mazda's view on advertising

Mazda has clear views on advertising and on the importance of maintaining a clear and consistent message in the market. However, Fields stresses that advertising is *not* brand:

> "Advertising is only one aspect of brand. It supports and illustrates our brand identity and makes it clearer to the market. You cannot

create a robust brand by advertising alone. Today's customer is far too sophisticated for this type of tactic. What advertising provides is the opportunity to project our brand to consumers in a clear and consistent manner worldwide.

"To ensure this, we have developed our 'Communication Philosophy'. It was developed to manage our overall communications, including advertising. To create tighter advertising consistency with our worldwide brand positioning, we have established a global tag line.

"In Japan, our tag line is the same as our brand positioning statement of *'Kokoro o Ugokasu shin Hassou'*; outside of Japan, it is: 'Get in. Be moved'. Our global tag line is used in all of our advertisements, and it helps us deliver a consistent message to different markets around the globe. Another innovation to develop a better alignment with our global advertising efforts is our visual identity ending tag, or what we refer to as advertising VI. I'm referring to the last two or three seconds of our TV advertising and how we illustrate our logo and mark at the end of the ad.

"This VI was developed and researched with customers to ensure that the visual cues are consistent in delivering the Mazda brand DNA. It is our intention to phase this VI into all TV advertising worldwide in the near future.

"Again, I would like to emphasize that our advertising portrays a crystal clear picture of the Mazda brand to convey a consistent emotional message. At its most basic level, our corporate message must support our Worldwide Brand Positioning, while providing relevance to our target customers.

"To bring our brand to life, we manage and control not only advertising but all of our communications, consistently guided by our Communication Philosophy. For example, our events, PR activities, and all of our press events and conferences are based on the brand strategy, with information, staging, and the format of press releases all consistent with our brand."

Brand management structure and internal communications

Following the development of the brand strategy, other initiatives were implemented at Mazda. One of the first innovations was to restructure the marketing organization to enhance the focus on branding. The brand marketing department was established as a part of the marketing division, in addition to the product marketing department. Brand marketing is responsible for consistent planning, implementation, and management of product development through the communication process under the brand strategy. Mazda believes that such an organization is indispensable for aggressive promotion of its brand strategy.

The second initiative was to communicate the brand strategy to every one of the company's employees. Fields says:

> "A brand cascade event was held for our 1,400 top managers. These managers were educated on basic knowledge about brand and our brand strategy, which in turn they cascaded when they went back to their respective departments and groups. Check-ups ensured that our message was communicated throughout the organization, and by doing this Mazda succeeded in spreading brand knowledge and creating improved awareness to implement the brand strategy to realize the Mazda brand. By maximizing internal communication activity, goals were shared globally."

According to Mazda, everyone is now reforming his or her daily tasks in pursuit of these common goals, and in this way the company is moving forward with its self-renovation. This provides assistance internally for everyone at Mazda to be responsible for brand development and execution.

A third innovation was a brand cascade kit, which was specifically developed and distributed for internal education. The kit was delivered to all divisions, and brand cards highlighting key words were distributed to every employee. As Fields says, "The brand strategy would never work without a total commitment from every employee. We believe that all of our employees needed to renew their thoughts, and let the Mazda brand direct their everyday job and assignments."

Summary of Mazda's brand philosophy and practice

Mark Fields summarizes the Mazda brand philosophy and practice as follows:

> "First, the brand strategy is about a relationship with the consumers. The brand should establish an emotional connection with them, and it is through this and other touchpoints that the brand is presented. Consumers who come into contact with and grow to love our brand become our assets, and their importance is in no way different from other assets such as profitability and our employees.

> "Secondly, it is a business growth strategy with a consistent management system, because branding requires two aspects – communication

and products. Both must work in conjunction, and that makes it a management system. Since employees, products, sales, service, and the company itself all come in close contact with customers, every aspect must be coordinated on the basis of brand strategy.

"Thirdly, brand strategy is a means to generate profitability. A brand with a strong emotional connection with customers can employ pull marketing, henceforth creating an efficient and highly profitable business environment. More specifically, this means increased conquest sales, enhanced owner loyalty, and improved market share.

"The next most important thing is the cooperation and commitment of management. They must understand and share the top management's direction, and promote coordination and cooperation among different functional groups in the organization, to develop products and services that fully relate to the brand.

"Finally, the will and commitment of top management is, above all, most important. Brand strategy is not a simple matter of image strategy and so senior management should take full responsibility and not let PR, marketing, advertising, and other communication groups act separately and inconsistently. Management must lead the entire organization to start brand building and promote change. It is senior management that must lead the organization to generate awareness and passion for the brand."

Note: More recently, the design philosophy has evolved to become, "Elegant and spirited, our KODO: Soul of Motion design is a true reflection of Jinba Ittai; the unity of horse and rider. Fascinated by elegance and fixated on creating an unbreakable bond between driver and car, our designers have worked endlessly to create a design philosophy that embodies the dynamic beauty of life. This can be felt both inside and out, transferring the energy of movement to those who see it and creating an irresistible urge to drive."[12]

I guess by now you know that I'm a Mazda owner!

The tough decision: brand deletion

Sometimes, there is no option but to kill (whether it is done quickly or slowly) or sell off a brand. In other words, the brand manager decides to remove the brand from the portfolio. This is usually a consequence of a negative reply to the question, "Can the brand be revitalized?" Killing a brand is often called *brand deletion*, and unwanted brands that are sold off are often referred to as *orphan brands*. A brand may be deleted for one or more of the following reasons:

- There is no foreseeable route to recovery when a brand is heading downhill fast.

- The brand is no longer profitable, and isn't likely to become profitable again.

- The brand has been totally outdated by market innovations.

- The brand doesn't rank highly enough in importance, relative to other brands, to justify a place in the future portfolio.

- The brand's customer base has eroded and is unlikely to return.

- Revitalization of the brand cannot be justified in terms of the return on investment.

- Inadequate brand management has caused the brand to move away from its true proposition and character.

Brands are expensive to manage, keep, and revive. In today's world of intense competition, it isn't economically feasible to hang on to a large portfolio. Unilever, for example, has reduced its total number of brands from 1,600 to around 400, to concentrate on what it calls its power brands. The financial problems intensify with a product branding approach, as opposed to a corporate branding approach, because there are no synergies in advertising and promotion, and every brand has to make its own way in the marketplace without corporate endorsement. But even when the parent brand is involved in endorsing a brand, markets are so dynamic and consumer tastes so fickle that it is very difficult sometimes to revitalize a brand.

Smart brand managers evolve their brands in line with such changes. Revolutionary changes are often not accepted by consumers and are difficult to sustain, as consumers don't connect with the drastic changes. The case of Oldsmobile is typical of a brand that became a casualty through a combination of market changes, inadequate brand management, inappropriate product development, and consumer attitudinal shifts (see case study below).

Case study 12: Oldsmobile

The final parking lot

Oldsmobile was a brand in the portfolio of General Motors (GM), when a decision was taken to phase it out – in other words, to kill the brand. The brand itself was over 100 years old, and possessed considerable heritage, but GM decided not to make any further attempts at revitalization. Previous attempts at breathing life into Oldsmobile during the 1990s had involved a large A&P expenditure and various product improvements. Why was the famous brand axed? There are four fundamental issues that GM had to address in this respect, which it failed to conquer.

1. The name issue

It isn't advisable to use the word 'old' in a brand name. One of the obvious problems for the brand is the name itself, which has proved to be a major consumer deterrent for a few decades, so much so that in the 1960s GM commissioned an advertising campaign aimed at changing the name to "Youngmobile". However, the problem persisted. In the 1980s, GM changed the tag line to "It's Not Your Father's Oldsmobile" in an effort to change the image that people had of a revered but old-fashioned brand. But despite GM's efforts, the brand still couldn't shake off the age association.

2. The product issue

From the 1940s to the 1980s the Oldsmobile brand heritage and image was one of sportiness and innovation. Its "Rocket" engines and the long, low designs were renowned and admired. But from the 1980s onwards, product developments moved away from this central brand character. Chevrolet engines were substituted and diesel engines given as an option. Even though these product decisions were tied in with the Arab countries' oil embargoes of the 1970s, when big cars were pronounced 'gas guzzlers', they nevertheless had the effect of helping to shatter the brand image of Oldsmobile, and triggered more brand dilution when added to the name problem.

3. The image repositioning issue

Attempts at repositioning the name as a luxury brand, accompanied by logo changes and product variations to match European competitors, failed, despite US$4 billion having been spent. Major discounting to boost sales worked against these efforts, and consumers were confused. They couldn't accept the widespread transformation of a brand that they perceived was "really not like that", and their associations with the old brand heritage ran deep. Brand sales consequently moved in the direction of fleet purchases and away from individuals.

4. The consumer issue

The result of all the above – which amounts to inadequate brand management – is that consumers fled from the brand in large numbers, seeing no benefits and no differentiation, and no longer feeling an emotional association. GM at last gave up and bit the dying brand bullet. But like all great characters, according to Hollywood lexicon, the Oldsmobile may not really die; it will fade away, but will still be remembered.

One wonders whether Oldsmobile might have survived if it had been consistent over time with its initial identity, and evolved as a sporty and innovative brand, leveraging on its heritage. The imposed schizophrenia of the brand personality through inconsistent brand communications and product development basically turned people off. Oldsmobile was no longer the trusted and believable personality consumers knew. The emotional association was destroyed.

Deletion by force

Sometimes, a company is forced to rationalize its brand portfolio and delete or sell some brands. This may, or may not, be a result of its own incompetence. In the case of General Motors, it was partly market forces and partly poor brand management. The process of restructuring the US automobile industry began in early 2009, brought on by the global recession. GM was one of the hardest hit, and filed for bankruptcy in June of that year. In order to survive, and gain government investment, it had to come up with a sustainable plan for a reduced brand portfolio.

The result was that, by June 18, 2009, only four brands remained – Buick, Chevrolet, GMC, and Cadillac; the rest were either sold or marked for deletion. Hummer was quickly sold to a Chinese company and Saab to a Finnish company. Famous brands, including Pontiac and Saturn, were among the victims. GM had too many brands that failed the test of relevance, with too little investment in them. And there was no focus. After the restructuring, Fritz Henderson, chief executive, said in an article published in *The Financial Times* of June 18, 2009, "100 percent of our product, technology and marketing spend will now be focused behind the four core brands and 34 nameplates. Each one needs to be a hit and that is our challenge/commitment." What GM will also need to do, if it is to avoid further survival crises, is to change the perceptions of consumers toward its somewhat jaded and irrelevant brand image.

Since this situation in the recessionary years, GM has recovered somewhat but is not yet back to its former glory. It now has the Baojun, Buick, Cadillac, Chevrolet, GMC, Holden, Jiefang, OnStar, Opel, Vauxhall and Wuling brands. [13]

When times are bad, only the really strong brands survive – unless they are bailed out by the national government.

Summary

While section one of this chapter discussed decisions regarding brand architecture that need to be taken and the fact that there are no rules or right answers to the questions that arise, section two of this chapter has dealt with some key decisions that brand managers face from time to time regarding managing the brand portfolio, and it shows what a difficult job this is.

Extending, deleting and revitalizing brands are actions that can be potentially highly profitable or, in the worst-case scenario, devastating and catastrophic. But this is what makes brand management such exciting work to be involved in.

Now that we know precisely what we are branding we can now proceed to look at how to build a strong brand strategy in Chapter 5.

CHAPTER 5

Brand Visions and Brand Personality

In the last chapter we looked at the important questions associated with brand architecture and before that how a clear understanding of the consumer is critical to brand success. I emphasized that the role of emotion was highly important in building a powerful brand. In this chapter I explain in more depth how important an emotional brand strategy is and how the world's best brands develop such strategies that culminate in the creation of brand visions and human-like brand personalities.

The rational and emotional sides of brand strategy

We must never forget that brand promises are often made in the world of commercial reality – in terms of exceptional quality, service, and, nowadays, innovation. However, this isn't where the source of success for brands lies. These elements are merely the price a company has to pay to get into the branding game, and the branding game is a mind game. As parity becomes the norm and brands match each other feature by feature and attribute by attribute, it is becoming harder to create a brand strategy through rational means. In the rational world, everything is equal. So, while consumers screen the rational elements of quality and other compelling product attributes as part of the buying process, the real decision to buy is almost always taken at an emotional level.

A brief excursion into modern science tells us why this is so. The notion that the rational, conscious part of the brain dominates the non-rational, more emotional parts has now been disproved. MRI scanning has revealed that people's decision-making is mostly quick and emotional, is often done subconsciously, and is much more intuitive than was previously thought. It is now an undisputed fact that emotion drives reason, and not the other way around. Our feelings happen with great rapidity and precede conscious thought. The emotional part of the brain is considerably larger than the rational part and outpaces it in terms of intensity, sending ten times as many signals to the rational brain as opposed to the reverse. What's more, recall and memory have been proven to be a result of emotional experiences.

The following questions and statements provide a simple example of how this takes place. The *rational* thoughts tend to be analytical, but it is the emotional statements that drive the purchase decision.

Rational	Emotional
Do I need it?	I want it!
What does it do?	It looks really cool!
What does it cost?	I'm going to buy it!
How does it compare to …?	I only want this brand!

Neuroscience makes it clear that brand managers need to employ emotional brand strategies, as the endgame for any brand strategy is trust and loyalty, which are emotional and not rational thoughts and behaviors.

Given the increasing scientific evidence of the power of emotion in people's decisions and actions, we can categorically state that without emotional brand strategies it is impossible to build great brands! If we look at the powerful brands around the world, we see that they elicit thoughts like those listed above in the right column. Great brands build tremendous emotional capital with their strategies.

Characteristics of power brands – emotional capital

Brand managers are increasingly turning to the emotional side of strategy in order to win and keep customers. Power brands develop emotional capital, because they:

- Are very personal – people choose brands for very personal reasons, whether they be self-expression, a sense of belonging, or other reasons.

- Evoke emotion – brands sometimes unleash unstoppable emotion, arousing passion and unquestionable excitement.

- Live and evolve – they are like people in that they live, grow, evolve, and mature. But luckily, if they are well managed, they have no life cycle and can live forever.

- Communicate – strong brands listen, receive feedback, change their behavior as they learn, and speak differently to different people, depending on the situation, just as people do. They believe in dialogue, not monologue.

- Develop immense trust – people trust the brands they choose, and often resist all substitutes.

- Engender loyalty and friendship – trust paves the way for long-lasting relationships, and brands can be friends for life.

- Give great experiences – like great people, great brands are nice to be with, good to have around, and are consistent in what they give to their friends.

Given these facts about the emotional capital that brands develop, we need to understand that brands are relationships. The founder of Starbucks, Howard Schultz, once said in a note to his employees, "I want to emphasize that the key to our success lies in our values, our culture and the relationships we have with our partners and customers. When we're at our best, we create emotional experiences for people that really enhance their lives." If this is true for all top brands – and I have no doubt about that – what is the process of establishing an emotional relationship with consumers? How do the top brands build such relationships?

The emotional brand ladder of success

In order to build an emotional brand strategy there are certain steps brand managers have to take, very much like climbing the steps of a ladder, as shown in Figure 5.1. To illustrate this let's think of a relationship that develops between two people, as opposed to between a brand and consumers. One person sees another across a room at a particular function, and wants to meet them. Following this awareness, an opportunity to meet may arise, and although the conversation may be short the two people do exchange information about each other and decide whether or not there is sufficient interest to carry the relationship further. If the interest is there, further meetings reinforce this mutual respect, and the two people become friends. If the friendship blossoms, it generates trust and loyalty between them. Close friends trust each other with information they wouldn't tell to others and with things they hold dear, such as their children. Close friends are loyal to each other, will protect each other against danger, and will forgive each other if either of them says something to upset the other. When relationships are very close it is then highly likely that they will become friends for life or have a long-lasting relationship.

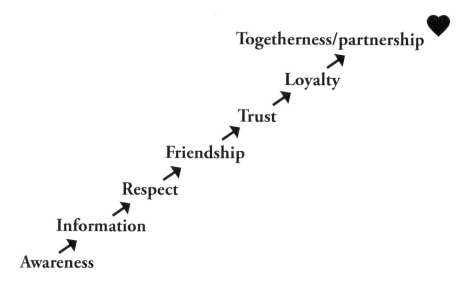

Figure 5.1: The emotional brand ladder of success (part 1)

The brand-consumer relationship grows in a very similar way. Awareness comes first, followed by involvement and purchase – a few meetings – which can lead to respect for the brand and then to the friendship and trust levels, which in turn lead to brand loyalty and lifetime customer relationships. The power brands get to and past the friendship and trust levels. Brands such as Starbucks and Apple understand that doing so isn't merely an option. If they *didn't* become friends with customers, and develop that sense of comfort, familiarity, and dependability, then they would never have reached power brand status. Companies that don't get to the critical friendship level often get stuck at the awareness stage.

Big spending on awareness often follows many brand launches, but the subsequent management of the brand may not take it up the ladder, as is shown in Figure 5.2 below. Lots of awareness may build a level of 'infatuation', but as we all know, true friendship and love go much further than the initial excitement. Building friendship takes a long time and has to be earned through consistency and dependability; without these qualities, there is no trust. Great brands develop such emotional relationships, but some brands sometimes forget what it takes, and consequently fail. For example, at an early stage in its history, Lastminute.com received 84% brand awareness ratings but only a 17% trust rating. Some brand managers spend millions on awareness – which is an essential step to achieve – but then neglect the emotional side of the brand-consumer relationship necessary for real long-term success. So the message here is that to climb the ladder, it is not good enough to try and buy your way to consumer hearts through promotions, discounts and other monetary incentives. Such activities will only cheapen the brand and commoditize it, making consumers think about it in rational ways. No, what is required is a well thought through, relevant emotional strategy.

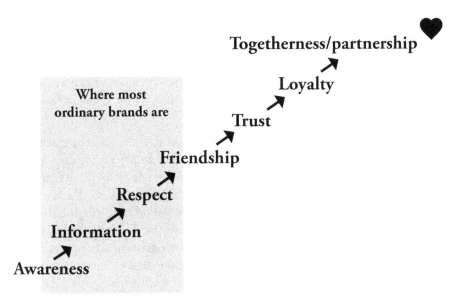

Figure 5.2: The emotional brand ladder of success (part 2)

Given this fact, how do we find the key to establishing a strong emotional association with consumers, and climb up the ladder so that we can move toward gaining trust, loyalty and long-term customer relationships? The answer is to focus intensely on emotions of universal appeal.

Finding the emotional brand driver and creating a brand vision

The most important part of any brand strategy is derived from what the brand stands for – or what it wants to stand for – *emotionally* in the minds of its intended customers. This must be relevant to both customers and the business, and be of universal appeal. If the emotional driver is not satisfying these three criteria, a brand will not succeed regionally, internationally or globally.

Many of the world's top brands choose one or two emotional words to fit such criteria. For example, Coca-Cola for seven years used the emotion of 'Happiness'. (From 2016 it has replaced this very successful emotional driver with a more product-focused approach, summed up in the call to action of "taste the feeling", which sounds like a backward step to me.)

Nike has always been associated with the emotion of 'Winning'. Despite its sponsorship of elite athletes and events, Nike has not ignored the attraction of the mass audience who cannot compete at elite levels. Nike's philosophy is well known and for many years the brand has used slogans such as "You don't win a silver medal you lose a gold", and "If you win a silver medal it just means you are the best of the losers". But it has widened the brand appeal to reach ordinary people by saying you can compete against yourself, you can always do better, there is no finish line, winning is a mindset, and in one advertisement featuring Roger Federer, "winning never grows old".

Orange, the telecom provider, when launched in the UK had the emotional driver of 'Optimism'. Coming last into the market with a higher price it had done some interesting consumer research, revealing that many people (around half the population) tend to be pessimistic and half optimistic. This tends to be genetic and we are born leaning one way or the other to varying degrees. Orange based its brand on this emotion, as everyone has hope inside them. From using this trait to attract employees, to communicating via advertisements that showed people having a good time (no phones!), to a meeting room in headquarters called 'Imaginarium' and a top management office labelled 'director of futurology', Orange lived the brand, captured market share and, prior to its takeover, became the number one provider in the market.

By contrast, but following the same emotional route, let's look at one of the world's best managed business-to-business (B2B) brands, BASF, the giant German-based chemical company. The interesting point to note here is that BASF makes mostly ingredients that are commodities and that are often incorporated into other products or items built by others. However, that does not mean that the company does not stand for anything, and its brand revolves around the emotion of 'Success'. It portrays itself in brand communications as helping to make things that are achievements and successful, such as arctic clothing and widespan bridges. And it has, in recent years, produced a brand vision statement that says, "We create opportunities for SUCCESS through trusted and reliable partnerships". This is, for a B2B brand, quite an emotional statement aimed at business customers and partners offering them opportunities for success through the medium of mutual shared trust and reliability. It demonstrates BASF's concern and care for partnerships and its commitment to helping partners do well.

Another brand that has really climbed the global charts is Tata from India, focusing its vision on the very word that every brand desires to possess – 'Trust'. Indeed, 'Leadership with Trust' is a part of the corporate logo.

Tata is the only brand I know that focuses its businesses consistently on trust. We have seen the importance of this element in brand building, for instance, in the Emotional Brand Ladder of Success earlier in this chapter. Without trust, you will never have a powerful brand. Tata is, in fact, a house of brands in terms of architecture, with lots of acquired brands such as Jaguar Land Rover, Tetley, and others. It operates across several industries across six continents with over a hundred companies.

Tata does not explicitly have a brand vision statement, but the emotional element of trust runs through all the company does. Tata does have a mission statement and a vision statement, which are:

- *Mission*: "At the Tata group, our purpose is to improve the quality of life of the communities we serve. We do this through leadership in sectors of national economic significance, to which the Group brings a unique set of capabilities."

- *Vision*: "The Tata name is a unique asset representing LEADERSHIP WITH TRUST. Leveraging this asset to unify our companies is the route to long-term success and delivery of returns to the shareholder in excess of the cost of capital."

Although these statements mix corporate and brand elements, the culture of trust is firmly placed at the forefront of all Tata's activities and those of the companies it owns but do not bear the Tata name. The important point to note is the reference to improving the quality of life for communities as this highlights the emotional benefit the company is trying to bring about.

Another splendid example of emotional branding comes from Hallmark.

Case study 13: Hallmark Inc. enriching people's lives

If you were to ask people what business they think Hallmark is in, most of them would likely say the business of manufacturing and selling greetings cards – and indeed, Hallmark is famous for that type of product. But this isn't what the Hallmark-branded business is all about. The Hallmark brand is focused clearly on the business of enriching people's lives. In a powerful brand vision statement, it has said that it wants "to be the very best at helping people express themselves, celebrate, strengthen relationships, and enrich their lives." Taking this view of its business has led Hallmark Inc. into a tremendous array of business opportunities that have proved to be highly successful and profitable.

The company, which has existed for over a century, generated consolidated revenues of US$3.7billion in 2015. Despite the rise of digital companies such as the online brand Moonpig and environmentally conscious consumers, the fact that Hallmark still has revenues in the billions as a privately owned company demonstrates the strength and sustainability of the brand.

Hallmark Gold Crown® has over 2,000 stores and makes up "one of the longest-lived network of specialty retail stores" in the USA "with a focus on helping consumers connect, celebrate and commemorate all of life's special occasions". *Hallmark Channel* is a leading producer/distributor of mini-series, TV movies, and home videos, and the *Hallmark Hall of Fame* has won more Emmy awards than any other series. The company is also involved in cable, TV, real estate, and the retailing of other relationship-building products such as Crayola Crayons, Silly Putty, party plates, gifts, wrappings, and more. But Hallmark says that these are really just business competencies and that it is what the brand means to, and does for, people that is important.

The whole of the Hallmark brand and its business are jointly built around emotion, and it genuinely cares for its customers. Indeed, the Hallmark corporate vision states that, "we will be the company that creates a more emotionally connected world by making a genuine difference in every life, every day." The Hallmark beliefs and values statement starts by saying, "Our products and services must enrich people's lives." Such statements to employees and the public at large are not just the foundation for good brands; they are a powerful driver of human emotion and behavior. Hallmark manages to build emotion into every touchpoint with the consumer, and it generates brand loyalty in return.

Throughout the management of the brand, Hallmark brings its vision and values to life. For example, Hallmark's strong corporate social responsibility program emphasizes its commitment to building relationships and enriching people's lives. The program involves, among other initiatives, employee volunteerism to assist community projects, and philanthropic contributions to various programs that will improve the lives of the underprivileged, helping people to connect with their loved ones who are far away. Hallmark also points out that "These beliefs and values guide our business strategies, our corporate behavior, and our relationships with business partners, suppliers, customers, communities and each other."

In summarizing its approach to brand strategy development, Hallmark says, "Our brand will continue to flourish because Hallmark is about what endures – that human need to connect emotionally with others. And that's what makes a genuine difference." By expressing its business objectives in a brand-related way based on enriching people's lives, Hallmark has found the key to becoming one of the world's top privately owned brands.[14]

We have now seen how world-class brands form brand visions through the use of relevant emotions. And that they use emotions that are relevant to their businesses and their customers based on universal appeal. This last element is important for international and global brands but we can see how it works if we ask ourselves, who wouldn't like to be happy, be a winner or perform better, achieve success, or have their lives enriched? Everyone would.

I would just like to mention one final point about how consumers are becoming a force for change in the creation and development of emotional brand strategies.

Meaningful and purposeful brands

The emotional dimension employed by brand strategists is, to an increasing extent, being propelled by the force of consumer demands. More and more brands are being 'forced' by consumers to demonstrate that they are making a difference to their lives. This view is confirmed by recent market research and brand health and strength rankings, such as those findings published by the Havas Group in 2017 entitled 'Meaningful Brands®'.[15] The last chapter of this book, concerned with tracking and measuring brand success, reveals more research but the main point I would like to make here is that consumers are intent on brands satisfying their *emotional* needs and will reward those that add value and meaning to their lives. In fact, according to this research, 75% of people interviewed expect brands to make more of a contribution to their well-being and quality of life, yet only 40% believe brands are doing so. And the research states that that the sample of people wouldn't care if 74% of the brands they use just disappeared. This is interesting reading and there is definitely a trend gaining traction where the purpose of brands is being questioned by consumers, and where brands are having to address this hunger for emotional associations between brand owners and supporters, driven by the latter group.

Brands that are emotionally driven and aim to make life better are sometimes referred to as purposeful brands, similar to the meaningful concept above. Many of the world's best brands are now focusing on this emotional dimension, concerning themselves with people's hopes and aspirations, inspiring them and encouraging them. They genuinely feel, and indeed can, make the world a better place, putting purpose as a strategic objective on par with the pursuit of profit, and sometimes ahead of it. They look for ways to add value and contribute to sustainability. The brands I have mentioned above and earlier in the book, including Unilever and Hallmark, are very much in this philosophical space. Nestlé is another global brand that has moved into this space, saying, "We're enhancing quality of life and contributing to a healthier future. Every day we touch billions of lives. We want to help shape a better and healthier world for individuals and families, for our communities and for the planet."[16]

Having looked at the emotional basis of brand success it is now time to move on to the next and closely related step in the brand-building process – brand personality. Let's start by looking at the psychology that lies behind this concept.

Brand personality

The psychology behind brand personality

Branding relies strongly on an understanding of psychology – how people think and consequently behave. Much of our understanding of how branding works stems from the work of Swiss psychologist, Carl Jung, who referred to four distinct functions of the mind, namely:

1. Thought

2. Feeling

3. Sensation

4. Intuition

Brand strategists and marketers have found that making a brand appeal to these four mental functions can give it a competitive advantage.

1. Thought

The thinking part of the mind concerns rationality and logic, often referred to as left-brain activities. The left brain is concerned with analysis, deduction, numeracy and other logical procedures. Rationality and logic can be powerful persuaders and can influence buying behavior because they provide reasons why a certain course of action should be taken. This understanding of brain function has resulted in brands being presented rationally and functionally to consumers. For example, a toothpaste with fluoride helps prevent tooth decay, which is a good reason to buy it. Projecting rationality and reason into brand communications can be useful but is not the only way by which minds can be influenced.

2. Feeling

Feeling is another powerful influence on human behavior, and it can be stimulated by advertising and promotional activities. Feeling belongs to the right brain, which is concerned with emotions, happiness, fear, anger, sadness and love. For example, images of a puppy happily playing with toilet tissue or of a sad, undernourished child can evoke emotional responses in almost everyone. Most brand managers now agree that building a strong brand that appeals to consumer feelings and emotions is essential, wherever possible. This can be largely accomplished by creating an emotional vision as explained earlier in this chapter and then using a brand personality to reinforce it.

3. Sensation

Sensation, as the word suggests, concerns the senses of touch, taste, sound, smell and sight. It is a right-brain function. Again, brand communications can stimulate desire by appealing to one or more of these mental sensory processes. As the sensors are connected to feelings and emotions they can be powerful persuaders. For instance, music from the past can evoke nostalgia. The Hovis bread brand's famous television commercial was so successful by appealing strongly to the sensory function. Shot using sepia-type photography the commercial showed a small boy, dressed in pre-second world war clothing, climbing a steep cobblestone hill, packed on either side with old-fashioned back-to-back houses, and bringing the loaf of bread back to his home. Nostalgic brass band music played as he walked up the hill. Brands can evoke lasting memories and gripping emotion.

Sensory marketing is used a lot by brands such as Chanel, Clinique and others placing fragrant strips in stores and magazines. Magazine statistics for this kind of sensory brand promotion show that 68% of readers buy the product after smelling a fragrance placed inside.

4. Intuition

Intuition is another right-brain function. It defies logic and rationality and is often acted out as impulsive behavior. Statements like, "I just knew it was for me" is typical of someone trying to justify intuitive and spontaneous behavior. Brand managers lock on to the intuitive process by studying the lifestyles and interests of consumers, analyzing in depth when and how people decide to buy.

An understanding of all four functions of the mind is essential to those wishing to build brands because these functions constitute the personality of every individual. Brand builders have learnt much about personality and have cleverly adopted much of this knowledge into brand strategies in an effort to get really close to customers and form deep, lasting relationships with them. As a natural corollary, one of the key skills in branding is to construct personalities for products, companies, and even countries. It is the personality of a brand that can appeal to the four functions of the mind.

The brand platform

Brand personality is one of the two major elements involved in brand building that underpins the brand vision, the other one being strategic brand positioning. Together, they form the basic platform necessary for any company to develop a powerful and sustainable brand.

For purposes of clarity, the brand platform identifies two concepts used; brand identity and brand image. Brand identity is concerned with how you want to be seen in the marketplace whereas brand image is actually how you are seen. If there is a difference between the two we call this a 'perception gap'. Perception gaps are to be avoided at all costs but sometimes companies don't really test the situation out with market research. This distinction between identity and image applies to people too and this is the link to the concept of brand personality.

We all want to be seen by others in a certain way and psychologists might associate this with 'self-esteem'. If we want to be seen as confident in an interview but are told afterwards that we lacked confidence it is not a good feeling. We must remember that my earlier definition posited that brands are relationships and as such they rely hugely on the perceptions of different target audiences, just as people do. In order to establish their identity and try to match this with their image, brands build personalities to build on the emotional attribute they have chosen for their visions. Having understood some of the basic emotional and psychological drivers behind great brands, it is now time to look closely at how brand personalities are developed and why they are of critical importance, starting with some additional psychology.

Personality, brand associations and symbolic meanings

Probably one of the most successful ways to build an emotional brand strategy is to create a personality for your brand. The people in the real world who stand out from the crowd always seem to have some kind of 'charisma'. They have a personality and attitude that others respect and are sometimes in awe of. They have a presence that almost commands people to follow without asking, and others always want to be around them. They aren't necessarily extroverted or introverted, but people feel good when they are around. Great brands are like great people in this respect, and the role of the brand manager is to manage the brand-consumer relationship by building a powerful and irresistible brand personality.

Like human relationships, whether they turn out right or wrong isn't usually a function of logic and rationality; rather, it is a result of emotional hits and misses. Given this reality, it seems strange that in many cases brand management continues to focus on the non-emotional side of the relationship, promoting features, attributes, price discounts, and so on, which have little impact on the growth of the brand-customer relationship. Such activities might bring in short-term sales increases, but they are open to imitation and won't attract and retain customers by developing an emotional relationship with them. In fact, they may well discourage this and 'cheapen' the brand in the eyes of consumers.

Relationships thrive on emotions; they survive or perish, depending on the emotional fit between people. Brands therefore have to reflect personalities that people like, and this means having an emotional basis or edge to them. Indeed, the best brands have personalities carefully crafted to suit them and their target audiences. People have a universal longing to be liked, given attention, and to be loved. But brand management often ignores this. Research clearly shows that companies lose 68% of their customers because they feel neglected or aren't given attention. This makes the emotional dimension of the brand-consumer relationship very important, and it is the personality and attitude of the brand that attracts and keeps people loyal to it.

Brand personality can strengthen the brand-customer relationship through the development of powerful emotional associations, and a strong brand personality helps support the emotional drivers and visions mentioned above. Building on the psychological underpinnings we have seen above, brands can create very strong emotional meanings that result from the pull of emotional appeal and they can symbolize several things to people, such as, what they stand for; what they believe in; what they care about; what they love; what they aspire to be; the type of person they want to be with; the kind of relationship they want; what they want people to know about them; and the kind of friend they like to have. People yearn to possess famous brands for all these reasons and more. The following classification illustrates just a few of these inner needs and associations that people find brands express.

The loyal friend

People sometimes feel lonely and need someone to talk to, and brands can become the friend that fulfills this role. The brand a person always buys can develop this relationship. It is a well-known fact that people talk to products such as cars and about companies, as though they are friends. Research elicits these thoughts by asking consumers to describe positive feelings about the brands they use, examples of replies being:

- "I miss you when you're not with me."
- "I have lots of fun with you."
- "I can't wait until we see each other again."

It is sometimes worth asking what a conversation between a brand and a typical customer might be like. A company might find that the relationship is going through a bad patch, as one disappointed customer revealed when she said, "You were never there for me," referring to a bank.

Brands can be friends of not just individuals but also of families. The usual cereal packet on the breakfast table can be a welcome and reassuring sight, and some people cannot actually converse until the first sip of their favorite coffee brand has been taken!

The trusted partner

As we grow up we share our lives with others and brands can fulfill a similar sharing role. Partnerships thrive on the feelings of appreciation and being valued by friends, family and partners. Brands often stimulate feelings of trust and familiarity as customers walk into a store, knowing that their brand will be there and that it will have the same outstanding quality when they buy and use it. Companies that work hard on brand service and product quality will reassure customers that they are valued, and the relationship will grow from strength to strength.

Business-to-business brands often use this angle for their brand strategy as they rely on a more limited number of customers than business-to-consumer brands.

The heritage link

The past is and always will be a part of our lives, and people feel immense loyalty toward their heritage. Some companies, for example Harley Davidson, include 'patriotic' as a brand personality characteristic. The power of heritage can be linked with the emotional pull of nostalgia as pleasant memories move consumer minds. The introductions of the new Volkswagen Beetle and Mini cars brought back fond memories of the 1960s for many people and have been extremely successful. Brands like Mont Blanc and Parker combine fashion and luxury with nostalgia, when past generations used lovely writing instruments to write important letters and documents.

The cult of belonging

Although every person is unique, each has the same need of wanting to belong or to associate with others, be it informally or formally. So we join clubs, get married, or become members of social or professional groups. Brands help satisfy this need by giving people the opportunity to join clans of their choice. Brand personalities provide the impetus for role modeling and for becoming one of a special crowd. The Body Shop provides the opportunity to be active in helping save the environment and protecting animals. Nike allows people to be a part of the sports club of their choice and be 'friends' with their heroes. When I was talking recently with the general manager of a listed company, he referred to the brand of clothing he was wearing as "my brand". He was proud of belonging to the group of people who bought and wore that particular brand. Brands provide instant membership of many fraternities.

The feel-good factor

Brands give everyone the chance to feel good in various ways and to express these positive feelings, thus reinforcing self-esteem. For example, someone might feel:

- Sexy, using Boss perfume.
- Rewarded, eating After Eight mints.
- Romantic, staying at a Banyan Tree resort in the Maldives.
- Youthful, taking a holiday at Club Med.
- Distinguished, driving a baby Bentley.
- Successful, wearing a Piaget watch.
- Confident, drinking Johnny Walker Blue Label.
- Trendy, buying the latest iPhone.

- Sporty, wearing Under Armour trainers and apparel; or

- Sophisticated, wearing Tiffany jewellery.

The main point we need to take away from this is that the feelings brands evoke in people can become self-fulfilling. For example, if someone feels confident, he or she will tend to act in a confident manner. Brands can give people new capabilities and behaviors.

The dream team

Brands can take people to the dizzying heights of success that are the stuff of dreams. You can dress like the Hollywood stars, be a part of the elite business community, or wear the same sports gear as the Olympians. Kids can be superstars just like their heroes. Nothing seems impossible when you buy the right brand. The use of real personalities, such as Usain Bolt and Roger Federer, bring a brand to life and help make people's dreams come true.

The real me

From aspiration to revelation, brands can reveal the real you. Brand choices reveal lifestyles, hopes, interests, and successes, and provide the opportunity for every person to express his/her own personality. The clothes you wear, the car you drive, the drinks you order, and the brands you buy paint a picture of the kind of person you are and the life you lead or aspire to lead. Sometimes there is a difference between the 'real me' as I normally am and the 'real me' I want to be. For example, at home I might just want to put on my favorite brand of jeans and T-shirt and relax – because I feel that is the homely me – feeling comfortable with my friendly clothes and chilling out with friends. For a dinner or cocktail party I might wear a really smart, eye-catching outfit because I want people to see the sophisticated part of me. Brands are the vehicles that allow everyone to show others what they are and can be like. Brands can help you say, "Hey, this is me!" in a variety of ways.

Because brands offer all these ways of helping people to bring out their own personality, it is not surprising that companies build brands with personalities that can facilitate this and build a strong brand-customer relationship.

Brand personality and not brand values

Before we look more deeply into some examples of brand personalities, I should explain why I (and many top brands) prefer to use personality traits instead of traditional brand values. Brand values tend to closely resemble corporate values, with characteristics such as 'quality-oriented' or 'global'. However, these are quite frequently replicated by other companies and can be confusing for employees and customers; a reason why personality attributes are preferred. Indeed, our minds with four functions use these to express ourselves. In driving employee behavior and brand communications they are particularly valuable as people understand people. Let me give you a true example to illustrate this fact.

One day I was walking through a shopping mall at lunchtime between meetings and passed by a shop that was selling pens, watches and gift items. As I walked by, two young ladies came out of the shop and I overheard one of them say to her friend, "I am not going in there ever again. They are so unfriendly." She did not say to her friend, "I am not going in there ever again because the service quality did not meet my expectations." Think about this. We compute things in our minds using personality-type words. We judge other people, events and many things that we experience in life, including brands, using personality traits.

It therefore makes sense to use personality as the main bridge between our emotional vision and our internal and external communications and behavior, particularly as it is the personality of a brand that can appeal to the four functions of the mind, as we have seen above. Given that this is true, how can a company create a personality for itself or its products and services? The answer lies in the choice and application of personality traits and characteristics.

There are about two hundred words that describe personality characteristics and that can be used for brand-building purposes. Examples include trustworthy, honest, caring, friendly, creative, fun-loving, professional, genuine, and curious.

If you build your brand identity using the personality concept it is immensely useful. Here is a really fast way to assess any perception gaps. All you have to do is to ask whichever stakeholders (customers, partners, agents, distributors, investors, employees or more) you are seeking views from one question, which is, 'If this brand was a person how would you describe it?' You know what? They really get it and will find it easy to answer.

Here's another real example of some research conducted with customers and people who had experience of two competing brands in the service sector (names hidden to protect the innocent). I'll call them Brand A and Brand B. Figure 5.3 shows the summary result of that research question. The important points to note here are that the brands are competing, and what the people in the research audience were describing was in reality their brand experience.

Brand A you will note has a mixed response with some positives and negatives, while Brand B is totally different with more positive perceptions. If these were actual people then it is likely that a relationship with A would at times be uncomfortable and not too easily sustainable, while a relationship with B would be much warmer, smooth and longer lasting. As these two competitor brands are in the service sector it is not surprising to learn that B is doing much better than A in terms of revenue, market share and profitability. A's problem is that it thinks it is behaving like B and delivering that kind of experience when it clearly isn't.

This one question – 'If this brand was a person how would you describe it' – is a fast and reliable indicator for anyone who wants to see what gaps may exist between their brand's identity (personality) and image.

Brand A	**Brand B**
• Sophisticated	• Easy going
• Assertive	• Modest
• Efficient	• Friendly
• Self-centered	• Caring
• Aloof	• Approachable

Figure 5.3: Competitive brand personality perception research

Creating brand personality

Whether a brand is a product or a company, the company has to decide what personality traits the brand is to have. There are various ways of doing this, one of which is to match the brand personality as closely as possible to that of consumers or to a personality they like. This process involves:

- Defining the target audience

- Finding out what they need, want and like

- Building a consumer personality profile

- Creating the product/company personality to match that profile.

This type of approach is favored by companies such as Levi Strauss, which researches target audiences fastidiously. For one of Levi's most successful products – 501 jeans – the personality that matches their desired customer profile is: Romantic, Sexually Attractive, Physical Prowess, Rebellious, Resourceful, Independent, and Likes Being Admired. This brand personality appeals to the emotional areas of people's brains – their feelings and sensory functions. Harley Davidson also carried out research into the personalities of 'big bikers' and used the characteristics of Macho, Male, Patriotic, Loves Freedom and Enjoys Heritage to turn around the brand in the late 1980s when it was losing market share to Japanese competitors.

This approach is not feasible for most corporate brands if the customer base is likely to be broader. For building a corporate brand personality the process can involve identifying behavioral strengths that already exist or ones they would like to have and are prepared to bring to life. This may well be influenced by the corporate or brand visions. For example, if a company wants to be seen as socially responsible, this might require a personality that is responsible, caring, resourceful, friendly and trustworthy. Standard Chartered has a brand vision or purpose of "Here for good" and uses the traits of International, Creative, Responsive, Trustworthy and Courageous. Thus from a corporate standpoint, the brand personality must be a good fit with the brand vision – the kind of person that would bring that vision to life. In this way, the personality becomes the brand's identity.

Another approach is to take a product's or company's rational strengths and move them into emotional expression. The Land Rover case study below shows how an established brand took itself to a higher level in light of increased competition, by creating an appropriate personality through transforming rational attributes into emotional ones.

Case study 14: Land Rover

Turning rational attributes into an emotional brand personality

The attraction of a strong personality is irresistible, and clever brand managers build personality into their companies, products, services, countries, and places. Land Rover agrees that the brand (or marque) gives products an identity, as well as authenticity and authority. But it also agrees that the rational traits and attributes that products have aren't powerful enough discriminators in the consumer's decision to buy.

Land Rover took the rational attributes determined by research and turned them into emotional personality characteristics, emphasizing that brands have to appeal to the heart as well as the head.

The rational attributes held by Land Rover were:

- 4 × 4 engineering and capability;

- heritage;

- robust; and

- individualistic.

Land Rover decided that these attributes weren't enough, and that more muscular emotional values had to be articulated and introduced into everything they did. This was especially important as competitors could copy the rational attributes through engineering, quality, reliability, specifications, performance, and styling. So, the following emotional values were created, based on the rational attributes:

- *Individualism* – as opposed to the quirkiness of "individualistic".

- *Authenticity* – as opposed to "heritage" with its museum-like, musty connotation.

- *Guts and determination* – as opposed to "robust".

- *Supremacy and leadership* – as opposed to "4 × 4 engineering and capability".

Land Rover then added the characteristics that its target audience could relate to, namely:

- the excitement of adventure; and

- the love of freedom.

These characteristics were felt to be much more powerful and expressive of the Land Rover marque, and differentiated Land Rover's products from the rest of the crowd.

Brands such as these manage not just to develop a personality that the target audience likes; they also have an 'attitude' toward life that attracts people, as can be seen with the Absolut Vodka case.

Case study 15: Absolut Vodka

A brand built on a powerful personality

Background

Absolut is a brand that dates back more than a century. When the product was introduced to the US market in 1979, it initially received a cold reception. In a crowded market with established competitors, no one expected Absolut to succeed in dominating the category. Nevertheless, it subsequently did and became a world-renowned brand.

Prior to 2007, the growing popularity of higher-priced vodka brands such as Grey Goose, Belvedere, Chopin, and others saw Absolut Vodka decline to mid-shelf status, which produced a substantial drop in sales. However, a new marketing campaign, "In an Absolut World", launched in May 2007, has seen a revival in popularity of the brand.

In 2008, the Swedish government, which owned the brand, sold it to Pernod Ricard for US$8.3 billion, far in excess of the value its investors had predicted.

Absolut's brand personality

Absolut's success can be attributed to the skillful management of the brand. It is a brand that invokes a strong emotional connection with its target customers through its distinctive and appealing personality, made up mainly of wit and humor. It is Absolut's wit, rather than its taste, that accounts for the brand's success. Former company president Goran Lundqvist described it thus: "Absolut is a personality. We like certain people, but some people are just more fun and interesting."

Absolut's brand personality projects wit, intellect, optimism, and boldness. And it has also been described as smart, stylish, contemporary, and creative. Through its previously well-known "In an Absolut World" campaign, it has created and projected statements that appeal to society in general. Some examples of advertisements from the campaign include the following:

- "In an Absolut World, currency should be replaced with hugs of kindness."

- "In an Absolut World, all of our conflicts would be resolved in peaceful and fun exchanges."

- "In an Absolut World, everything is wheelchair accessible."

- "In an Absolut World, the moon wouldn't just light up the night."

In addition to conveying the brand's personality through the traditional print and broadcast media, Absolut uses the Web and new media such as Facebook. Its website invites visitors to the site to share their visions of how things might be "in an Absolut World" and to comment on others' visions. This initiative provides a platform for stimulating the imaginations of its online community. "Our consumers are intelligent, and we hope they have a gut reaction that sparks conversations and challenges them to think about their vision of an Absolut World," Tim Murphy, former senior brand director remarked. Similarly, Absolut has used Facebook to extend its advertisements that communicate its personality traits.

The brand's latest venture is into the gaming world with Absolut deadmau5, "an immersive journey for gamers and music fans alike with one amazing aim – to help you experience an #AbsolutNight like no other", giving consumers a unique virtual experience of an amazing night out with top vodka brand Absolut and Canadian electronic music producer deadmau5.

Through all these cleverly executed communications, and with its famous bottle packaging, Absolut has developed a highly differentiated personality, and one with a consistent attitude to life that people like.[17]

Here are some other examples of major brands that project well-defined personalities. Caterpillar has built a set of personality traits that match its business products. So successful has this been that it has extended the brand into totally different categories such as clothing and mobile phones, but all products are based on these same traits, which are Hardworking, Tough, Resilient, Determined, Bold, Rugged, Independent and a Good Friend. BASF has the personality characteristics of Innovative, Successful, Responsible, Competent and Open. And Hallmark's personality has been seen as Creative, Caring/Loving, Personal, Elegant, Traditional and Emotional.

You will no doubt have realised by now that famous brands build and project personality-based identities that fit well with the emotional drivers or visions they have established. The acid test for determining what should be the personality of your brand is would this be the kind of person that would deliver your brand vision?

Brand personality is long term

Human personality changes only slowly over time, having been largely formed at a young age. Similarly, brand personality should only evolve slowly and not be subject to rapid or frequent changes. We think it very odd if our friends are unpredictable in their behavior, and in general, society views people with changing or alternative personalities as bipolar or schizophrenic. Consumers are much the same – they like consistency and predictability when they develop a relationship with a company or product. Establishing a friendship with customers is the main aim of a brand. People can get very attached to brands, sharing much of their lives with them. Powerful bonds can be forged when brand and customer personalities merge.

Brand personality must be simple

A brand's personality must not be too complex. Although human personality is extremely complex and difficult to understand, it would be futile to project a brand personality that matches human complexity. Although there is no precise answer as to how many characteristics a brand personality should have, ideally, there should be no more than five characteristics, and seven is the limit, as beyond these numbers it is difficult to communicate the personality. In addition, for corporate brands, getting employees to understand the personality and bring it to life, it is necessary to keep the list short and explain clearly what the characteristics mean, an aspect that will be discussed further in the chapter on employee engagement. Flexing the brand personality is a technique used quite often to promote several characteristics.

Flexing the brand values

Some brands cleverly mix the rational and emotional characteristics of their brand's personality, so that they can flex the brand character to suit the audience they are addressing. By having several brand personality characteristics, they can emphasize different aspects of their character to different target audiences. So where, for example, a large telecommunications company brand has a set of characteristics that are Friendly, Innovative, Trustworthy, Understanding, and Contemporary, it can put across all these characteristics to each of the two main target audiences, but emphasize Friendly, Contemporary, and Trustworthy a little more than the others for the residential consumer, and emphasize Innovative and Understanding more to the business community. In brand communications, the attitude of the brand personality would thus appear more emotional to the residential audience – because they are more attracted by an emotional attitude – and more rational to the business audience, because this is their attitude toward decision making. The brand-consumer relationship will still be based on emotional strategy, but the degree of emotion exhibited is controlled according to the needs of the consumer group with whom the brand is trying to build a relationship, and is represented by the attitude of the brand when communicated. Further mention of the personality flexing technique is given in Chapter 7 on brand communications.

So, brands often mirror consumers' thoughts, feelings, attitudes, behaviors, lifestyles, and personality. Several successful brands have achieved global status because of brand management's ability to relate to and keep in touch with consumer emotions, mirroring their minds. Brand managers must be specialists in 'coaching'; bringing out the best of the relationship between all the players – the brand and consumers. And there is no better way to do this than by managing attitudes, feelings, and emotions. In some ways then, we can say that brand management is in the reflections business – anticipating what consumers want to see reflected back at them through the brand mirror.

Personality and brand attitude

Brand attitude for the consumer is based largely on what the brand stands for, and in particular, how the brand personality is communicated. Brand attitude is a product of brand communications – how the brand talks to the consumer. It is contained in the visuals and the copy of advertisements, for example. If a brand has a personality constructed around the words 'warm', 'friendly', and 'approachable' and communicates this well, it will be perceived as having a 'caring' attitude. The words 'knowledgeable', 'trustworthy', and 'professional', when brought to life through communications, suggest a more businesslike attitude.

The key to the way in which the brand should be communicated is often found in matching the attitude and personality of the brand to that of the consumer, so the importance of understanding what makes a target audience tick shouldn't be underestimated. If that understanding isn't there, then the attitude of the brand may turn off the emotional relationship process. It may either 'invite' or 'alienate' consumers. So, for example, if a brand's character exudes confidence, it may make some consumers feel inferior and others smart. An ambitious or sophisticated brand attitude can invite those with ambition, but turn off those who think they will never be able to climb to those heights. A fun brand might make some people feel shy and others really good about themselves. A reliable brand could make someone feel either secure or bored, and a tough brand might attract the active but turn off gentle people, and so on. Attitude is a two-way street, and brand managers have to manage these inner thoughts and self-directed feelings of consumers.

Summary

For brand managers in the 21st century, there are many complex tasks to undertake, but achieving brand loyalty and lifetime relationships with consumers are the true goals, because only when these are achieved will the brand last and grow in value. Brands are at their most powerful when they determine business direction, and when they bind themselves to consumers through emotional associations.

The power of emotion has been present since life began – it is the great motivator and the prime driver of the human spirit. Although rational attributes may attract, emotional attributes sell. In building powerful brands, emotional associations are greatly enhanced through strong, emotionally-based brand visions underpinned by charismatic brand personalities.

Brand personality is the driving force for both communications and employee engagement as will be seen in later chapters. It humanizes the brand, creates the identity and strengthens the brand-consumer and brand-employee relationship through the development of powerful emotional associations related to the functions of the mind.

In the next chapter, I will discuss positioning and many of the strategies available to brand managers. An emotional positioning strategy is one of them, and you will see how this can, and should, be linked with other strategies chosen. While reading the next chapter, keep in mind that all great brand positions stem from a well thought through brand vision and a charismatic personality, often based on consumer insight.

CHAPTER 6

Brand Positioning

Positioning is vital to brand management because it takes the basic tangible aspects of the product and actually builds the intangibles in the form of an image in people's minds. It focuses on the chosen target audience(s) and influences their thoughts about the brand in relation to other brands, thus bringing the competition into the brand strategy equation. Through the strategies described in this chapter, positioning seeks the best way of convincing people that a particular brand is both different from and better than any other brand. In order to do this, positioning brings in the competitive dimension, pitching the business and the brand against competitors for particular target audiences.

This chapter explains the critical role played by the positioning process in helping to make the strategic leap from being perceived as an ordinary brand to being seen as a leader, with all the rewards this brings. Strong, or even world-class, branding is impossible to achieve without powerful positioning.

The positioning process

If *personality* is the main part of brand identity, *positioning* is the other pillar of a brand's strategic differentiation platform. It is partly to do with how the core brand values are projected to the outside world. Someone can have a great personality, or a company can create a unique personality for itself or its products, but unless people see it and perceive it as such, it will have little effect. Conversely, positioning can be much more successful if it is personified, because personality is a differentiator in itself. However, as will be seen below, even personality isn't enough to completely differentiate a branded business.

Mind the gap! Avoiding the perception gap

All brand managers aspire to build a great image for their brand(s). Brand image, however, may not turn out to be the same as the identity and personality we want the brand to be perceived as having, because image is subject to perception – the way in which people think about something, or even imagine it to be. So, if we project the identity wrongly, or not strongly enough, the people whom we want to acknowledge our identity might view it as something entirely different. They might not see us as honest, or might think our packaging looks cheap. Image can be based on fact or fiction, depending on how people perceive things. Differences between identity and image are often called *perception gaps* and these must be avoided at all costs.

To avoid the perception gap between identity and image, we must ensure that what is offered is what is acknowledged; what is promised is what is delivered; and that the target audience sees and relates to our brand personality/identity, which will depend on consumer perceptions. There is no difference at all, as with the other steps in formulating a brand strategy, between positioning for B2C or B2B organizations.

Two key questions

Positioning is also about creating a perception of *difference*, and brand managers use a variety of strategies to answer two key questions:

1. Why is our brand different?

2. Why is our brand better?

It is absolutely critical for brand managers to convince and persuade people that they are both different from and better than the brands of their competitors. Simply put, the main goal of positioning is to create and own a perceptual space in people's minds that differentiates one brand from all others.

Positioning is more than just differentiating a brand on personality, although this is important. In positioning a brand, the brand's actual performance can be introduced, as well as its personality. This brings into play competitive business dynamics, as well as brand attributes and values. The idea is to portray a brand's strategic competitive advantage, and positively influence the perceptions of the target audience(s) so that the brand stands out from the crowd.

One major point to note is that unlike brand visions and brand personalities, which tend not to change over time very much at all, positioning may change on a more frequent basis. This is because market dynamics change and so does competitive behavior. Ongoing research is therefore necessary in order to track how well your brand is perceived versus competitors, on what dimensions, and to what impact. And all this has to be done on a thorough understanding of the needs and wants of your target audience(s). I will give some detailed explanation on how to formulate a positioning statement and what to look out for later in this chapter.

There are several broad types of positioning strategy available and here are some of the most effective ones used by companies.

Thirteen power-positioning strategies

There are 13 main strategies that can be used, either individually or in a combination, to establish a powerful position. The fundamentals of these strategies are described below, together with some of their advantages and disadvantages that need to be given consideration.

1. Features and attributes

This is probably the most obvious strategy and is traditionally the most frequently used in many industries. With this strategy, the focus is on those brand attributes that can be used to endorse the perception that here is something that is different, or better, or both.

The motor vehicle industry is a typical user of this strategy, and most car manufacturers either do this now or have had to do this in order to stay in the forefront of people's minds. Volvo is one of the best examples, having for many years positioned its vehicles as being the safest on the road, even though it may not be and has not been the brand to develop many safety automobile technologies. However, go around the world and ask people which brand of car is the safest and over 80% are likely to name Volvo. It is interesting to note that although Volvo is now owned by Chinese company Geely this perception has not changed (Chinese brands often have difficulties with country-of-origin quality perceptions but this ownership change has not been widely publicized, probably for this reason). Service companies can also use this strategy, an example being the Ritz-Carlton hotel group advertising its uncompromisingly high service-quality standards. It gets its staff to think in this way by saying to them, "We are ladies and gentlemen serving ladies and gentlemen."

Advantages: With this strategy, there is the potential to own it for a long time, as with Volvo, or it might last only for a short period of time, as in the case of laser jet printers, or 3M with nasal dilatory strips. In either case, it can result in the creation of a rapid market share, particularly if your product is first into the market with a new or distinctive feature or attribute.

Disadvantages: Features and attributes can be copied sooner or later (with increasing speed as technology advances), and this will erode market-share gains. Competitors may produce enhancements that cause your offer to be obsolete quite quickly, and repositioning might consequently be difficult. Technological change is militating against this strategy by increasing the speed with which products can be copied, and by reducing product life cycles. Smartphones are typical victims of the feature/attribute never-ending race with several hundred products released by just a few competitors each year.

2. Benefits

This strategy takes features and attributes to the next stage by describing what benefit(s) the customer will receive as a result – for instance, a toothpaste containing fluoride (a feature) helps fight decay (a benefit).

The benefits positioning strategy really answers the question consumers have in their minds regarding "What's in it for me?" Consumers are looking for emotional benefits.

Advantages: This strategy helps give a company and its products more appeal by allowing people to see clearly what the brand attributes actually mean. Like features, benefit positioning can establish short-term competitive advantage, and can lead to market leadership and quick gains. It is a reasonably flexible strategy, and can be extended in a clinical, logical way (aimed at the left brain) or in a more emotional way (aimed at the right brain).

EXAMPLE		
Feature	**Rational Appeal**	**Emotional Appeal**
Whitening toothpaste	Clinically proven whiter teeth	A more attractive smile and increased self-confidence

Disadvantages: As with the features strategy, the benefit positioning strategy can be somewhat short-lived, and what is a benefit and competitive advantage today may be part of tomorrow's basic product. It is based around the concept of a USP (unique selling proposition) that is vulnerable these days to easy replication, further enhancements, and technological innovations. I can buy a laptop computer today with a huge processing speed, currently the state of the art, only to find six months later that there is a new industry standard for that product category.

3. Problem–solution

This is another widely used, and often highly effective, strategy. It is based on the premise that consumers don't necessarily want to buy a product or deal with a company strictly for that purpose. What they really want is a *solution to a problem* they have that can be provided by the product or company. Here are some examples.

People often regard some banking products as a necessary evil. It is highly unlikely that they will wake up one morning gleefully shouting, "What a great day for an overdraft!" It's more likely that they will lie awake at night worrying about how they are going to solve an immediate financial problem to which an overdraft might be the solution. Many technology companies use this strategy, and Ikea says it offers "affordable solutions to better living".

Advantages: This strategy is clearly appropriate for industries such as financial services, IT, and communications, but it is also more widely applicable. Because problems always have an emotional consequence or impact on the consumer, it is a useful strategy because emotion can be built into this positioning, often being accomplished by suggesting an emotional benefit attached to the solution.

EXAMPLE: LIFE INSURANCE		
Problem	**Solution**	**Emotional benefit**
What happens to my family if something happens to me?	Life insurance	Peace of mind; my family will be looked after if a tragedy occurs

Disadvantages: Other competitors can also solve the same problems consumers have, perhaps even improving on the solution. In technology-led industries, this strategy is now becoming so overused that other means of differentiation are essential.

The big crunch can come if you claim the solution approach but don't deliver – for example, with warranties that don't perform. Also, to maintain brand credibility with this strategy (particularly in technology-driven industries), new product development is vital because life-cycle compression means the rapidity of new product innovations makes today's problems disappear fast. The pace of change also creates different problems for consumers. You have to stay on top of the game at all times.

4. Competition

Every company must always be aware of the competition – what it is doing and what it intends to do. Depending on competitor strategies, it may be necessary to change your position – a reactive strategy. On the other hand, it is possible to be proactive and change your position and thus disadvantage the competition. One of the biggest business wars, which has been ongoing for years now, is between Internet software and hardware suppliers. In a full-page advertisement in the *Far Eastern Economic Review* of July 19, 2001, Oracle claimed that it ran SAP four times faster than IBM. Using a large chart to emphasize the point, Oracle also claimed, "that's why SAP customers choose Oracle over IBM 10 to 1. Interesting." In a similar vein, HP and Oracle ran a co-branding campaign in 2009. The front-page advertisement in the *Wall Street Journal* of June 19–21 had the headline, "Runs Oracle 10x Faster", followed by, "The World's Fastest Database Machine. Hardware by HP. Software by Oracle."

A simple, neat, but aggressively to-the-point advertisement was this print ad run by Durex some years ago: "To all those who use our competitors' products: Happy Father's Day." The Durex logo was placed in the bottom right-hand corner of the page. You can't get much more direct than that.

Advantages: Competitive strategies tend to be more effective when used for positioning companies rather than products. Corporations tend to have more unique characteristics in the form of personality, culture, size, and visual identity that people can more readily associate with, and an image that can help keep a company one step ahead when managed well. However, with products there is often less to work with in terms of differentiators, especially in today's increasingly cluttered markets. Notwithstanding this, if a positioning strategy is based on facts or statistics it is possible to own a position, as long as consumers believe the figures!

Disadvantages: Competitive positioning can invite retaliation, and in some countries this is prevented by legislation. It can lead to a lot of wasteful expenditure and embarrassing public incidents, as in the case of ambush marketing. The message here is that you had better be sure your product or company has something to offer to your target audience that others cannot match.

5. Corporate credentials or identity

Some companies rely on the strength of their corporate name to endorse products, positioning them by the house-brand reputation. This can be very powerful, as demonstrated by companies such as Sony, IBM, and Nestlé. The sheer power and ubiquity of the parent brand name can make life very difficult for would-be competitors trying to establish their own position. The famous phrase, 'You never get fired for buying IBM' is an example of brand strength.

Advantages: The power of the corporate name can help strengthen or make a strong position for even an average product. A well-known name can cross different markets and, in some cases, create global product positions, as in the case of Sony moving into the entertainment industry from consumer electronics.

Disadvantages: If the company goes through a bad time, so does the product, and the position can lose its credibility. A badly managed corporate image will make life very difficult for products positioned around the strength of the parent's name and reputation. It can also work the other way round, as was the case with Firestone tires, which became a major cause of anguish for parent company Bridgestone and caused huge problems for the end-user, Ford.

6. Usage occasion, time, and application

This strategy can be an effective differentiator, but it is appropriate for products and services, rather than companies and larger institutions. The strategy gains its value from the fact that people not only use products in different ways, but may do so on different occasions and at different times. For instance, some people eat Oreo cookies for a between-meals snack (time usage). A nutritious chocolate drink is used by some people before going to sleep (time usage), and by others as a food supplement at various times of day (application). Champagne is usually enjoyed only at celebrations (occasion usage).

Advantages: Products and services can gain a market position that is more easily defendable, and the strategy is as flexible as the capability of the product's possibilities for different usage situations.

Disadvantages: Products with more effective usage may usurp the position, and as consumer behavior changes over time, the time or nature of usage might also change. Also, strong positioning here may limit opportunities, as is the case with champagne producers who are trying to widen their usage base.

One really good example of a brand that uses this across many consumer segments is Tiger Balm, the tag line for which is, "works wherever it hurts". This ointment product can be used for muscle sprains and aches for young and old, for athletes' muscle rub and sports injuries, joint pain in older people, headaches and cold relief, and so on.

7. Target user

The target user positioning strategy is a very good example of focus in marketing. Companies that know their target audiences well can be effective in positioning a generic product to many customer groups, as is the case with Nike, which has trainer footwear dedicated to each sports group, and Red Bull, the global energy drink that targets mainly active young people who like extreme sports. In 2016 it sold over 6 billion cans and since it started 30 years ago it has sold over 62 billion cans, and is available in 171 countries. Needless to say, it has the highest market share of any energy drink in the world.

Advantages: This strategy is good for getting into, and defending, niche markets, and for building strong customer relationships. It is clearly a winner for developing a product range where a wide range of customer groups exist for a generic product, but where slightly differing needs or applications allow a wide low-cost product range. In 2016, Nike had revenues of around US$32.4 billion, and produces around one in every two trainers sold in the United States.

Disadvantages: The strategy relies on accurate segmentation and, therefore, research. Companies that know the market structure and dynamics, but don't understand customers' real needs and wants, may well come unstuck. The strategy can be limiting, and user profiles will change over time. Nike, for instance, found it relatively easy to go from trainers to sports apparel, but failed to move into leisure apparel for older people.

8. Aspiration

Aspirational positioning can be applied in many forms, but the two most common ones are concerned with:

- status and prestige (related to wealth achievement); and
- self-improvement (related to non-monetary achievement).

In both cases the strategy relies on self-expression, and as most individuals have a need to express themselves in one way or another, associating themselves with companies or brands that facilitate this is helpful.

With respect to status and prestige, Rolex and Rolls-Royce are power brands that people use to make a statement about their financial achievements in life, among other things. On the self-improvement side, Adidas's "Impossible is Nothing" platform taps into the sports lifestyle and sporting achievement.

Advantages: Everyone has aspirations, and they are always emotionally linked. By appealing to these universal feelings, brands can quickly become global players. When combined with other strategies, this one can be immensely powerful.

Disadvantages: Not everyone sees himself or herself as a winner, and thus this strategy can be a turn-off for under-achievers. It is essential, therefore, to know your target audience.

9. Causes and ethics

This positioning strategy is also linked to emotion, and focuses on people's belief hierarchies and their need to belong. Avon, Benetton, and other companies target customer groups whom they believe will subscribe to a certain philosophy or who want to relate to a specific group or movement. Avon targets women and supports women's causes; for instance, it once conducted a survey of 30,000 women in 43 countries to discover what they feel are their greatest challenges, what is needed for personal happiness, and what things are most important in their lives. The Body Shop has always used this positioning as it campaigns against the testing of cosmetic and other products on animals, and works toward environmental protection.

This strategy is becoming more widely used and important, as it relates to freedom of thought and speech, environmental responsibility, democracy, the liberation of women, and other social trends. It is also a positioning strategy that is extending its use and appeal through the concept of ethical branding, a good example of which is Innocent Drinks.

Case study 16: Innocent Drinks

Ethics and social responsibility can mix with fun

Innocent Drinks, a UK-based company best known for its smoothies and quirky brand messaging, is actively involved in several cause-related marketing initiatives. It says very clearly on its delightful, refreshing website: "We want Innocent to become a global, natural, ethical food and drinks company, always remaining commercially successful and socially aware." The brand promise is, "Tastes good. Does good". The brand values for Innocent Drinks are:

- Natural

- Entrepreneurial

- Responsible

- Commercial

- Generous

Each year, Innocent donates a minimum 10% of the company's profits to charity. The majority of this is channeled to the Innocent Foundation, which aims to improve the lives of the rural communities dependent on sustainable agriculture in those countries where Innocent sources its fruits. In September 2007, Innocent became the first company in the world to launch a bottle made from 100% recycled plastic. This had to be lowered to 35% temporarily, in 2011, as the quality of the plastic had become poor and unacceptable. They are now back up to 50% for their juice and smoothie bottles, and continue to work at making the most out of their plastic. Other sustainable characteristics in Innocent's packaging include using the least possible amount of material per pack, using materials with a low carbon footprint, and using materials for which there is a widely available sustainable waste management option.

Innocent's ingredients are also sourced in a responsible manner. Buying priority is given to farms that look after the interests of both the environment and the workers, For example, since 2005 all of Innocent's bananas are Rainforest Alliance certified. Innocent also aims to be a resource-efficient business by paying close attention to its carbon and water footprints, and actively seeks to lower both in its business activities.

Although Innocent sold a 20% stake in its business to Coca-Cola in 2009, it says it will not change its ethical positioning. Co-founder Richard Reed said in an article in the *Guardian* of April 6, 2009: "Every promise that Innocent has made, about making only natural healthy products, pioneering the use of better, social and environmentally aware ingredients, packaging and production techniques, donating money to charity and having a point of view on the world will remain. We'll just get them to do even more."

Do have a look at its website and social media posts, as this is a brand that enjoys having some fun too. From its corporate headquarters, named 'Fruit Towers', to an area on the website for bored people, Innocent proves that being an ethical and socially aware brand doesn't mean that you have to be serious all the time.[18]

Advantages: Companies can own a strong position through this strategy. It can be very powerful when linked to other strategies concerning applications, target users, and emotion. Ethical and socially responsible practices are now demanded by consumers, especially younger ones, and few companies can get away without using this in their positioning and brand management action plans.

Disadvantages: Causes can go in and out of fashion, and while being welcomed by some, others might be offended; thus, proper targeting is vital. Additionally, while a cause is in vogue, the 'bandwagon' effect often occurs, as is the case now with literally hundreds of companies giving us steadfast promises that they will do everything they can to protect the environment. If you embark on this strategy with your brand, you are also committed to the long term and to a high marketing budget in order to prove to the core audience that you really mean what you say.

---

10. Value

Value is often related to what people pay, but this strategy isn't to do with price. There are two main elements of value positioning:

1. *Price/quality* – that is, value for money, a positioning used by Virgin, Aldi, Lidl, and McDonalds.

2. *Emotional value* – that is, the associations people have when they own, for example, a Mini car. BMW has brought back these memories and emotions with the highly successful Mini car range, fighting on the nostalgia platform in selling nostalgia.

Advantages: This is a good strategy when it combines the two elements, and can also be used tactically via promotions. The key is to concentrate on *value*, not *price*.

Disadvantages: It tends to be commodity-oriented when it concentrates on price, and not suitable for those building a power brand and looking for high premiums.

11. Emotion

As a positioning strategy this can exist on its own, but it is often used as an overlay position, adding value and strength to other strategies, as previously mentioned. It is highly important because, as research shows time and time again, emotion sells. Häagen-Dazs ice cream is a case in point, and the brand's success has been phenomenal. It broke into a market dominated by giants such as Nestlé and others, and sold its products at prices up to 40% higher than its competitors. The key to its success was the creation of a unique positioning around the concept of sheer luxury and the enjoyment of the moment. Some of the advertisements for the product portrayed this with romantic and sexual imagery, or by using fantasy.

Advantages: Emotional positioning strategies move people to want and do things. Emotion creates desire, and can be very powerful indeed. Positioning without an emotional element tends to be less persuasive and to lack motivation.

Disadvantages: As a strategy on its own, it might not sway the minds of the 'cold fish' – the more calculating, careful-planning, thrifty types of people. For those who are very price-sensitive the cost will be the decisive factor, overpowering their emotional feelings.

12. Personality

As mentioned in the previous chapter, brand building based on personality creation can be extremely effective, being frequently used by companies to build world-class brands. But people won't respond to a personality they see as being either not relevant or not likable.

Personality characteristics such as the following have proven to be extremely attractive to most people, although this is by no means an extensive list:

- caring;
- modern;
- innovative;
- warm;
- independent
- strong;
- honest;
- experienced;
- genuine;
- sophisticated;
- successful;
- inspiring;
- energetic;
- trustworthy;
- reliable;

- approachable; and

- fun-loving.

Advantages: People are very responsive to this strategy, and, when combined with others, it can produce high market share, loyalty, and profitability. It is the only way really to gain and sustain a strategic competitive advantage.

Disadvantages: The strategy relies on a very clear understanding of the target audience, and a great deal of investment, to ensure that the customer experiences a consistent personality on all occasions. Building a corporate personality, for instance, demands that the entire culture of the organization be changed so that all staff live that brand personality in their everyday work.

13. Claiming number one

This is an enviable position to have, as it generates perceptions of leadership. In the hi-tech field it can work wonders for the brand and provide a perception of difference, even though product service and quality may be similar between major players. This is essentially what has happened to Amazon.com, which remains the brand leader in its field, even though other companies offer similar products and services. Accenture, the consulting firm, was the first company to position itself as a technology consulting specialist, and has remained number one in this category ever since.

Advantages: Your brand is widely perceived as the market leader, and if you can maintain constant innovation you could own this position.

Disadvantages: The obvious concern here is keeping ahead of the pack when innovation is happening all the time. You will need to invest considerably in research and development.

Gaining power from combining strategies

The power positioning strategies discussed above can be combined in various ways as companies and people wish. Two well-known examples of this are the home furnishing specialist Ikea, one of the top global and still privately owned brands, and the sports shoe and apparel manufacturer Nike, one of the world's most admired brands.

Case study 17: Ikea

Using multi-positioning to establish global niche leadership

Ikea is a good example of a company that successfully uses a combination of positioning strategies that satisfies the needs of a particular segment to find a distinctive global position in a competitive market. Ikea is a Swedish company that retails home furniture and fittings around the world. It uses demographic and family-based segmentation to target primarily young people, especially young married couples, who cannot afford to buy expensive furniture but have aspirations for a nice, fashionable and comfortable home.

Ikea uses consistent brand visuals both outside and inside its stores and carefully considers the needs of its consumer market segment by keeping costs low and providing good service. It limits the number of sales staff but provides enough people who can answer all questions concerning the sections to which they are attached. This is supported by a sophisticated computerized system that informs customers of stock and, where appropriate, delivery times. Smaller items can be purchased and collected to take away at the end of the journey around the store. So it appears like a giant supermarket with staff. Customers can assemble all larger items themselves or have delivery staff do this for a small additional charge.

Furniture and furnishings are displayed in room format so that customers can see how various combinations would appear together in their own homes. Each store has a cafeteria and a children's play area to support the needs of young families. Opening hours are adjusted to suit working customers.

Ikea understands that its customer base has not got a lot of disposable income but desire the best home they can provide for themselves and their loved ones. One of their slogans that summarizes their key position is, "Affordable Solutions for Better Living". This lets the target audience know that Ikea understands their situation and the challenges they face. The words give a brand promise that Ikea will provide the solution to their problem. This is a smart move as most people appreciate others who help them to, or actually provide the solutions to, their problems. Furthermore, it demonstrates to customers that Ikea knows they are looking for a better life for themselves and their families.

Other messaging includes sentences that help build the emotional connection with customers including, "Your partner in better living. We do our part, you do yours. Together we save money." This positions Ikea and the customer as partners, working together to achieve desired results. And in an emotional sign off in brand communications to reinforce this promise, Ikea often says, "Live your life, love your home", which also introduces the emotional dimension.

In terms of multi-positioning, Ikea uses target user, value for money, aspiration, features and attributes, benefits, usage occasion, problem-solution, and emotional strategies. All of these are combined to generate a great customer experience.

Nike is also a global brand that uses a powerful combination of positioning strategies.

Case study 18: Nike

Multi-positioning strategies

Nike, one of the world's best-loved brands, elegantly employs a combination positioning strategy, allowing its brand to be differentiated across its multi-product lines, sub-brands, and business interests by drawing on the best benefits of each relevant positioning strategy. These positioning strategies include features and attributes, benefits, cause-related/ethical marketing, emotion, personality, and aspiration.

Features and attributes

Nike has taken the marketing of features and attributes to a higher level with the introduction of NIKEiD across both its online and retail channels. NIKEiD gives consumers the power to design, personalize, and customize the features and attributes (such as choice of colors, sole, inner lining, etc.) of selected Nike performance and sport culture footwear, apparel, and equipment. It is the beginning of a consumer-driven, Nike-supported community whose members share ideas, concepts, and a passion for NIKEiD. Each shoe designed will have the name of the creation, the designer's name, their country of origin, and the date it was designed. According to Nike, the NIKEiD business has more than tripled since 2004, with more than three million unique visitors visiting the NIKEiD website every month.

This positioning strategy also allows Nike to reach out to new users (see 'Target user' positioning strategy, above) who may be seeking customized designs as a way to express themselves and differentiate themselves from the mass majority.

Benefits

Nike Free (into its 13th phase with the RN series) is a good first example. Promising the benefits of barefoot running while wearing a shoe, it allows the foot muscles to gain strength by providing less constriction. Various features of the shoes are adapted to provide this end benefit. The latest technology presents new outsole geometry that enables the shoe to flex, expand and contract in smooth conjunction with the foot. Models offering different degrees of 'barefoot running' and shoe support are also available to ensure consumers get the right fit.

Another example of Nike's positioning by benefit is the development of Flywire (much like the theory of a suspension bridge), which allows fibers to support the shoe at key points instead of using whole layers, which increases weight. With Flywire, shoes can be made extremely light, yet not compromising support, a benefit especially relevant for sports such as athletics, basketball, and football (soccer).

Cause-related/ethical marketing

Since 1993, when Nike introduced its footwear recycling program Reuse-A-Shoe, sustainability has been a key area of development for the brand. This initiative was timely, given consumers' growing expectations for brands to embrace a greater sense of environmental consciousness. Together with Nike Grind – a palette of the resulting recycled materials – Nike has recycled old shoes and pre-consumer waste to create, resurface and transform courts, gyms, and other sports-related areas and products. Nike Grind is used in 71% of Nike footwear and apparel products.

Nike Considered line, which combines sustainability principles with innovations in sport, is a natural extension of Nike's sustainability initiatives. The goal is to create performance innovation products that minimize environmental impact by reducing waste throughout the design and development process, the usage of environmentally preferred materials, and the elimination of toxins. Nike has also developed a Considered Index, which measures the predicted environmental footprint of a product prior to commercialization. Only products scoring significantly more than the corporate average are designated as 'Considered'.

Nike Considered eventually brought about Flyknit in 2012, a material technology that dramatically reduced the use of glues and other hazardous materials that were needed to build products. One example is the Flyknit Racer – compared to other low-profile runners, its production process creates 80% less waste.

Emotion

Nike embraces the emotional aspects of its brand very well and this positioning strategy is frequently used in an overlay position, adding value and strength to the other strategies employed, particularly personality and aspiration. The ads for the brand frequently show a range of emotions, often revolving around the various expressions of winning, courage, and the call to "Just Do It". For example, the "Courage" campaign that debuted in 2008 celebrates the 20-year anniversary of the "Just Do It" campaign by presenting an inspirational collage of some of sport's most-loved athletes in their finest moments. Thirty-plus athletes from 17 different countries are featured, including Michael Jordan.

"The TV ad celebrates quite frankly what we felt is one of the most inspirational brand statements of all time – Just do it," said Joaquin Hidalgo, at the time Nike's vice president of global brand marketing. "It's at the core of an athlete's persona whether they are a professional or amateur. It's a call to arms to do better, to get to the next level."

Personality

Nike has become well known over the years for using celebrity athletes to endorse its brand. Some of these famous names include Michael Jordan and Roger Federer. They are more than Nike spokespersons; they add credibility, and their popularity, personality, and influence within their respective domains augments Nike's brand personality.

These personalities speak to consumers emotionally and seek to inspire consumers to be like them, to excel in their sporting achievements, to "Just Do It" in their Nikes.

Aspiration

Nike's mission statement is to bring inspiration and innovation to every athlete (if you have a body, you are an athlete) in the world. And they have delivered on both inspiration and innovation exceedingly well. Product innovation aside, Nike has religiously and consistently communicated the inspirational aspects of the brand, best summed up by their trademark swoosh and the tag line "Just Do It", through brand activation events and campaigns.

The Nike + Human Race was a wonderful example of inspiration delivered. Held on August 31, 2008, the world's biggest ever one-day running event offered around one million runners across the globe the chance to compete together. The 10km event was staged in 25 cities, including Los Angeles, New York, London, Madrid, Paris, Istanbul, Melbourne, Shanghai, São Paulo, and Vancouver.

"The Nike + Human Race is about inspiring and connecting a million runners worldwide," said Trevor Edwards, Nike's vice president for brand and category management. "We are offering runners new ways to compete and race, courses through legendary landmarks, each ending with a headlining musical act. It's an unprecedented way for us to bring an entirely new running experience to consumers around the world."[19]

Capturing hearts and minds

Whatever strategies are used, the key to positioning is capturing people's hearts and minds, by appealing to both the rational and emotional aspects of their psychological make-up. Astute brand managers understand this and know how to combine strategies that satisfy the emotional and rational needs of consumers.

Summary: Choosing a positioning strategy

Whatever strategy or combination of strategies you eventually choose, there are certain points you need to remember:

- The position must be salient or important to the target audience you are trying to reach and influence. It is no good communicating messages to them that are of no interest, as they will either ignore them or forget them quickly.

- The position must be based on real strengths. Making claims that cannot be substantiated can cause enormous loss of credibility.

- The position has to reflect some form of competitive advantage. The whole point of positioning is to inform and persuade people that you are different from and better than the competition, so whatever that point of difference is, it must be clearly expressed.

- Finally, the position must be capable of being communicated simply, so that everyone gets the real message, and of motivating the audience. The aim of positioning is to provide a call to action to the target audience, and communications must be created carefully.

Repositioning

As mentioned at the very beginning of this chapter, most positioning is *repositioning*. Unless you have a new company or product that no one has heard of, you will already have an image in the marketplace; consequently, you will need to reposition if you want to change it. In most situations, therefore, it is very important to understand what your image is and whether it actually matches the identity you are trying to portray.

Eight reasons for repositioning

There are eight main reasons why companies attempt to reposition themselves or their products. They are where there is a:

1. poor or tarnished (or outdated or inconsistent) image;
2. fuzzy or blurred image;
3. change in the target audience or in their needs and wants;
4. change in strategic direction;
5. new or revitalized corporate personality/identity;
6. change in competitor positioning or new competitors;
7. momentous event; or
8. rediscovery of lost values.

1. Poor, tarnished, outdated, or inconsistent image

For whatever reason, the image you have may not be all that is desired. The automobile brand Rover had a clear problem here, and even when taken over by BMW, with millions of dollars spent on the brand, it never regained its former glory. BMW was forced to admit failure and sell the brand for a token sum to a Chinese manufacturer, which has also failed to resurrect the brand.

2. Fuzzy, blurred image

Sometimes the perception people have of your company or product isn't clear. It's not that it is poor; it may be that people don't think strongly about it one way or the other – they are indifferent, if you like. This is usually caused by unclear positioning and/or lack of brand communications support.

3. Change in the target audience or in their needs and wants

If the marketing focus changes, then repositioning is a must. Theoretically, this might prove difficult to do, depending on how close the new focus is to the previous one. So, for instance, if Coca-Cola decided to target the over-sixties age group, repositioning would not only be necessary, but would also be a major challenge in convincing those people that the product isn't a drink made for the younger set. When considering extending the marketing of your company or product to new market segments, it is imperative that a reality check be carried out through market research to see whether or not a new position could be a reality, or whether the task would be too large and costly, perhaps even damaging the perceptions held by existing customer groups. If Coca-Cola tried to access the over-sixties segment with the major advertising that would be necessary, how might young people respond?

Another case in point is British horse racing. In an effort to stop the decline of interest in the sport, a branding project was initiated in 2008. The problem that activated this was that the main customer base for horse racing was aging and declining, and younger people didn't share the same interest. In addition to this, other sports were capturing people's attention and wallets. British horse racing therefore had the task of broadening its appeal in order to penetrate new target markets.

According to a report published in the *Guardian* on May 12, 2009, research by a branding agency revealed that: "Roughly 10% of the British population goes to the races at least once a year. Roughly a third of these attend on a regular basis, while the other two-thirds are once-a-year race goers. The aim of the rebranding project is to convert irregular race goers into more regular ones, while also reaching out to at least some of the remaining 90% for whom the sport is effectively invisible. In particular, there is a concern that unless at least a proportion of the Internet generation is recruited to racing to some degree, the sport's popularity and prosperity will inevitably decline. The 18–30 age group, and young women in particular, is seen as a key target group, along with over-55s."

4. A change in strategic direction

As mentioned, one type of directional change is when there is a need to move from one category to another. This situation usually arises when the category a product is in becomes too crowded, and symptoms of high competitive pressure, such as the erosion of sales and margins, occur. Categories exist in consumer minds and shouldn't be defined by a company. They depend on how people organize information about the things they see, be it by name, usage, attributes, or other descriptors. Successful category repositioning depends on possession of the attributes necessary for acceptance by consumers in the new category, and this should be tested out prior to relaunch as slight product modifications or enhancements and repackaging may prove to be necessary. Care should be taken to ensure correct definition of perceived categories. IBM has successfully repositioned itself away from being perceived as a seller of computer hardware to being seen as a solutions-based information technology company.

5. New or revitalized corporate personality/identity

This is the corporate equivalent of plastic surgery. Some companies find it worthwhile to change their identity completely – not just with a new logo, but possibly also with a name change, a new structure, and a new personality – in order to overcome problems of the past or to take advantage of new opportunities. The name change of Lucky Goldstar to 'LG' is one example of a company that has attempted with reasonable success to move more upmarket with its image and to target more profitable customer groups.

Another example of this kind of repositioning is TAG Heuer, the well-known professional sports watch brand. It launched several expensive global advertising campaigns using sports personalities in an effort to move away from its former cold, mechanical, technically efficient image to one that is perceived as warmer and more human. The basic position of mental attitude overcoming adversity and being in control of oneself is still present; however, the company says, "Through the association of the brand with these key players in sports, who have succeeded through sheer physical and mental effort, we hope to make a comeback to a more humane face." The brand itself was also given a new personality, and the strategy worked. TAG Heuer's success has been so great that it has now been taken over by the LVMH Group (see more on TAG in Chapter 7 concerning the role of brand ambassadors and personalities).

6. Change in competitor positioning or new competitors

Sometimes the competition moves its positioning closer to yours, and you may feel it is best to move away and reposition. BMW, in the United States, had to do this when Lexus encroached upon its position and started to erode its customer base. Another example is Bentley. Although owned and produced by the same companies for many decades, though not now, Bentley cars were perceived as a cheaper version of Rolls-Royce cars. This was thought to be a position that endangered the sales of both vehicles, but particularly of Bentley, now owned by the Volkswagen group. The repositioning of Bentley cars, through the creation of a sportier image supported by product development with high-performance engines, moved it away from the 'poor relation' perception into a powerful position as one of the world's most luxurious sports vehicles. For example, the affectionately named 'Baby Bentley' has been bought in large quantities by English Premier League football players, and this has started somewhat of a craze for the car among celebrities and 'wannabees'. Overall, sales have soared, making it a highly successful example of repositioning.

7. Momentous event

Occasionally, a momentous event might occur that demands repositioning. A momentous event could be a sudden, unexpected crisis. The media usually seize on such crises as opportunities to highlight the failings of a brand. For instance, when Coca-Cola endured another ignominious public revelation in March 2004, the UK's the *Guardian* newspaper wrote of it on March 20:

> "First, Coca-Cola's new brand of 'pure' bottled water, Dasani, was revealed earlier this month to be tap water taken from the mains. Then it emerged that what the firm described as its 'highly sophisticated purification process', based on Nasa spacecraft technology, was in fact reverse osmosis used in many modest domestic water purification units.

> "Yesterday, just when executives in charge of a £7m marketing push for the product must have felt it could get no worse, it did precisely that. The entire UK supply of Dasani was pulled off the shelves because it has been contaminated with bromate, a cancer-causing chemical."

The article went on to say, "Coca-Cola said it was voluntarily withdrawing all Dasani 'to ensure that only products of the highest quality are provided to our consumers'." Consumers might not have found much consolation in that statement.

This rather problematic situation led the company to embark immediately on major corporate social responsibility campaigns and activities concerned with water scarcity and other global water issues.

Another example of a momentous event was the public relations disaster resulting from the British Airport Authority's delay in opening its new Terminal

5 at Heathrow Airport. As the media were quick to point out, "The chaotic scenes as the new Terminal 5 at Heathrow opened yesterday were a classic example of a British public relations cock-up. Instead of being met with a high-tech, hassle-free travel experience, passengers were faced with overcrowding, delays, cancellations, ill-trained staff and baggage chaos."[20]

In 2017, the failure of BA's IT system at a holiday time in May left thousands of would-be travelers with no flights, no baggage and nowhere to stay for up to several days. Thousands were affected and the queues of people went outside the airport. This was later described as a human error in re-booting the system. It cost BA a huge loss in market capitalization and compensation, not to mention consumer confidence in the airline that may take years to remedy. Ryanair is currently addressing another calamity after cancelling flights affecting hundreds of thousands of people due to a lack of available pilots.

The lessons for brand managers are clear: first, don't advertise what you can't deliver; second, don't make claims that aren't true; and third, never compromise on quality.

8. Rediscovery of lost values

Sometimes when a brand has reached a point where consumers are almost taking it for granted and sales are stagnant or worsening, instead of trying to create an entirely new position, it might be worthwhile looking at successful strategies from the past, or evoking nostalgia for past values. Kellogg's once ran a campaign for its Corn Flakes product with the tag line, "Try Them Again For The First Time". Such a strategy, based on brand heritage, can be very successful, especially when competitors are relatively new and the target audience is open to the emotional value of nostalgia. Consumers can easily answer in their minds why that company or product is different and better.

Repositioning and change – the new paradigm

Ten to 20 years ago repositioning was a fairly unusual event, driven mainly by the factors described above, but today it is becoming more frequent as companies seek to keep up with the pace of change and innovation. As constant innovation becomes mandatory for success, so repositioning follows in an equally mandatory manner. Repositioning of brands is now the norm rather than the exception, taking place on a much more frequent basis. This means that brand managers have to take a different view of how they sustain and improve their market leadership and/or ambitions.

Here are some factors to consider in repositioning your brand in the world of change:

- Accept that repositioning is an essential part of brand development.

- Ensure you don't alter the personality of your product/service/company, as this will place your brand in the 'schizophrenic' category.

- Gather market intelligence on what the changing needs of your customers are, and the competitive response.

- Remember that you are dealing with the management of perceptions, and this means that you must budget for it. Repositioning means cash outflow in image and product communications to change perceptions and make people *think* you are still, or are now, different and better. The more entrenched the perceptions, the more you will have to spend.

- Bear in mind that all the products/services you have in the pipeline have to be changed according to your new positioning; if this is difficult, then your repositioning may encounter problems. In the case of motor vehicles, for instance, this can take up to seven years, as products are in the pipeline that will slow down major repositioning.

- Get buy-in from everyone who can make an impact on the brand in your company, or the repositioning effort won't work.

- Remember the basics: in order to reposition, you either have to add more value to the brand proposition or change the target audience.

Should positioning be revolutionary or evolutionary?

Revolutionary positioning is a term that tends to be applied to a situation where you are starting from square one, say, with a new product, company, or personal goal. In such a situation there is no current image, and a position has to be created for the first time. In other words, once you are nowhere, you have to go somewhere. In this case, positioning has to be revolutionary. You have to choose a powerful position amid all the established competitors, and make an impact.

Evolutionary positioning, on the other hand, is about developing your image gradually. Here the issue is that once you are somewhere, you have to decide where to go next and not be left behind. This is a repositioning problem and it can be extremely dangerous. The danger lies in suddenly stepping completely away from the position you have been occupying, and to which consumers, particularly existing customers, are accustomed, without alienating them and losing your unique identity.

In most cases, brand managers have the dilemma of balancing the two approaches. For example, Giorgio Armani, in an interview with CNN, described his biggest problem as keeping his classic design stylish while at the same time adopting fashionable change. He saw it as a true dichotomy. On the one hand, the existing customer base expects to see his classic style; on the other, fashion is moving faster due to technological advances and media hype. Armani said that the media are now less sensitive to individual style and more attuned to what mass designers are producing. So, if the latest mass-designed fashions include the color red, everyone (Armani included) is expected to deliver something in red. If not, he said, he would be left out of media support for that season. The dilemma for designers such as Armani, therefore, is how to remain true to his distinctive style – that is *positioning* – and yet incorporate the latest trends. His answer is: evolutionary change, not revolutionary change. He has to position his products to satisfy the conflict of identity versus modernity. He must remain constant to his customers and meet their expectations both of classic style and contemporary fashion.

Positioning for equality

Time passes quickly, and people's wants, needs, and aspirations change over time. Sometimes you just have to accept the fact that you are falling (or already are) behind the pack, and have to catch up. You have to convince people that you are 'with it', not out of touch with the latest trends, are up-to-date, contemporary, and can match what others offer. This means positioning for equality – showing people that you aren't disadvantaged.

Quite often this type of positioning is concerned with the more basic competitive elements of features and benefits, and keeping up with the needs and wants of the people you are trying to retain or acquire as customers. It is also mostly confined to positioning against the competition in specific categories, such as personal computers. With this category the life cycles have shortened so much that when customers start to use their left brain and analyze and justify which particular brand's features and benefits will both do the job and give value for money, the next range of upgraded models has already made the choice obsolete. Positioning here, then, is aimed at giving your customers the message that you have the necessary elements to be a legitimate competitor in that specific area of interest. So, as a computer manufacturer or retailer, you have to have models with the latest chips, hard disk sizes, memory capabilities, speed, and so on.

Positioning for superiority

Everyone likes to be superior, the best, everyone's choice, but this position is difficult to create and maintain. It goes far beyond equality positioning by seeking to create inequality, a differential advantage, and an image of being a cut above the rest, an undisputed leader. Some companies, including several of the world's leading brands, have already done this. Others have it firmly placed on their boardroom agenda.

Positioning for superiority is only achievable once the target audience acknowledges equality. In other words, you have to demonstrate that you are at least as good as the competition with whatever it is you are offering, and only then can you persuade people that you really have something extra or special to give.

Companies that gain a superior position can be said to have achieved a sustainable competitive advantage (SCA), being the most preferred choice in their field of competition.

The need for positioning statements

Unless you are in total control of all aspects of creating your image through communications, which is most unlikely, there needs to be a communications brief for people to follow. This is one of the main reasons for having written positioning statements. If positioning statements aren't in writing, there is a real danger that the ideas might be misinterpreted, the strategy warped, and the key messages not expressed clearly. The result could well be confusion in the minds of the audience. Positioning statements are essential if you are to keep messages clear and develop a consistent image and position.

What are positioning statements?

Positioning statements are internal documents, not meant for public consumption. They summarize strategy, and act as a guide for strategic marketing and brand management. They state specifically and briefly what you want people to think about you, your product or company, or country. They not only spell out the desired image you wish to have, but are also a good test for strategy, as they quickly tell you whether the perceptions you wish people to hold are believable, credible, and achievable. Positioning statements aren't easy to write, and often need several attempts. It is best to write them with inputs and agreement from other people. In companies, for instance, a corporate positioning statement would need to be considered by as many senior managers as possible to gain consensus agreement and buy-in, and to ensure execution. Product managers would also need to seek other opinions and endorsements.

Before writing a positioning statement, it is vital that there is a complete understanding of the following areas:

- *Your brand*: this seems obvious, but you have to be very clear about what you can really offer that will attract the people you are trying to influence. With products, this will mean looking closely at all the features and attributes, and the benefits that people will derive from them. All the time you should be looking for factors that will help differentiate what *you* have to offer from what the competition is offering. The same goes for services. What service standards can you present that will give you the opportunity to suggest a competitive advantage? Companies themselves often have distinguishing characteristics, such as global stature, track record, personality, and other unique features that can be highlighted and used as differentiators.

- *The target audience(s) you want to influence*: knowing what people need and want is critical, and there is a difference between the two. I might *need* some food to eat, but what I *want* is a curry. More than that, I might want a *vegetarian* curry because that kind of food fits in with my belief structure. It becomes important, therefore, to understand people's intangible requirements as well as their more tangible ones. Unless there is precision in customer understanding, the messages we send may be irrelevant and lose us credibility.

- *The competitors you are up against (competitive set)*: no strategy is complete without a thorough understanding of the competition, whether you are a football manager, marketing manager, entertainer, managing director, or prime minister. Some of the questions to ask might include:

  - Which competitors do customers consider?

  - What positioning strategies are the competitors using, and why?

  - What key messages are they sending?

  - What appears to be their competitive advantage and the key points of difference?

  - Why do customers buy from them?

  - What image do they currently have?

  - What differences do customers see between them and us?

- What competitor would they switch to if they moved from us? One of the major problems that can arise here is deciding just who the competition is. This issue is particularly relevant for fast-moving consumer goods, where the definition of categories becomes extremely important, but it does need to be considered in any positioning situation. For instance, if we were to ask whether Elton John and Rod Stewart are in the category of 'rock music entertainers', we would almost certainly answer 'yes'; however, if we were to ask whether they are competing with The Rolling Stones, we would probably say 'no'. Definition of the product category is therefore a critical first stage in competitor analysis, and is vital to the positioning effort.

- *Why your brand is different from and better than the competition (strategic competitive advantage or SCA)*: analysis of the above areas will allow you to make some accurate judgments as to what position to choose and which positioning strategy you need to employ in order to influence the perceptions of the target audience(s). This is the most important part of the positioning process, and should be considered in relation to the above areas concerned with the needs and wants of consumers and competitor analysis. If you do not have a SCA then it will be difficult to win and working to achieve one becomes paramount.

- *The emotional and rational benefits you expect people to receive as a result of choosing your brand*: if you put yourself in the shoes of customers, there is a greater likelihood that you will understand how they think and be successful in managing their perceptions, and you will find it easier to track whether you have achieved the intended image.

When you write your positioning statement, certain things contained in it may be aspirational in nature and some factual. This doesn't matter, as these statements are for internal purposes only. However, the aspirational or desired consumer perceptions must be worked on hard in order to deliver on the promise. Communicating parts of the positioning may have to be delayed, therefore, until the brand can actually do what the statement says it can.

Some of the above analysis might entail commissioned research if you don't have the internal resources to carry it out, and it may take some time, but your communicated position will be much more focused and accurate as a result. Once you are ready to write the positioning statement, try to be as concise as possible.

How to write and use a positioning statement

There are many ways of writing positioning statements, but they should all contain certain elements. From past experience I have found the following template to be the most practical.

A POSITIONING STATEMENT TEMPLATE

BRAND X

is better than

COMPETITIVE SET

(The main competitors your brand is competing against in your category, industry, etc. It is always best to name the main ones.)

for

TARGET MARKET

(The customer group or groups you are aiming for stated, if possible, in terms of their needs and wants and not just demographics. For a master brand this might be broad, but for each customer segment it would be more clearly defined.)

because it

STRATEGIC COMPETITIVE ADVANTAGE (SCA)

(The SPECIFIC advantage(s) your brand has, compared to others, in meeting those needs compared to the named competitors.)

with the result that

KEY PROPOSITION

(The real emotional and rational benefits that will be experienced by your target audience derived mainly from the SCA.)

The brand personality (character)

This is the personality your brand has, as discussed in earlier chapters. This can be stated separately at the end of the positioning statement, or more usefully, the words that describe the personality can be used in the text of the positioning statement itself.

If you work methodically through this statement, you will achieve answers to the two critical questions:

1. Why are you better?

2. Why are you different?

These two questions are of the utmost importance to consumers, who want to know why they should buy your brand in preference to others on offer. Only if these questions are answered truthfully and adequately will you be able to persuade customers that you should be their preferred choice. Great care must therefore be taken to ensure that the content of positioning statements is credible, believable, deliverable, and relevant to the wants and needs of the audience whose perceptions you are trying to influence.

You will find that writing positioning statements is a difficult process. It takes time and usually several iterations to get these accurate and acceptable to everyone involved in business and brand management. But it is well worth the effort as positioning statements are used as one of the documents given to research, advertising and other agencies as a part of their brief.

Example: a positioning statement for an airline

In this particular example, you will see the master brand personality for an Asian airline, which differentiated it from other international long haul carriers. You will also see how this was transferred down into positioning statements for each target audience. It is important in positioning statements to go into detail for segments, because their needs and wants are different, and so your total proposition will be different. However, the segment positioning statements take direction from the master brand statement to ensure consistency, while also ensuring relevance.

This is a real case in which all major segments of the market are addressed. For purposes of confidentiality the airline is not named nor are competitors, but in the real situation they were. Also, in the master brand statement the customer statement was necessarily broad.

The main things consumers look for when choosing to travel with airlines are safety, comfort, convenience, and a great brand experience via service, whether pre-flight, in-flight, or post-flight. You will find this reflected in the statements. You will also notice that the brand's strategic competitive advantage, Asian service quality, is carried throughout the different statements.

MASTER BRAND POSITIONING STATEMENT

AIRLINE BRAND X

is better than

Other international carriers

for

All users of airline services

because it

Employs state-of-the-art systems and technology, with global presence, complemented by the naturalness, warmth, and traditions of service of a national personality that represents the very best of all of Asia

with the result that

Every customer can have complete confidence in the understanding of their personal needs and wants and the natural, genuine willingness of Airline X people to care.

ECONOMY CLASS POSITIONING STATEMENT

AIRLINE BRAND X

is better than

Every other international carrier

for

Those seeking a comfortable, safe, convenient journey that offers new standards in air travel with a fascinating cultural dimension

because it

Employs state-of-the-art systems and technology, complemented by the naturalness, warmth, and traditions of service of a national personality that represents the very best of all of Asia

with the result that

Their voyage becomes a unique experience and a lasting memory.

BUSINESS CLASS POSITIONING STATEMENT

AIRLINE BRAND X

is better than

Every other international carrier

for

Business Class travelers seeking a vastly enhanced experience of
pure enjoyment

because it

Offers all the Business Class space, luxury, and special features expected of a
sophisticated global airline, made truly special by the naturalness, warmth,
and service traditions of a national personality that represents the very best
of all of Asia

with the result that

They arrive happier, more refreshed, and more relaxed, having enjoyed a
superior form of delivery of all the privileges and attention they deserve.

FIRST CLASS POSITIONING STATEMENT

AIRLINE BRAND X

is better than

Every other international carrier

for

Those seeking absolute luxury, convenience, privacy, and
individual recognition

because it

Offers unique First Class privileges and, in the naturalness, warmth, and
service of their attendants, an incomparable experience of Asia

with the result that

Their flight becomes 'a journey' in indulgence – given color and excitement
by the fascinating traditions and combined personalities of the world's most
exotic continent.

When you have positioned the company in this way, these statements must then be applied rigorously to product, service, staff, communications, etc. This part of brand management will be covered in later chapters.

Here is another example, originally written for Innovation UK.

Case study 19:
Creating the 'Innovation UK' brand

In the 2000s, the UK government developed a brand strategy and subsequent campaigns designed to address the issue of the UK's negative perceptions in certain markets, such as Japan, that were hampering trade and investment. Initiated in Japan and developed by a Civil Service cross-departmental team, the issues and strategy are described below.

The UK was not seen as an 'innovative' nation in key markets, and this was seen as unhelpful for the development of international trade and the UK economy.

A comprehensive brand strategy was seen as an important solution to this issue.

The strategy was developed by a team of stakeholders, including the PM's office, trade, foreign office, private sector etc.

The brand was launched in Japan and rolled out in Asia and other key markets; workshops were held for global UK trade representatives.

A set of brand values in the form of personality characteristics was created that were deliverable and which should be used to bring out the tone, manner, look and feel of all the Innovation UK communications. (Rational traits = Creative, Resourceful, Intelligent; Emotional = Visionary, Passionate, Inspiring, Open and Happy about sharing ideas/knowledge.)

The emotional ones were designated to take preference as they were likely to have most impact and at the same time act as a brand differentiator.

A broad positioning statement was crafted to define why UK Innovation was different and better than its competitors, as follows:

INNOVATION UK POSITIONING STATEMENT

UK INNOVATION

is better than other countries

for

Governments, investors, businesses, R&D institutions and technology professionals, students, and any organizations looking for inspiration, technology breakthroughs and visionary ideas that will shape the world in which we live

because

Not only do we have proven authenticity* as a source of scientific and technology ideas, products and innovative practice, we also have a passion to share our ideas and breakthroughs with others in order to enrich the quality of life for all citizens of the world

with the result that

We offer hope, optimism, opportunities and excitement to those who want to make a real difference to people's lives and tomorrow's world.

*Justification for this included facts such as:

- UK approaching 120 Nobel prize winners (about 100 in science), second only to USA

- Tradition of leadership and innovation in science and technology

- Newton's gravitation and laws of motion

- Darwin's work

- Faraday's electricity applications

- Fleming's discovery of penicillin

- Watson and Crick – discovery of DNA

- Hodgkin's discovery of cholesterol and insulin

- Cloning of animals

- Inventions of radio, TV, computers, Internet, fiber-optics

- UK domination of music and musical innovation

- UK prominence in running global fashion houses etc.

The brand strategy was launched in Japan via a video message given by then Prime Minister Tony Blair at a reception for over 400 people. At all Innovation UK events, the positioning was reinforced by consumer satisfaction surveys using the latest technology. The brand strategy and localized events were rolled out to other countries, such as Singapore, with considerable success, and a workshop was held for global UK trade officials to explain the brand strategy and help them to plan how to use it.

The success of the project led to significant gains for UK business, as the following quotes testify.

UK Trade and Investment

"Innovation drives economic progress. For businesses it will mean sustained or improved growth. For consumers, it will mean higher-quality and better-value goods, more efficient services and higher standards of living. To the economy as a whole, innovation is the key to higher productivity."

UK Foreign and Commonwealth Office

"Defining our brand strategy was an essential prerequisite in promoting the UK as an innovative country. Setting out a clear proposition helped us to ensure that our activities were targeted at the right audiences in the right way. Paul Temporal helped greatly in this process which has resulted in tremendous gains in terms of stronger business relationships and international collaborations."

Note: I worked closely with the British Embassy in Tokyo on developing the Innovation UK brand strategy, in particular with Robin Ord-Smith MVO, currently Her Majesty's Ambassador to the Kyrgyz Republic, Bishtek.

Development of tag lines

Tag lines are phrases that normally appear consistently after the brand name, supporting its personality and positioning. They are never used in isolation, always being prefaced by some form of communication. They cannot (and, indeed, don't have to) say everything. Rather, they have to be broad – able to lock down several messages, the thrust of which may change over time. They should, however, impart a sense of direction and provide the penultimate 'full stop' – representing the final impression and, ideally, call to action, conveyed to the viewer, listener, or reader. Once created, they can be very successful in connecting the brand with the minds of target audiences, and in cementing the emotional association. Tag lines need to firmly present 'difference', claim superiority, effectively cover personality, service, and technical sophistication if necessary, cope with change, and be equally relevant to local and foreign markets. Most of all, they have to convey a sense of promise, excitement, and experience. All in just three or four words!

With respect to the positioning statements for the airline given above, here is one of several tag lines suggested: "Your World of Difference". Does this tag line pass the test? Here is the justification:

- This line powerfully highlights the promise of difference, reinforcing the personality-based positioning and related, differentiating product development.

- It attracts interest and a desire to know more.

- It communicates what the airline's developmental process is all about – a quest to be different and better – both to consumers and their own staff.

- It implies superiority.

- It is broad, able to encompass and lend power to a host of messages. No specific promise is inherent.

- It becomes a most effective 'full stop' for any and all specific messages conveyed in communications, reminding consumers that the benefits featured are not available elsewhere.

- 'World' communicates globality, coverage, size (and, therefore, sophistication), yet in a way that supports the personality position.

- 'World' communicates the feeling of a 'cocoon', removed from the chaos and inconvenience that can accompany the air travel experience.

- Given the context in communications, a "World of Difference" becomes a reference to the country's cultural diversity, representative of the very best of all Asia.

- 'Your' puts the emphasis on the customer. It encourages a sense of relationship. It conveys the impression that the airline puts the customer first.

- The line has a 'softness' in tune with the brand personality traits.

- It is tight, simple, with ease of recall.

- It is confidently in tune with the strategy of outflanking and enveloping key competitors.

- It is safe. Should a radical change in market circumstances require a shift from the position, this statement will still apply to what has become an essential process of differentiation.

The following case concerns the Chinese company Haier. Haier has bravely created a niche position for itself in the United States and avoided the country-of-origin quality perceptions that might have arisen. However, positioning itself in a mature and sophisticated market was no easy task for an unknown foreign company.

Case study 20: Haier

Positioning an Asian brand in a sophisticated Western market: those who dare win

As a great deal of my time is spent within Asia, I often advise would-be global brand players from Asia how to get to the number one position in their home market, then dominate their region, then go global if need be. The rationale behind this is simply that few global brands have ever become global without first being number one in their home market. Second, while researching foreign global markets, the common-sense approach suggests that you then go for number one in your region. This second step is tough enough, as Asia represents around half the world's population, but the task is a little easier for Asian companies as opposed to Western ones, as the understanding of cultures isn't a big problem. Finally, when you have size, volume, an established name, and experience, go for the global market if you feel you can support it and can make it into the top two or three.

Fast track

Founded in 1984, Haier is a Chinese multinational consumer electronics and home appliance company with its headquarters in Qingdao, Shandong Province. It has a wide range of products, the main ones being refrigerators, air conditioners, televisions, microwave ovens, and washing machines. However, it is undergoing huge transformation. According to the company, "the Haier Group is today the world's leading brand of major household appliances and is now transforming from a traditional manufacturer to an open entrepreneurship platform. In the era of the Internet and post e-commerce, Haier will extend its ecosystem to social networks and community economies while enhancing the user value of Haier products and services and instilling integrity as a core competence throughout the Group. Haier aims to become a global leader in the era of the Internet of Things." Currently, the Group's brands include Haier, Casarte, GE Appliances, Aqua, Fisher & Paykel, Leader, Goodaymart, DCS, and Monogram. Each brand has its own market position and provides outstanding user experiences for end users.[21]

Looking back, as China's top white goods manufacturer, Haier, has taken the fast track, in contrast to the normal progression suggested above. CEO Zhang Ruimin took a non-driven state enterprise making poor-quality goods, made quality the imperative, and turned it into a company that is now the world's fourth-largest white goods manufacturer, churning out 43 million products annually that span across 15,100 varieties of appliances. Haier is ranked number one in the China market and generated US$17.8 million in worldwide sales revenue in 2008. In that year, it sold 12 million refrigerators, becoming the world number one in this category. So popular is the Haier brand in China that people pay a premium for it, according to Carrefour in Qingdao. In fact, its washing machine cost more than a similar US Whirlpool-brand model. Global revenue for 2015 had risen to approximately US$27 billion.

Zhang started with the goal of being a top-five maker of white goods in the United States by taking Western companies such as GE and Whirlpool head-on, despite his brand still not being a household name in Asia. However, the quality dimension first had to be addressed, as no brand can survive without first-class quality, with which Asian companies traditionally haven't been associated. Zhang has always realized the importance of quality. Such is his passion that, as a senior manager in the 1980s, he once gathered his staff together at the end of the day in the factory street and smashed 76 defective refrigerator products with a sledgehammer to get across his point on the vital importance of quality.

Country-of-origin issues

One of the most critical problems facing Asian brands in recent years is the perception of 'cheap and poor quality'. This perception has persisted for many decades, and has proved difficult to shift. It took 30 years for the Japanese brands to shift a similar perception, but Chinese goods are still in the 'poor quality' perception category, which is why Haier chose just this issue to fight its battles. And the chief executive really has taken the fight to the commercial 'enemy' – the US – where quality begins at home.

The strategy

The strategy for Haier wasn't to build at low cost and export products to the US that would be seen as 'made in China'. The company realized that while the top brands in the world – because of the power of their brand names –

could market products made in Asia, the Haier brand name would suffer from the home country labelling.

Instead, a strategy was used to reverse the conditions of manufacture so that Haier was made in the US. The company bought land enough for several factories in Camden, South Carolina, and spent US$30 million on its first refrigerator plant. This was an important part of 'managing perceptions' – what brand management is all about – and establishing a secure base for the future, albeit at an increased cost of production. Staffed mainly by local people, Haier now uses the label "Made in the USA".

Haier claims to have helped grow the market in certain categories. Since its entry into the US, Haier has established itself as the top-selling brand for compact refrigerators and home wine coolers; while being ranked number three for freezers. In fact, Haier has been instrumental in growing the compact refrigerator market by 50% a year after the brand's entry into the US. Haier is also sensitive to the needs of different markets, and it is keen to give consumers aesthetic value. The introduction of the wine cooler in the US is a good example of this understanding, with its sophisticated smoked-glass door, curvaceous lines, soft lighting, and chrome racks. It is very much an upmarket product and has been featured on the cover of the International Wine Accessories catalogue. This innovation was also brought to the market quickly, with less than a year from product conception and design to retail availability.

Haier recognized that the price-commodity trap was waiting, and tried hard to avoid competing on price and promotions through a focus on quality, design, innovation, and giving consumers what they really want. One of the key initiatives that Haier has taken to improve its image is by demonstrating its concern for the environment. Using innovation and technology, it has started to introduce eco-friendly appliances that help project the image of a company that cares for the environment, as well as its customers' concerns. For example, in 2008 Haier, with GE, developed environmentally-friendly washing machines that have the latest energy-saving technology, low noise emission, and more user-friendly features.

Partnership and structure

Haier America Trading sought strategic partnerships that would give its brand both recognition and credibility, and managed to secure Wal-Mart, among others, to carry some of its products, mainly small refrigerators and freezers. Haier adds value to its retailers by providing logistical assistance, inventory management, and stress-free customer service.

Speed to market and product innovation are essential items for Zhang, who claims, "In this information age, whoever is the fastest to meet customer demands wins. I work with whoever can give me the information and technology to meet consumer needs." For this reason, Haier has teamed up with renowned brand names such as Ericsson, with the intention of using Ericsson's Bluetooth wireless technology in its products. Such alliances are giving Haier access to a valuable R&D base that it currently doesn't have. As far as innovation goes, Haier has been known to have up to 400 new products hitting the market each year. By 2008, Haier had already accumulated 8,333 patented technology certificates under its name, and its dual-drive washing machine technology was included in the IEC standard proposal. This demonstrates that Haier has acquired world-class innovation capabilities in product R&D. All these developments are consistent with Zhang's vision of making innovation a key driver in his business model.

Haier's failure/success rate isn't known, and one wonders if the company can keep up with this rate of change. Zhang's response is, "Wherever we go, the strategy is always to break in with one product, then introduce more and more along the way. The strategy has worked in every market". Zhang says that Haier uses niche marketing and can produce a run of around 30,000 units of one product before moving on to the next. Some of them are clearly *very* niche – for example, a washing machine featuring a virtual fish tank! Currently the company is in dozens of product categories and is practicing mass customization.

Haier has learned from the mistakes of others in managing its brand. Typically, Japanese companies operating in the US have a wholly owned subsidiary headed by headquarters' executives. Zhang has a different philosophy: he is smart enough to recognize that his staff are still many years behind their counterparts in developed countries, and he actively encourages the joining together of foreign experts and his managers. In the US, Haier America Trading is a joint venture between Haier, which has the majority shareholding, and a small group of US investors. The Haier parent company is involved only in corporate and brand strategy while the US stakeholders, who understand the market, run the operations. They are given a great deal of autonomy, and this enables both speed and flexibility in decision making. Michael Jemal, a president and CEO of Haier America Trading, once said it is "the opportunity of a lifetime to launch a brand, to build a brand, to create a market."

Brand culture

Lexus, the company and brand created by Toyota to break into the luxury car market in the United States, sent its Japanese managers to the country well ahead of start-up time in order to gain a better understanding of the market and US consumer behavior, by staying with American families. It then placed these executives in charge of operations. Haier, however, has again taken a different route. The top managers are American.

The brand culture is important to Haier, and prospective employees must successfully complete a four-hour initiation program before they are appointed. The program emphasizes teamwork, safety, and the importance of quality. On the factory floor, memorabilia from the Haier heritage are displayed, including a photograph of the sledgehammer incident. Employees can earn a trip to China to help them appreciate the values of the company and to experience Chinese culture, which for some is a once-in-a-lifetime experience. Thus, Haier attempts to blend the best of East and West in its employee relations.

The future

Haier wants to be a global brand. The number one white goods company globally, in 2012, Haier Group bought the New Zealand appliance manufacturing company Fisher & Paykel, and in January 2016 it acquired General Electric's appliance division for US$5.4 billion, but it has a positive transformational view of the future, recognizing the impact of the digital age and the Internet of Things. Its strategy so far has followed the path illustrated below in Figure 6.1.

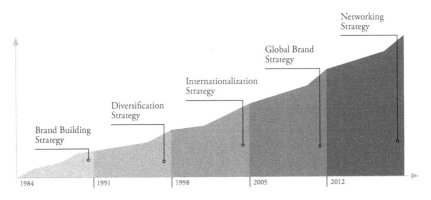

Figure 6.1: Haier Group Strategy

Haier says on its website, "The advent of the Internet Age has disrupted the development mode of traditional economies, while the basis and operation of the new mode finds expression in networking, with the market and enterprise demonstrating features of networking. From Haier's perspective, the way of implementing the development strategy of a networked enterprise is embodied in three respects: border-free enterprise, manager-free management and scale-free supply chain."

Zhang Ruimin's view of the future is, "I want to turn Haier into an Internet-based company, a company unrestricted by borders… We believe that there is no 'inside' the company versus 'outside' anymore." It certainly looks as though the next stage of transformation is underway.[22]

This is just one Chinese company. More entrepreneurs like Zhang, with ambition, passion, and flair, and controlling huge companies such as Haier, will emerge from this tremendous country. And the Chinese government's new policy of moving from 'Made in China' to 'Branded in China' will almost certainly mean the end of the domination of global branding by Western companies in some basic consumer goods categories over the next few decades.

Summary

I would like to conclude this chapter by emphasizing that good positioning brings about differentiation and brand strength. When a brand occupies a distinctive position in consumers' minds, it is difficult for competitors to gain the advantage. The more salient that position is to consumers, the stronger the brand will be.

Positioning is strategic and not tactical. It is one of the four elements of a brand strategy, along with architecture, vision and personality. Having said this, positioning may need to change from time to time as customer wants and needs, competitor activities and market dynamics change. Frequent research is therefore necessary in order to monitor how your brand is faring as these elements come into play.

The main aim of positioning is to highlight the point(s) of differentiation between your brand and those brands that compete with you. It seeks to establish a strategic competitive advantage and manage the perceptions of your target audience(s). As such, any positioning strategy should be based on real brand strengths of importance to customers and not just be aspirational. The image and reputation of your brand will depend on how well you can establish a favorable, strong and sustainable position and deliver on its promise.

All chapters so far have dealt with various aspects of brand strategy and I will now move on to look at strategy implementation via brand management.

PART 4

Activation and Management of Brand Strategy

So far, this book has dealt with the critical components that need to be addressed in building a powerful brand strategy. It is now time to turn to an examination of the elements of strategy activation and how they are managed.

There are five main elements that fall under the heading of brand management, but sometimes they are carried out by different departments or cross-departmental teams, and can involve outside agencies and consultancies. They are:

1. Brand Communications

2. The Digital World

3. Internal Brand Engagement

4. Brand Planning and Control

5. Measuring Brand Success (including Brand Valuation)

These five areas are more tactical in nature as opposed to the development of a brand strategy, which I have previously discussed. They have to be tactical in order to react to changing dynamics in markets and competitor activities, and to ensure they remain relevant to the changing needs and wants of consumers. As we will see in the following chapters, it is sometimes difficult to keep locked in to strategy while reacting tactically at the same time and discipline is required.

In the chapter on brand communications I will discuss the importance of an integrated communications strategy and consistent key messages, selection and briefing of agencies, and the projection of brand personality.

The chapter on the digital world will follow as this is partly concerned with communications but also offers a fresh take on the changing world of customer engagement and e-commerce.

Regarding internal brand engagement, this chapter will emphasize the role of the whole workforce in delivering the promise made by communications. The customer experience is only as good as the people that deliver it, and the vision, personality and positioning of the brand strategy must be brought to life at all levels in an organization. Sometimes also referred to as internal branding, employee branding, or employee engagement, this area is often overlooked by organizations.

Fourthly, I will devote a chapter to viewing brand management from a planning and control perspective, with all the components that have to be considered in managing the customer experience to a consistently high level. This will include touchpoint analysis, brand action planning, and a discussion of the need for a brand management structure to ensure all aspects of brand strategy implementation are successful.

In the final chapter I will look in some depth at how success can be measured by brand owners and managers, focusing particularly on the fast growing specialization of brand valuation.

The first of these chapters follows and is concerned with brand communications.

CHAPTER 7

Brand Communications

Introduction

A total communications strategy is of critical importance to brand building as it determines the effectiveness of image creation. Communications deliver the promise of the brand that consumers will experience. The tone, manner and style of communications reflect the brand personality, and the choice of media impacts the target segment penetration.

In this chapter I will discuss the trends and forms of brand communication. Communications practices are changing rapidly, and the days where advertising agencies were given a brief and produced a media plan are fast receding. As markets become more fragmented, audiences more sophisticated, and technology develops so quickly, the opportunities to communicate with consumers for a brand become almost endless. Linked to this is increasing evidence that traditional advertising messages do not work anywhere near close to the effectiveness with which they used to. So one has to be very careful with the use of advertising in its traditional forms and should put together an integrated communications plan that makes use of a variety of ways by which to bring the brand and its key messages to people's attention. Traditional communications channels are well known by practitioners and consumers as vehicles for conveying messages and propositions about what the brand stands for, what it is offering and so on. But the traditional ways of communicating with target audiences are transforming rapidly due to the fast-changing world of digital technology.

But older means of brand communication are still heavily used and in this chapter I will cover the more traditional aspects of brand communications that are still relevant, with examples to cover aspects of segmentation and consistency and personality projection. I will only briefly touch on the digital world, which is now beginning to outpace traditional channels and in some ways join with them. Digital communications and online transactions are growing fast and represent the future. Brand owners ignore them at their peril, but the digital world offers so much more than just opportunities to communicate that I will devote the next chapter to discussing the Internet and its broader brand-building capabilities.

Traditional communications channels

There are many options for communicating the key messages you want to be positioned in people's minds; however, the effectiveness of each method is changing very rapidly, as this chapter will show. The main channels of communication are:

- advertising;
- direct marketing;
- sales promotion;
- sponsorships;
- public relations;
- the Internet; and
- integrated communications.

Let's look at how each of these channels can be used in brand management.

Advertising

Advertising is a part of what is called paid mass communications, generally meaning space paid for in a publication, or time on radio, television, or cinema screens, although it may also be taken to include posters, billboards, and other outdoor advertising. Its main purpose is to persuade an audience either to take some action or to develop an attitude toward what is being advertised. Advertising is most frequently used for positioning brands.

Advertising achieves image differentiation mainly through repetition of a particular message, which leads to recognition, recall, attitudes, preferences, and action. It is frequently used by companies, but is also becoming more widespread in its application, being a part of global, regional, and national campaigns where information is less important than the need for exposure and positive perceptions. A good example of advertising-driven brand building is Absolut Vodka, where the personality of the product (intellect, wit, sophistication) has been consistently marketed and advertised around the world, and positioned so that it appeals to the target audience in terms of exclusivity. The brand has enjoyed a successful campaign relating it to different parts of the world. For instance, one advertisement for the product shows the usual clear bottle, but one that was enormously big and fat, with the caption "Absolut Texas".

Advertising can be executed through the various types of media described above, all of which have their advantages and disadvantages; however, creative repetition is the key to its success. The nature and cost of commercial advertising space means that only a limited amount of information can be placed, and so the frequency of an advertisement is also a governing factor in how effective it is. Little perceptual change will be gained by a limited number of exposures. Often, companies complain about the lack of advertising effectiveness, when the real reason is that the campaign was too short in terms of the message frequency. Managers in charge of brand communications need to appreciate that it takes time, and a great deal of repetition, for key messages to strike home and change human perceptions, which evolve relatively slowly. Image advertising, in particular, needs a long-term commitment. When carried out properly, with good emotional and creative input, it can be a powerful aid to positioning.

The use of emotion in advertising: appealing to the heart and head

There is no doubt that emotion sells. Emotion is still somewhat of a mystery, as far as our understanding of mental processes is concerned, but we do know that it originates in the right brain and manifests as a state of arousal. We also know that emotions trigger the brain 3,000 times faster than do rational thoughts. Emotion can also be positive (as in a state of happiness) or negative (as in a state of fear). As far as brand image is concerned, it is important to establish an emotional relationship with the people who are to be influenced. If positive feelings and emotions can be associated with what we are positioning, there is a much greater chance of attracting people, and altering or producing the perceptions we want them to have.

Emotion is increasingly being used by many organizations, especially service companies who are finding it more and more difficult to differentiate themselves from each other. Life insurance companies, for instance, are not just talking to consumers about the rational aspects of having a policy in terms of investment and returns, but are using emotional questions and statements in their advertising, such as "What will happen to your family if something happens to you?" and "We are offering you peace of mind". Financial services companies are typical of the many service organizations that are trying to persuade consumers that they are different from and better than their competitors in markets that are becoming increasingly commoditized. Fidelity Investments, in the United States, launched a series of advertisements that presented the company as being human and warm, with analysts saying why they like to work for the company and being very helpful to small investors seeking advice. In this age of technology, companies such as Fidelity, with large, dispersed customer bases of millions of people, most of whom they might never meet, have to show that they are not just cold, impersonal bureaucracies, but have a human side that cares about their customers.

Some of the ways in which advertising can tap into people's emotions include the use of:

- drama;
- shock;
- fear;
- humor;
- warmth;
- aspiration;
- music; and
- sex.

All of these have their advantages and disadvantages. Any agency creative must be examined very thoroughly to ensure that the emotional response it aims to achieve is in line with the overall position and desired image. *Appropriate* is the key word in creative selection.

Drama

Drama can be powerful in positioning. One brand of coffee ran a series of advertisements that showed a young couple meeting over a cup of coffee, and followed them as the relationship developed through its ups and downs. It was like a mini soap opera, and audiences loved it. The coffee was always present, being a part of their everyday lives. Drama was created by means of a story, but demonstrations and narrative can also attract audience attention and brand recall. However, care must be taken not to offend. In 2008, Snickers ran a TV commercial featuring Mr T of the TV series *The A-Team* saying, "Speed walking. I pity you, fool. You a disgrace to the man race. It's time to run like a real man!" Although the ad was intended to be amusing, the gay community in the UK found it offensive and Snickers eventually removed it.

Shock

Shock tactics can also be powerful influencers, but the line between a positive and negative response can be fine. Some non-profit organizations use images of starving children and distressed, abused animals to boost their position, but these tactics can easily alienate viewers. In 2012, Transport for London launched a series of adverts for their 'Stop. Think. Live.' campaign. These depicted teenagers lying dead on the ground, and captions included "My friend saw the text, he didn't see the truck." and "My friend heard the truck, he didn't hear the van." These shocking posters were an effective way of communicating to teenagers the importance of staying alert when on the road.

Closely related to the above is the use of fear. Volvo has used images of people who were involved in horrific car accidents, but who lived because of the car's safety features. The "Volvo Saved My Life" club helped the company to establish its position as the safest car, a position it still owns today.

Humor

Humor can be a double-edged sword. Ethnic and minority jokes can offend, even though many people enjoy them. Care must be taken to ensure that the surprise element of the humor is followed by pleasure, not pain. Humor, when used well, relaxes audiences and reduces their resistance to key messages. Cadbury's 'eyebrow' advertisement from 2009, which shows a young boy and girl moving their eyebrows in rhythm with the soundtrack, has attracted a lot of favorable attention around the world. Following this they produced another advertisement of office people dancing and lip syncing in their chairs to 'Yes Sir, I Can Boogie!' as a way to show that Cadbury can #freethejoy.

The meerkat adverts from comparethemarket.com continue to be hugely successful, using humor to play on a pun and entertain with their furry characters, and Warburtons used the much-loved Muppets for their 'Giant Crumpet Show'. The use of likeable and memorable 'mascots' help the brand to engage with their target audiences.

Warmth

Warmth also relaxes audiences and creates positive mental attitudes. Images that project love, patriotism, friendship, caring, and other warm behaviors can be of great assistance to positioning. Johnson & Johnson's advertisements for baby and other products have built an amazingly powerful and unassailable positioning of gentleness, care, and love, which is represented in the company's global market share.

Aspiration

Aspirational advertising can be a great motivator. Nike's 'Just Do It' campaigns are all about self-improvement and success, and advertisements featuring successful sportspersons such as Roger Federer help to reinforce this position. Aspiration as a means of bringing out people's emotions is often executed in advertisements through the use of children and well-known personalities.

Music

Music is frequently used in advertisements on television and radio, whether as jingles or background. If memorable, it can aid recall of the commercial, but it can also be a source of irritation. Up to 50% of all advertisements include music in some form. It may be used to arouse sentimentality, as was done so successfully in advertisements for the Hovis brand of bread where an English brass band played a very sentimental tune; or to illustrate fun, excitement, seriousness, and other emotions that fit the desired positioning and perception.

Music is liked by every possible segment and can be used to stimulate emotions in all age groups, but it is particularly appropriate for younger audiences. Marks & Spencer have used modern songs to help revamp their brand, making them more relatable to a younger audience.

Music can become iconic for the brand, such as in the Go Compare adverts: now it is hard to imagine any advertisement of theirs without the opera singer, and it may be difficult to stray from that motif. It can, however, be a non-differentiator, as is the case with so many car television commercials playing the same kind of dramatic, classical music as the products weave their way through hills, rain, and difficult terrain. A lack of creativity in both scenes and music can cause consumers to take the opportunity to briefly leave the room.

Sex

Caution should be exercised when using sex to sell a product. Subtlety is key to the use of sex in brand communications. There are no adequate guidelines here, but research indicates that sexual images should be linked clearly to the product benefits, and are received better by consumers if linked also to humor and respect, and are used suggestively rather than explicitly.

Sometimes, brand management steps over the mark and risks damage to the image of the brand, as Protein World did with their billboards featuring an attractive blonde woman in a bikini and the caption "Are you beach body ready?" There were more than 300 complaints submitted to the ASA about it, saying that Protein World were body-shaming women and suggesting that there is an ideal to aim for – that being the woman in the posters.[23] Jack

Wills was also recently criticized for sending their target audience the wrong message, with their overly-sexualized images of teenagers drinking and partying in underwear or pyjamas. This advert was shortly banned by the ASA.

Though when used consistently across a market, such as the perfume or cologne market, it becomes hard to differentiate between them and, as a result, sex does not really help to sell the product. In fact, recent research seems to suggest that sex does not sell. University of Illinois advertising professor John Wirtz and co-authors found that not only were participants no more likely to remember brands that used sex in their adverts, but that they were also likely to have a negative attitude toward such adverts. So maybe sex really does not sell and brands who use sex should aim to change their marketing strategy.

Direct marketing

Direct marketing is where consumers deal directly with manufacturers or suppliers when buying items, with no intermediary such as a retailer involved. Techniques used here include:

- direct mail;

- telephone selling; and

- press, television, and radio advertising.

To be effective, direct marketing has to be clearly targeted or it can damage a company's image through unwanted solicitation, as with junk mail. If done well, it can be highly effective, not just in sales terms, but also in building a strong position. Its specific advantages are:

- It is effective in targeting well-defined segments.

- It can help build relationships over time.

- It is interactive, thus involving the consumer.

- It is easily measurable in terms of responses.

- It is easily customized to provide specific messages to specific people.

It is critical for positioning and image building that the personality and identity of the company is visible and consistent, and that the correct values are projected. Dell Computer has built its entire brand identity and position through this means, establishing a first-rate image with low-cost, high-quality products and speed of delivery.

Sales promotion

While advertising tends to occupy a large part of the communications budget for many companies, especially those involved in consumer goods, sales promotion techniques are often used to get new products off the ground and establish positions, to acquire new and lost customers, or to speed up the buying process. Included in sales promotion techniques are:

- free gifts with purchases;
- redemption coupons;
- contests;
- samples;
- price reductions;
- discount coupons;
- self-liquidating premiums;
- 'buy one, get one free' offers;
- gift packs; and
- privilege cards.

The danger with sales promotion activities is that consistent promotional activity may weaken brand image. Some experts argue that they shouldn't be used for brand building for this reason, but companies such as American Express, Citibank, Carlsberg, and others have found them to be useful in increasing their customer base (mainly by getting people to switch brands), increasing individual customer spend, and speeding up the purchase decision. As a general rule, it is better to avoid the price discount type of promotion and go for the added value type. Adding more value to the brand offering, rather than subtracting from price, gives consumers good perceptions about value without losing quality perceptions. Perceived value for money is rarely a reflection of price alone.

Sales promotion activities are liked by retailers and salespersons, and can provide a company with a short-term competitive advantage, but there is always the tendency for competitors to wade in with their own similar promotion, so the results may be short-lived.

Sponsorships and endorsements

Sponsorships and endorsements are now becoming a fact of life for many brand managers, as more and more companies try to boost their brand images by tying up deals with celebrities. The main things to watch out for in this area of brand management are that they are relevant to the audience you are targeting, and that they are appropriate to the personality of your brand. The following examples are mainly from the world of sport, but many other examples, including celebrities, can be found in different sectors.

Brands and sports sponsorships

Sport has universal appeal. It is one category that attracts people from all nations – a universal audience. Sports sponsorships give corporate brands an advantage over advertising, by offering them a better chance of standing out from cluttered communications and addressing huge, targeted markets. It is little wonder, then, that the big brands are equally attracted, and want to be in on the major sporting events and activities that can give them global reach – and that they are willing to pay the substantial prices necessary to get there. An example is Barclay Group. Becoming the name behind the change from the English Premier League to the Barclays Premier League (BPL) cost Barclay Group US$130.65 million between September 2006 and the end of the 2009/2010 football season. Though no longer a part of the league's name, Barclays remains the official bank and one of the major sponsors of the Premier League.

Arguably the world's largest and most valuable football brand – Manchester United (MU) – signed with Adidas for a 10-year sponsorship worth £750 million, starting in 2015/16. The deal with Adidas more than doubles the old one with Nike.

No mention of sports sponsorship would be complete without reference to the Olympic Games. Predicted revenues for the Rio Games exceeded US$9 billion, and a great deal of this comes from the power brands. The turning point was the Los Angeles Olympic Games held in 1984, when the cost of sponsorship and broadcasting rights accelerated tremendously. ABC paid US$225 million for the US rights, and the number of brands allowed to become official sponsors was limited. As a result, a payment of US$4 million got sponsors exclusivity in their category. Coca-Cola paid US$12 million to be the official soft drink of the Games. Nowadays the premiums are far higher, and the big brands compete savagely for global exposure at the world's greatest sporting event. For example, Adidas became the third sponsor of the 2012 London Olympics when it signed a deal in 2007 worth more than US$201 million. The deal also covered sponsorship for clothing and equipment used by British athletes for the 2008 Beijing Games, the 2010 Vancouver Winter Games, and the 2012 London Games. When six billion people are watching, it's worth it.

Sports, sports personalities and brand ambassadors

Sport and sports personalities have become very popular with companies seeking global exposure and recognition, boosting the image of the brands (but not in all cases, as shown below) with their endorsements. Indeed, there are funds that invest in sport in a major way. The £4.2 billion CF Lindsell Train UK Equity Fund has invested substantially in Manchester United believing that the football club and world's most valuable sports team (*Forbes*) could be eventually worth more than the £2 billion it was valued at in 2017. Many other funds are also investing in sports-related industries and brands.

Sports personalities are inextricably bound up in the massive financial market as will be seen below. Their heroics in different sports encourage business growth in a phenomenal way. Sporting successes in the last few years have led to huge growth in sales of bicycles, tennis racquets, trainers and 'athleisure' products. For this reason, many companies are keen to get world-class athletes to endorse their brands.[24]

However, relevance and appropriateness are everything when it comes to personality (brand ambassador) endorsements. Most of the big brands get involved in this form of promotion, and not just the sports brands; TAG Heuer is one such example that has successfully managed its brand and its ambassadors.

Case study 21: Tag Heuer

Consistent campaigns driven by personality and brand ambassadors

TAG Heuer has many brand ambassadors, all outstanding in their sports, such as Cristiano Ronaldo, Tom Brady and Dan Carter. TAG Heuer is a brand I have always admired. For as long as I can remember it has demonstrated an unswerving focus on the delivery of its strategy in what is the crowded marketplace of watches, and in particular, luxury watches. It has carved out a very distinctive position in its category and is truly global.

> "For more than 150 years, TAG Heuer has faced down every challenge, and then pushed past it. By defying the time-honored conventions of Swiss watchmaking, it has led it to ever higher levels of precision and performance. It makes its own rules, chooses its own path, never quits moving forward, never compromises, never cracks under pressure."

So reads the short description given by TAG Heuer. It is this description of what the brand stands for that has led to some of the world's greatest and most consistent brand communications campaigns over many years focusing on the "Don't crack under pressure" symbolism.

The brand has a rational and emotional set of attributes that drive communications and personality endorsements. The rational side contains sturdy, robust, versatile, durable, resilient, technical and the emotional side has precise, challenging, dashing, dynamic, risky, tough, and heroic.

An example of messaging that has appeared alongside photographs of famous sports stars and legends is as follows. "The superiority of certain champions as well as certain sporting legends is derived, not from their physical strength, but from their capacity to mobilize their human emotions and place them in the service of the goal they have set themselves."

Talking further about its Ambassadors, TAG Heuer says, "They're athletes and actors, models and surfers, divers and drivers. They come from all corners of the earth. They're all under intense pressure every day on the field, at sea, on camera or on stage in front of millions of fans. They never stop. They never run. They never crumble. They live every 1/1000th of a second of every day to the max." Within the sports section the brand says, "There is no finish line, no quitting, no hiding. Our athletic ambassadors all share the same obsession: defying the boundaries of time by pushing themselves past their limits. They break records, but never break. They live their passions out loud and invite the whole world to cheer on their victories."[25]

Other personalities: the good, the bad, and the ugly

Apart from reminding us that there is big money in sport these days, the following examples show how the branding of sports products revolves around brand personality, and the personalities who represent the brands.

Usain Bolt

The world's fastest man, Usain Bolt, has recently retired from athletics following the IAAF World Athletics Championships 2017. The BBC announced him as Overseas Sports Personality of the Year in 2012 and many brands over the years such as Gatorade, Visa, Virgin, Puma have signed him up to be the face of their products. Puma have sponsored Bolt since he was a teenager and now he is the highest earning athlete in track and field, with a large proportion of his wealth stemming from his sponsorship deal with Puma. In 2013, Bolt and Puma renewed their deal to last until the end of his career, which was worth

US$10 million each year.[26] Bolt has also partnered with Virgin, and featured in a number of their ads that spanned from comedic to inspirational.

Even with retirement, brands still want Bolt to be their ambassador. Puma, of course, is one such brand but in November 2016 he signed a three-year agreement to be the brand ambassador for forex broker XM Group. "I'm happy to enter into a partnership with award-winning forex and CFD broker XM," said Bolt. "XM and I have similar brand values and aim to be the best at what we do. Their reputation has helped them to become an industry leader. Similar to XM, my focus has always been to be the fastest."[27]

Serena Williams

Serena Williams has dominated the world of tennis for years, and it is no surprise that she is the world's highest paid female athlete.[28] Beats by Dre, JPMorgan Chase and Nike are just some of her current endorsements.

Williams has proven to be an inspiration; she even won the Australian Open while pregnant. So, with the anticipation of her first child, there were expectations that this would attract more endorsements and sure enough, she signed a deal with Tempur-Pedic and featured in advertisements where 'Sleep is Power'.[29] Williams later returned to the courts, saying the pregnancy had given her a new power.[30]

Roger Federer

Roger Federer is another star who has fielded huge endorsements and sponsorships. He is the highest paid tennis player in the world and a number of his deals have been running for at least a decade. The largest being that with Uniqlo, which pays Federer approximately US$300 million over 10 years starting in 2018. Other brands include Wilson, Rolex, Credit Suisse, Lindt, Moët & Chandon and Mercedes.[31]

He has consistently provided these brands with a great image, as well as building himself a fantastic personal brand image; he has been a Goodwill Ambassador for UNICEF since 2006 and even has his own charity, the Roger Federer Foundation.

For any brand considering the use of well-known personalities it is important to choose carefully.

Personalities can step out of character

With the correct endorsements, the returns are there; but if things go wrong, the brand reputation may suffer. When it was revealed in 2012 that Lance Armstrong had been taking performance-enhancing drugs, he lost seven Tour de France jerseys and valuable deals with sponsors such as Nike and Anheuser-Busch InBev. Tiger Woods' infidelity scandal and a problematic back injury forced him out of the golfing world for a while, and this caused many brands such as Gillette, AT&T and TAG Heuer to pull their endorsements. Even now, having returned, he struggles to compete consistently with the best, and only a handful of deals remain – though Nike and Rolex do feature in his portfolio."[32]

Basketball superstar Kobe Bryant was charged with rape while under contract to McDonald's. Michael Phelps, the hero of the 2008 Olympics US swimming team, lost his endorsement contract with Kellogg's after a photo of him smoking marijuana was made public. Ben Stokes, the England cricketer lost his £200,000-a-year contract with New Balance after his arrest in September 2017 following involvement in a street brawl. The sportswear firm said, "New Balance does not condone behavior by our global athletes that does not match our brand culture and values, and therefore we have ended our relationship with Ben Stokes."[33] England stopped selecting Stokes as well, pending the results of a police investigation.

Of course, you can never tell what will happen when famous personalities are intertwined with the brand, and the public does tend to forgive and forget, but care is essential when choosing the 'face' of the brand. It is sometimes easy to grab at opportunities to reach millions of people through personality endorsements without taking the time to look at the possible downside. And even thorough analysis cannot predict how people are likely to behave in the future, so there is always an element of risk in this strategy.

This subject leads us naturally to what is arguably the most stressful part of the job for all top and brand managers: public relations and crisis management.

Public relations and crisis management

I often think of public relations (PR) as the 'Cinderella' of brand management, because it works so hard but receives few accolades when brands are successful. While advertising and sales promotion are very visible and tend to get the spotlight, PR is often the unsung hero, capable of achieving a great deal of perception change, yet getting very little recognition for the role it can play.

PR departments are often referred to by a variety of other names, including 'corporate affairs', 'corporate communications', and 'public affairs'. The basic work of PR is communicating and developing relationships with various target publics, including:

- the media;

- employees;

- shareholders;

- business partners;

- industry analysts;

- local and foreign investors;

- governments;

- the general public; and

- customers and potential customers.

Advantages of PR

PR is heavily media-related and communicates to these audiences through press releases, press conferences and interviews, advertorials, newspaper/magazine columns, receptions, sponsorships, and other events. Because PR can speak so widely through so many channels, it is critical to the brand-building process, although, surprisingly, many companies don't purposefully use it to do this. I would suggest that more brand managers use PR in a strategic way to build and protect their brands, as opposed to relying on it in a reactive way, as happens with crisis management.

It is surprising that PR isn't used more widely in brand building and management. Although it often uses mass media, unlike advertising, it doesn't pay for the space, a fact that might be of great appeal to the thrifty. In many cases it is free, and can both influence public opinion and build/maintain brand reputation and image at zero cost! It is for this very reason that PR often has more credibility with the public than does advertising. I am not suggesting that PR is a total substitute for A&P activities, but that it should be in every brand manager's armory, as it can provide valuable support to those activities, just as they can act as a support to PR.

Another advantage of PR is that, unlike advertisements, news tends to be read. The proliferation of advertisements in newspapers and magazines tends to result in readers largely ignoring the messages they contain, merely giving them a cursory glance. Similarly, television commercials are often given short shrift by viewers, sometimes because they are of poor quality, but mostly because they have no relevance to them. The tendency of advertising to irritate and alienate people, via whatever medium, is well known. But PR presents messages in a more engaging, newsworthy way that captures people's attention.

Disadvantages of PR

The work of PR is no easy task; it involves a lot of time invested in meeting and talking with the target audiences, and persuading them to listen to a certain point of view, and to adopt particular attitudes toward a variety of situations and circumstances. It also involves managing the media; getting people such as journalists, in particular, to report or say favorable things about the client when many competitors are also seeking comment, especially at times of great importance, such as new product launches. PR is an ongoing process, as opposed to a one-off campaign.

The stories that are generated by PR and sent to the media must be significant and newsworthy. Nine out of ten releases/stories that journalists receive never get into print – they are just not different or interesting enough. PR contributions must therefore be both timely and interesting, and the more expert PR practitioners will generate what in reality are releases that contain ordinary information, but also give the material a special twist to make it rise to the top of the editorial in tray.

Because of the above, the PR professional must have well-honed skills. In fact, the success of the PR effort depends on the strength of the PR practitioner's networks and oratorical skills – how they convey their ideas creatively and persuasively.

Points to note

Most large companies have corporate communications departments whose tasks include looking after public relations. Some companies and individuals hire agencies to do this for them, whether on a retainer basis or for particular projects, or in times of crisis. Some points to note that have relevance for brand management include:

- Most press releases never see the light of day in the media, and should be used sparingly. Inundating journalists with them isn't going to get results. They look for really newsworthy items, and routine releases are usually filed immediately in the wastepaper bin. Journalists only consider press releases when there is something significant to say that consumers will want to hear about. They are only interested in stories that sell and have a human-interest angle.

- Treat journalists as strategic partners in your business. Relationships are very important, and good relationships are only earned over time. Buying journalists the odd lunch won't buy you media space. It is more important to listen to their views, because they are the ones who are constantly in touch with the public and know what they will want to read, see, or listen to. Also, don't try to be everyone's friend. Choose carefully those few journalists who you believe will, in the long run, be the best choice for your strategy and future situation, and be prepared to invest a lot of time in talking to them.

- Make the best of opportunities that present themselves. An important development in the industry can give you the chance to comment and make your name known. One bank positioned itself as the 'Knowledgeable Bank' and managed to get a regular column in an influential newspaper, where it wrote about financial developments affecting people around the world.

- If events are being planned to boost the image of the company or its brand(s), ensure that they are a good 'fit' with the company's positioning strategy. The same applies to sponsorships: they have to be appropriate to, and in character with, the brand personality or identity to be projected. When Mattel organized The Barbie Doll World Summit event for charitable purposes, it brought together children from over 27 countries – an event that was totally in line with the brand's personality and positioning strategy. When Rolex sponsors sporting events, the company chooses only those top tournaments that reinforce the status and prestige of the brand name. And, of course, with both these examples, they were and are sure of getting the right media coverage targeted at the right target audiences.

Public relations and crisis management: you can expect the unexpected, but can you prepare for it?

Every CEO and brand manager fears a crisis that can influence market and consumer opinion in such a way that it sends the share price rocketing downwards and does serious long-term damage to the brand image of the product or service and the company that owns it. It is also a nightmare for PR specialists, because, when a crisis occurs, everyone else in the organization suddenly seems to distance themselves from the problem and to hand the 'hot potato' over to PR. Poor handling of a crisis can spawn more crises and ruin a brand's image. A good response, on the other hand, can save and even enhance it.

PR specialists are skilled in handling awkward and potentially image-damaging situations, and some are capable of turning a crisis into an opportunity. The problem with a crisis, of course, is that you don't know when it is going to materialize. Nevertheless, many companies are wise enough to develop crisis management manuals and procedures that try to anticipate every disaster situation and prescribe what the response should be. However, although crisis scenario planning is carried out by many leading brands, it is nevertheless simulation, and often doesn't resemble the real event when an actual crisis occurs. However good these preparations are, there is always the chance of something unexpected happening.

Unfortunately, there are no rules for crisis management. But we can look at some unfortunate situations that companies have had to face, and glean from them valuable information about what can go right and wrong, and what can be done or should be avoided.

The speed factor

In crisis management, the speed and type of response is critical to maintaining brand image. Sometimes, the public initially knows more about a problem or disaster than the company itself, as news teams tend to be quick on the scene. In such cases, the company is faced with a lack of information, and yet hard questions are being asked which require answers. As a brand manager, it is imperative that you put out a media statement of some kind as soon as possible, acknowledging what has happened. You may not have all the details, but you must say what you know. Failure to do so can seriously damage your brand image.

In times of crisis, brand managers have to move swiftly, and yet it is surprising how often avoidable mistakes are made, even by the famous brands. Coca-Cola made a huge PR error in 1999 when it failed to make any media statement for three days after a poisoning scare occurred at its canning/bottling plant in Belgium. While the media all over Europe were drawing damaging conclusions, Coca-Cola's head office made no attempt to communicate with the public. By the time it issued a statement, it was too late. This wasn't only poor PR and brand management; it was irresponsible. Had the crisis happened to a brand of lesser stature and power, it could have suffered permanent and fatal damage. There is little doubt that this decision, taken at the highest level in the company, was partially responsible for changes in management not long afterwards, and that it caused considerable damage to the reputation of the world's most famous brand.

In August 2008, melamine-contaminated milk produced by China-based dairy producer Sanlu caused the deaths of six babies in China, while another 300,000 fell ill. New Zealand dairy giant Fonterra, which had a 43% share in the joint venture company, made no comment for several weeks after learning of the contamination. Angry consumers finally forced the company to take responsible action and recall the product, but the delay damaged its reputation with its customers.

A more recent PR disaster from 2017 is that of Equifax after it emerged that a security disaster gave hackers undetected access to 400,000 British consumers' details for two months. Warnings about this prospect were given to Equifax in March 2017 but it did not admit that these details had been stolen between May and July until September. Other cases such as Toyota's major problems with car recalls in the USA after many accidents, with no quick response and the President being hauled up before Congress, are also worth learning from.

Other companies have demonstrated a quick response, as in the famous case of Tylenol – Johnson & Johnson's leading analgesic brand. The speed of withdrawal of the product from the market after poison was found in some of the product probably saved the company from catastrophe and demonstrated how concerned it was about public safety. Its re-entry into the market with tamper-proof packaging reinforced the critical attribute of "We Care".

The 'ostrich syndrome': denial

One critical issue with crisis management is whether or not the crisis should be denied. Many companies opt to deny that there is a crisis until either they work out their response or things become so much worse that they have to admit it. This is the fastest possible way to destroy a brand image that it has taken time to create. Generally, the best advice is not to deny that there is a crisis situation, even if you think it isn't really significant. What must always be remembered is that you are dealing with human perceptions, and these are very fragile, easily influenced, and difficult to change once entrenched. The message for PR here is that if consumers *think* there is a crisis and that it is important, then there *is* one and it *is* important, especially if those people are from the media. Perceptions can be fact or fiction, but they exist in people's minds; and to those people, their perceptions – which cumulatively form the brand image – are reality.

Maintenance of trust

The world's most powerful brands enjoy the trust of their customers, and this trust creates brand loyalty. In a crisis of any proportion, maintenance of that trust is vital to continued brand loyalty. Reassurance is an essential part of the PR response, and failure to quickly regain trust can mean that the brand image fails just as fast.

Whenever disasters occur, there are always PR opportunities at both the national and corporate levels. Out of sadness can come hope and resolve; for companies, a crisis can offer opportunities to improve their brand strength.

Integrated brand communications

The Internet is now a vital component of brand management and market communications, as discussed in detail in Chapter 8. Often, however, outside assistance is needed for Web-based and other communications. The trend now is toward integrated communications being offered by single agencies, which can provide companies with assistance on various fronts.

In the past, brand managers have had to rely on different agencies, or parts of agencies, to deliver brand communications via a variety of means, but this inefficient and often inconsistent approach has given way to new ideas on integrated communications that bring consistency to the way in which the brand is presented. Brand managers I have talked to welcome this trend, because consistency builds great brands. A really great example of integrated brand communications was that developed by Tourism Queensland.

Integrated, innovative communications: 'the best job in the world'

Campaigns should stay true to the brand and not become brands in themselves, as mentioned above, and brands should be evolutionary rather than revolutionary, but campaigns supporting brands can indeed be both revolutionary and very innovative. One of the best examples of this that I have come across is that created by Tourism Queensland, which was 'The Best Job in the World' campaign. This not only demonstrated real creativity, but gained amazing results through an integrated marketing and communications approach. It also showed how a public sector brand can take strategy and research through to implementation.

Tourism Queensland linked its brand to the master brand of Australia with a brand tag line of "Queensland – Where Australia Shines". In the global recession at that time (2009), with a saturated tourism market, the challenge was for the brand to reach out to more people, get more visitors, and generate more brand awareness of the 600 islands that Queensland has instead of just being known for the Great Barrier Reef.

The big creative idea was to offer 'The Best Job in the World', a six-month assignment to become a Great Barrier Reef Island caretaker, cleaning the pool, feeding the fish and collecting the mail. While looking after the island the successful applicant was also expected to explore other islands and write a weekly blog reporting on the adventures. Compensation included round-trip travel from anywhere in the world, room and board, all expenses while in Queensland, with a total package of AUD$150,000. Anyone in the world could apply.

Some interesting facts include the budget, which was only US$1.2 million, and the use of integrated media. As well as offline and online advertisements and mobile marketing, there was coverage gained on CNN, ESPN Sports and even *Oprah*. Incredibly, the BBC produced a one-hour television documentary on the campaign. Social media were used extensively to great effect. The estimated value of global publicity created was US$200 million, the campaign reached a global audience with 34,684 entrants from 201 countries, and it won three awards at the Cannes International Advertising festival in 2009. And the bottom line was a tourism increase of 20%. Not a bad return on brand investment![34 35]

New global marketing and media realities

The marketing and brand communications industry has seen some significant shifts over the last decade, driven by the managers of brands and the consumers that actually build the brands. First, there are many more competitors, and many more media opportunities, than before – for instance, there are now hundreds of cable TV channels in the United States. Second, more money is now being spent on promotion, as opposed to advertising, than in the past. Mass media is becoming less impactful, and therefore less fashionable. Brand managers are realizing that in the world of mass customization, mass-media approaches are less successful. Third, consumers are much more discerning and fickle, and less tolerant of traditional media attempts to influence them.

The traditional agencies have responded to these global and media realities by producing communications solutions that give brands and consumers more choice and relevance. The latest developments in brand communications are concerned with bringing together many communications platforms to create a bigger impact on target audiences, and to add power to the projection of the brand identity. Many agencies are combining their separate units and divisions to create improved and more cost-effective 'packages' for their clients.

Interactive, integrated communications

Television and print are significant media for advertising, but the growth of the Internet and the digital world promises to give companies more opportunities for targeted and one-to-one advertising. The power brand companies are now developing interactive strategies that cover all possible consumer communications touchpoints. For example, as well as carrying out all the traditional means of advertising and promoting its watches, Swatch has its own club, with an online community, for whom it provides social networking opportunities and a means to share common interests and photos, and to engage in discussion forums. It has blog features where Swatch club members can share their brand experiences and opinions. Through this experience, Swatch generates many more touchpoints with consumers and ensures that its brand communication is a two-way street and not a one-way dead end.

The increasing shift toward the use of digital as well as traditional media ensures that the brand receives maximum exposure. Such interactive strategies also ensure that consumers are involved with and can communicate with the brand. While Chapter 8 discusses the digital world in detail, it is appropriate to mention here that there is an interesting innovation involving traditional and digital technologies in brand communication, an example of which is the development of smart billboards.

Yahoo! has been awarded a patent that describes technology for a smart billboard where sensors, cameras and microphones work together to collect information about passers-by. For example, for drivers the sensors could monitor the day or time of day someone drives by and tell if they looked at the billboard, while the microphones and cameras could capture images or videos of vehicles approaching the billboard, which then could work with advertising exchanges to push advertisements to people's devices. Furthermore, it is envisaged that smart billboards could tailor the ads to drivers.

Other research involves work on 3D billboards using laser systems that send beams in different directions thus projecting different pictures to different angles. Eye tracking technology can collect data when someone looks at the ad and microphones could listen for conversations concerning ads. This is all beginning to get rather scary, but from a brand perspective the whole point of this is, of course, to make advertisements more precisely relevant to different target audiences. Watch this space. (Or perhaps you'd better not!)[36]

Whatever kind of communication is used to attract customers it is important to ensure that the copy is kept both simple and relevant.

Communications copy – simplicity, relevance and consistency

One important element of brand communications is the copy used. Brand managers need to be able to distinguish between creative that is 'on brand' and that which is 'off brand'. Too often, the tone of a company's brand communications copy fails to match the personality of the brand.

It is critical to speak to the audience in the way the brand as a person would speak to people. I would suggest that any advertising copy that is proposed to be sent out to consumers, via whatever means, be subjected to a critical analysis of whether the brand personality is actually doing the talking. And here are two more tips, remember that less is sometimes more, and that emotion sells.

Emotional brand communication: example of a simple, emotion-packed advertisement: Mercedes-Benz

Some of the best advertisements are those that use few words, but are filled with emotion in both pictures and copy. The following is an excellent example.

Longing.

Source: Courtesy of Mercedez-Benz. Used with permission.

The product attributes are clearly shown and referred to, as is the element of human desire. The advertisement is headed:

"The New C-Class Sports Coupe. Let your feelings go."

The copy says:

"How wonderful it is to dream. Of capturing the rush of youth. Of accelerated heartbeats and boundless enthusiasm. Of butterflies in your stomach. Of the pure driving pleasure of a lowered sports suspension that brings every curve and corner to life. Of the commanding power of a supercharged Kompressor engine. Of giving in to temptation."

This advertisement, although somewhat dated now, is a great example of how a brand makes the emotional connection with consumers and slips in rational areas of competitive advantage. It has a wonderful visual and terrific copy and it is not full of clutter. In brand communications less is more.

A challenge to simplicity: expressing multiple personality characteristics

Some companies have several personality characteristics or values, rational and emotional, and this can present a problem as to how to project them all. There are two ways of dealing with this challenge.

First, if the brand is targeted at more than one segment then it is very likely that different segments will have different needs and wants that can be expressed as emotional associations or desired personality image characteristics. This is especially relevant to corporate branding. For example, a telecommunications company will have many segments to communicate to, but for purposes of simplicity let's assume there are just two – domestic households and businesses – and that the brand personality is Caring, Dependable, Innovative, Resourceful, Confident, and Knowledgeable.

It is not easy to put every one of these six characteristics into, say, a 40- or 60-second television commercial or any other type of advertisement. But if we look a little closer at the two segments and, subject to checking the company personality against the desired characteristics of consumers, we would probably find that the kind of telecommunications 'person' the company communicates with is different in nature. Hence, the priority characteristics to focus on for business customers might be Innovative, Resourceful and Dependable while the priority characteristics to emphasize for families might be Caring, Dependent and Confident. In this real example, all six characteristics were relevant to all segments but the emphasis varies to 'dial-up' those of most interest to each customer group. In this scenario, it would be wise to brief the advertising agency on the emphasis to be placed on the personality to produce two brand communications campaigns each presenting the overall corporate personality in a unique, attractive and appropriate way to specific target audiences.

An alternative challenge faces companies that want to express several personality characteristics to one segment in different cultural settings. Companies targeting large global segments such as youth or millennials are frequently faced with this issue. For example, Levi's, a great corporate brand, has used eight brand personality characteristics to address its global audience.

In this situation, with communications campaigns running globally, Levi's played what it calls its "Brand Chord". The personality traits are like musical keys on an electronic keyboard where chords are formed by combining various notes (traits or brand values) in different ways. And, like electronic keyboards, some notes can be pressed hard to produce a louder noise than others that are pressed more softly. For Levi's, the brand traits are Masculinity, Rebelliousness, Sexiness, Individuality, Originality, American, Freedom and Youth. What the

Levi's brand does is to play all the 'notes' in various combinations over different campaigns, playing up some characteristics at certain times and in certain media placements, and others on other occasions. In this way, it insures that all the brand personality traits get a hearing with repetition over time. This method also gives the brand flexibility to play down some characteristics at times to cater for cultural sensitivities. For example, the French are less sensitive about sex, but in an Arabic country this value would not be appreciated so much. In Germany, rebellion is tolerated more than in Japan. The 'brand chord' can cater for these nuances and many commercials might be made for the duration of the campaign over a couple of years. This brand personality also links to the personality created for each Levi's product and they too play their own brand chords.

For example, Levi 501's – one of Levi's most successful products – has a brand personality of Romantic, Sexually Attractive, Rebellious, Physical Prowess, Resourceful, Independent and Likes Being Admired. It is basically impossible to express these all at once and so the product brand plays its own "Brand Chord". So one six-month campaign may play up Romantic and Sexually Attractive while another may play up Resourceful and Independent. Over the two years and four campaigns all the personality traits are projected.

But it is not always the case that corporate brands have to communicate several personality traits. The famous Marlboro brand communicates just two main characteristics, which are Strength and Independence, and has consistently projected these for over half a century. With the Marlboro country (wide open plains with mountainous backgrounds), the 'tough looking' Marlboro cowboy (always on his own) and the red and white distinctive chevron packaging, the consistency of the brand's communications has never been in doubt.

The message here is that the more you know about the target audience the more effective your brand communications will be, as shown in Case Study 22 below.

Relevance: what you say, and how, depends on what you know

It is probably clear to you by now that it is critical to understand the target audience well before attempting any communication with them. Some brands go to extraordinary lengths to get to know their customers, and base all their communications on the insights they gather. Once they understand the way the target audience thinks and behaves, then they tailor what they say, and how they say it, to that audience.

Case study 22: Procter & Gamble

Cross-cultural insights shape brand communications

Procter & Gamble (P&G) has global brands with the same brand positioning and central message. It manages to communicate this single message, while also localizing it for each distinct market in which it operates, by really understanding each country's socioeconomic situation and the aspirations of its consumers. This gathering of consumer insights is critical to how P&G tailors its communications to local audiences, while at the same time projecting a consistent brand proposition. This case is a good example of a brand that adapts *what* it says to its consumers – and *how* it says it – based on what it knows about them.

Targeting women

Many of P&G's brands are targeted at women, and we will look at two examples of its women's brands, Pampers and Always. But first, P&G regularly takes a long, hard look at its target market, to see if there is anything changing in the lives of its prospective customers that must be reflected in its brand communications.

P&G says that women, as a target market, are changing in many ways. They are reinventing themselves. They are becoming more independent, more demanding, more questioning, more self-reliant, more aware of their power, and more connected. And the increasing pace of globalization, driven largely by technology, has united them in how they live their lives, using social networking and mobile media. P&G found that the use of mobile text messaging is ubiquitous and used particularly where young women and teens have little privacy at home. In Saudi Arabia, for instance, teens use Bluetooth technology to bypass the laws that prevent them from communicating with the opposite sex.

Technology is now a vital part of women's lives, and they use it in different ways, but women as a whole have one ideal in common – personal fulfillment. As with the use of connection technology, P&G found that the expression of this ideal also differs in different cultures and markets. In Western markets, women see the pursuit of independent non-work activities and passions as their gateway to happiness; whereas women in emerging markets seek to find a balance between achieving their potential and gaining financial independence, and complying with traditions and the obligations of family. These insights have led P&G to look closely at how women's basic ideals are shared, and how different expressions of them, filtered by cultural norms, can influence their decisions to purchase its women's product brands, such as Pampers and Always.

Pampers brand

Pampers is what P&G and other brand owners call a 'power brand'; it is their largest brand and has seen more than US$10 billion in sales worldwide.[37] The brand has a presence in almost every country in the world. Pampers has become the generic name for diapers in its category, similar to Colgate in the toothpaste category, and consumer understanding is the secret of its success.

Although motherhood is universal, and a mother's concerns are similar wherever in the world she might be, P&G targets the Pampers brand based on women's different aspirations. The brand stands for the same central idea everywhere in the world: caring for a baby's development. However, according to P&G's Nada Dugas, who has held positions of brand communication director of Europe and IMEA and Geneva-based communications director for baby and feminine care:

> "The way we communicate differs with respect to who we are addressing. There are mainly three groups of mothers that exist in all countries, but the predominance of each group depends a lot on the socio-economic situation and the economic development of the country.

> "The first group is more related to developed countries and affluent classes (but is not limited to them), and their aspiration is to have achievers (children such as the early music learners and experimenting kids). The key motivators for a mother belonging to this group are:

- Self-reliance, and creating a nuclear family:
  - seeing herself as a person – not just a mother
  - having contact with people outside the family, but
  - with a sense of belonging that comes from a smaller circle
- Enabling development, tracking progress, and coaching for success:
  - the mother sees herself as a coach
  - is able to track development goals
  - seeks a competitive edge to reach her milestones
- Discovery, seeing the child as an individual, and building independence:

- sees the child as a little person; a 'self'
- views the world as a safe place, if one is prepared
- teaches children to make their own choices
- learns through experience and discovery

- Newer and better, looking forward, and being prepared for the future:
  - views things with a longer time horizon
  - believes in progress; wants the newest and the best
  - focuses on tomorrow, and has a plan to get there

"For this group our communication focuses on 'hero-ing' the baby, showing his progress and development.

"A second group is focused on relationships and the physical and emotional contact with the baby. This segment is focused on:

- Building bonds, belonging, and the extended family:
  - her world is defined by the extended family
  - she lives in a community of families
  - traditional, generational influences (her mother, her grandmother, etc.)

- Being there today:
  - of life goals, 'Mom' eclipses all others
  - more likely to be a stay-at-home mother
  - wants to enjoy every day while her children are babies

- The desire to protect:
  - sees the child as very dependent on her
  - the world is different from the one in which she was raised
  - may fear the day her child leaves the nest

- Everyday moments:
  - focuses on 'now'; not eager for separation
  - memories made of the missteps as well as achievements
  - enjoying the 'roller coaster' of life

"For this group, again, we tailor our communication to reflect the closeness of the mother to the baby and her caring for him.

"Finally in the less affluent countries, what matters is being practical, healthy, and buying a product that performs and represents good value for money. Women in this group are motivated by:

- Healthy development, day-to-day living, physical health:
  - illness is more likely
  - baby's physical health is an accomplishment
  - can impact on emotional and economic status
  - puts family at risk
- Value, responsibility, balance, and practicality:
  - life happens
  - solo parenting
  - makes trade-offs
  - takes pride in making good choices
  - each choice is important
- Positive self-image, confidence, and the belief in good:
  - optimistic outlook makes today happier
  - gets confidence from the black and white
  - stands up for herself… and especially for kids
  - believes in things that are 'good' and 'right'
- Hope and a better tomorrow:
  - dreams are free
  - for her children, she wants happiness, health, education, and 'to have it better'
  - feet planted on the ground, but can indulge in fantasy
  - believes things can change at any moment

"For this segment, we target our communication by showing the performance of our product and its value."

The role of consumer insight in brand communications is to enable brand managers to address the target audience in terms that are relevant and suitable to them.

Another example of P&G's discerning insights into consumer thinking is the Always brand. Nada Dugas explains:

> "The Always brand stands for women's empowerment, but empowerment is perceived differently, and so our communication differs accordingly.

> "For example, in countries like Pakistan, Egypt, and the Arabian Peninsula, women's accomplishment is through family status: marriage and children. In this case, our communications focus a lot on the married woman and her family environment. In Russia and other countries, women's self-realization is through a good job and economic independence. The external signal is very important. In this case, we focus more in our communication on the role of the woman as an independent and self-assured woman."

So, although P&G has global brands and global communication, it constantly adapts its marketing to suit local needs and the nuances of local cultures. What it says and how it says things to people depends very much on how well it gets to know them.

Attracting customers with brand stories

I would like to emphasize the importance of developing brand stories. Rather than just talking about business, many brands are now telling stories about what they stand for, what they are, their heritage, culture, and people. Brand stories provide an opportunity to express the brand vision speaking through the brand personality. Engaging people who visit their websites and other materials through the use of stories really brings the business to life in a non-hard-sell way, and the distinctive personality of the brand can lead to the development of trust and belief. If people develop belief in the brand they will become customers and become a part of the story.

One example of a brand that tells its story and expresses what it stands for in this way is TOMS.[38] A highly emotionally driven brand TOMS' tag line of "One For One" sums up its philosophy. From its beginnings as a shoe company, TOMS says it exists to improve lives, and for every pair of shoes bought the brand gives a pair to someone in need. The website is simple but highly effective in providing visitors with a story they can believe in, as TOMS says, "Through your purchases, TOMS helps provide shoes, sight, water, safe birth and bullying prevention services to people in need." The site interweaves explanatory stories into the main one by illustratively explaining what is meant by "Improving Lives", "What We Give", "Thoughtful Partnerships" and "Beyond One For One". It invites the reader into the ways in which it helps people and the impact it makes, being "committed to more than just giving". It is not packed with products like many company websites, although there is a tab for shopping; the story is the upfront and main point of focus and it is compelling reading.

However you communicate to your target audiences the key to success is to keep the messages not only simple and relevant but consistent too.

Consistency is key

Consistency in brand communications is very important. Getting one message across to target audiences consistently is much better than having a variety of messages that lose impact and may confuse consumers.

One of the best well-managed brands I have ever seen is BASF, the world's leading chemicals company, based in Germany. Apart from being a B2B brand it is a brand that sells ingredients, chemicals that most people would never normally see. So how does a company brand ingredients?

Well, BASF looks at this question from the end product point-of-view, where its ingredients are used in the production and manufacture of many different categories of things that are a part of people's lives, such as widespan bridges, automobiles, sports and leisure equipment, sun protection applications and clothing. (This strategy is a little like 'Intel Inside' in that you never see its products but they are used to help change the world in which we live through enabling other products and processes to exist.)

The BASF brand has many times in the past indicated that it plays its part in helping these achievements come to fruition – it stands for success and achievement. This moves the brand away from its commodity status by adding an emotional element to its identity. What the company is saying is that we do not just sell chemical ingredients; we actually stand for something and help shape the world around you.

The most famous of its brand communications campaigns used the key message of "Invisible Contribution. Visible Success" and BASF mastered the consistency challenge with a series of advertisements featuring end products such as a widespan bridge, a car, a surfer on a surfboard, a man in cold weather arctic clothing and other shots, But it only had one key message that was displayed consistently and creatively, placed with the product featured, and the bar on the side of each advertisement simply explained in two simple paragraphs what "Invisible Contribution" and "Visible Success" meant. No other words were necessary and the template for each advertisement was the same.

Summary

This chapter has dealt with the more traditional aspects of brand communications and has introduced some new ways of communicating. As mentioned briefly, there are some radical changes taking place in the way brands communicate with customers such as the spread of brand storytelling. These changes tend more and more to be driven mainly by innovations in the use of the Internet and new technologies but one thing that does not change in successful communications is the need to have an emotional brand strategy with associated key messages that invite people into the brands' world. And however the brand messages are delivered they need to be simple, relevant and consistent. The next chapter looks in more detail at the impact of the digital world on brand strategy and communications and at some of the new kids on the brand block.

CHAPTER 8

The Digital World

By the time you read this chapter, new digital businesses will have been born and some will have faded away (possibly including some I have mentioned); such is the pace of change in digital technology. This chapter discusses some of the changes that are taking place, some of the companies that are riding the wave of technology, and some that are still looking to survive. Social media, online business and digital services are among the areas discussed and there is a brief look at the future and where markets are moving. It is important to note that some observers view the emergence of digitally-based brands as a triumph for the companies that create them. My view is that they are only responding to the demands of consumers, whose mantra seems to be, help me find what I am looking for and give it to me now. Looking for the hidden needs and wants of consumers is the best opportunity for businesses in the digital world and it is as well to remember that there is no longer a digital divide.

In the years since the publication of the first edition of this book, the gap between people who were frequent users of the Internet and those who had little access, skill, or willingness to use it has largely disappeared. Now, nearly all age groups are computer-literate and Internet-savvy, from four-year-olds to adults in their golden years. As a result, the volume of traffic on the Internet is now huge and rapidly increasing. In 2017, every day over half a billion tweets, almost four and a half billion Facebook entries and over half a billion YouTube hours of footage were transmitted, posted, and uploaded. The growth continues with a massive overload of content and it is more difficult than ever for brands to stand out.

The Internet and its applications have revolutionized the way in which humanity communicates and does business. A company would fail without a website or an online shop. Many individuals have their own personal websites or blogs (web logs, or diaries), and some people are or aspire to become YouTube stars, whether they advise on the latest make-up or are musical sensations.

But for hundreds of millions of individuals who use the Internet, social networking sites such as Facebook do the job just as well of telling the world who they are, and enabling them to communicate with potentially millions of others. Privacy settings allow users to choose who can see their details or contact them. An increasing number of sites, not just social networking sites, allow users to post vlogs (video blogs, often taken with a mobile phone camera). Reality TV no longer has a monopoly on instant viewing (seeing things happen in real time) as viewers can do their own reality programming via their own chosen channels. This isn't just a one-time digital revolution that has taken place; it is ongoing, with more and more sophisticated services emerging that make life easier and enable us to do things faster.

Brands such as Google, YouTube and Facebook have become legendary in less than eight years, and are transforming everything from politics to personal relationships, from finding things to finalizing deals, as we will see in the case studies in this chapter. Google, Facebook, Amazon and Microsoft dominate the digital world. In the second quarter of 2017 they generated US$74 billion between them. This has led some politicians and media to suggest that these Silicon Valley titans are monopolistic and should be broken up, with some also suggesting they should be regulated as utilities companies. Despite this grip on markets at the top there are still many opportunities for smaller, entrepreneurial companies. And the fact is companies that haven't yet embraced the Internet will find themselves at an increasing disadvantage, as nowadays an online brand strategy is just as important as one that is offline.

The speed factor

It took 89 years for telephones to reach 150 million users, television 38 years, mobile phones 14 years, the iPod seven years, and Facebook just four years. This new digital world is characterized by enormous and increasing speed; not just marketing speed, but the speed of innovation and availability. The development of the Internet has made commercialization so fast that it is hard to keep up. It is both a brand manager's dream and nightmare: you can become a star overnight but a has-been a short while later. For some, an idea may be good, but it may take too long to make a profit before the idea becomes obsolete. For example, MySpace and Bebo are relics, discarded and forgotten in social media.

The on-demand society of today means that technology is being churned out at a rate never seen before. Instead of a digital divide we simply have a digital world. However, with the continuous production of ideas and breakthroughs in technology, staying competitive is a daily challenge for tech companies. Even giants such as Facebook have to push for a new product, service and competitive edge continuously to survive.

Fundamental change

Technological innovation of the kind referred to above is producing game-changers in all areas of the Internet. In the case studies that follow, we will see how this fundamental change is playing out. We will see how, in a relatively short time, social networking has made its entrance and totally changed the global communications landscape. These new channels are providing everyone with the opportunity and ability to know instantly what is happening around the world, and to get involved. The new digital world allows users to be interactive with anyone, anywhere, and at any time in *real time*.

This chapter is about this new digital world, and about some of the companies that are changing the way we live. We will look at the world of online business, and the multitude of digital services that are helping make everyday life easier, but first we will look at the rise of social media.

The rise of social media

Over the past two decades, one of the most dynamic developments related to digital media has been the rise of social network sites, such as Facebook, Twitter, Google+ and Instagram. Since the launch of the first social applications in the late 1990s, Facebook for example has attracted over 2 billion monthly users worldwide, many of whom have incorporated digital social interactions into their everyday lives. Social media has created global communities as well as the best opportunities for creating global brands if successfully tapped. The ability of Facebook to bring together communities has provoked CEO Mark Zuckerberg to say that the social media website can take over from churches and offer users a sense of community.[39]

Nor is social media a western-dominated branding domain as consumer products have always been. Chinese company Tencent Holding's social media platform messaging app WeChat has 600 million users who send an amazing 38 billion messages a day! It is the first firm in China to pass the US$500 billion valuation mark, putting it ahead of Facebook, and is Asia's most valuable company. (In 2017 it reached a valuation of £391 billion compared to Facebook's £387 billion.)

Tencent is extremely innovative and has its own WeChat Pay service for its customers and has big plans to enter markets outside China. Not content with the success of its own service, Tencent has a majority stake in Finnish mobile games maker Supercell and stakes in Snap (owner of Snapchat), ride-sharing app Lyft and electric vehicle manufacturer Tesla.

The challenge of social media for brand managers has always been the fact that it is based around people talking to friends and others who have common interests, and brands are not invited into these conversations. Brand owners and managers have therefore had to be extremely innovative in trying to have an online social media presence that attracts consumers to their sites. They have to exercise care with these initiatives as generally, and especially with millennial consumers, people do not want brands to be selling to them in direct ways. Social media analytics are now improving so that brands can understand what people are saying about them on a 24 × 7 × 365 basis and what they do and do not like, and the frequency of comments and views etc.

The dark side of social media

But there is a darker side to social media. The targeting, bullying and predatory uses of sites like Facebook are the subject of regulation discussions with governments and this is proving difficult to resolve. Not only is freedom of speech an issue in this debate but there is an open admission that Facebook was deliberately designed to be addictive. The founding president of Facebook, Sean Parker, has talked openly about how Facebook exploits human 'vulnerability' by making users crave validation, using the term "social validation feedback loop". One of the early design questions for the company was, "How do we consume as much of your time and conscious attention as possible?" Comparing 'likes' to little dopamine hits he said this was "exploiting a vulnerability in human psychology". Facebook now has over 2 billion users and Parker added that it "changes your relationship with society, with each other" and indicated that Twitter, Instagram, Snapchat and all other major social media sites were doing the same thing. Much food for thought.[40]

While all these debates as to the degree to which social media companies might be evil in intent or practice are proceeding, they continue to battle it out as new innovations excite customers and fuel the craving. Symptomatic of this is the case of Instagram and Snapchat.

Case study 23:
Facebook's Instagram versus Snapchat

Snapchat was created in September 2011 as an app that lets users share pictures that delete themselves once they have been viewed. Snapchat has since evolved its product offering, adding even more creative tools to enhance the camera and chat functionality, resulting in 2.8 billion Snaps being created each day.[41] It also then introduced Snapchat Stories, where users collect Snaps together in chronological order. This allows individuals, brands and media companies to tell their stories to larger audiences, and it's a key area for selling advertising.

Despite it looking a bit like a media or messaging company, Snap describes itself as a camera company, something it reiterated in the IPO filing in February.

> "In the way that the flashing cursor became the starting point for most products on desktop computers, we believe that the camera screen will be the starting point for most products on smartphones. This is because images created by smartphone cameras contain more context and richer information than other forms of input like text entered on a keyboard."[42]

It's impossible to talk about Snapchat without also talking about Facebook. Facebook tried to buy the messaging service for US$3 billion in 2013, but Snapchat turned the offer down. Facebook's response was to build a similar app called Slingshot, which didn't take off. The social networking giant has since been relentlessly experimenting with incorporating many of Snapchat's popular features, such as ephemeral messages, photo-editing tools, face-altering filters and scannable personal barcodes. The approach appears to have finally succeeded: with reports suggesting that the Facebook-owned Instagram's cloning of Snapchat Stories may have led to Snapchat's user growth stalling.

"Facebook has started to take a very experimental and incremental approach to try to counter Snapchat. Instagram Stories has been massively successful," said Dawson. "It's sucked some of the air out of Snapchat's sales over the last few months."

However, even if Snapchat continues to grow, there's a long way to go before it could start to outshine the dominance of Facebook, as Snapchat only has over 160 million daily active users, whilst Instagram proudly announced a whopping 250 million users for their Stories feature.[43] Snapchat's shares took a 3% hit following Instagram's announcement.

In the ongoing features battle, Snapchat has recently integrated a map to track friends or 'hot' activity around the world. This is similar to Find My Friends, and is an additional way to keep up-to-date on your friends' activities, but whether this will really take off is undetermined, as many users can find this a violation of privacy as well as encourage stalking and bullying.

To try and create a further edge over its competitors, Snapchat has controversially ventured into hardware through the creation of Spectacles, smart glasses that record and upload 10-second videos. The staggered launch of the product through colorful vending machines dotted around the US was a PR masterclass, with queues of 'Snapchatters' waiting hours to buy a pair and some reselling on eBay for thousands of dollars.

Although Spectacles hasn't yet been raking in huge profits, it signals a move into the rapidly expanding and exciting realm of virtual reality devices. But whether this revolution in communication can translate into Facebook-level success is yet to be determined.

It all comes down to the bottom line of course. When Snapchat, which floated with a value of £18.5 billion, revealed its maiden results as a listed company in May 2017 its shares plunged by 23% in just 45 minutes after it reported slowing user growth on sales of just £115 million first quarter losses of £1.7 billion. The hype around digital services companies and amazing valuations often are not matched by monetization of products and services, leading some analysts to worry about another Internet bubble building up.

The big brands that dominate the digital world, such as Facebook, naturally try to take over various sectors of the industry. Facebook's Instagram battles with Snapchat, while Facebook Messenger competes with the likes of WhatsApp and Apple's iMessage.

Twitter is still going strong as it provides its unique feature of keeping updates short and sweet. Many people use Twitter to keep up-to-date with their favorite celebrities such as Katy Perry, Justin Bieber and Barack Obama (who are the top three users with the most Twitter followers as of 24 July 2017[44]). Cristiano Ronaldo evidently has over 55 million followers. Given its ability to send messages worldwide in seconds, some regard Twitter as the ultimate instant public relations medium. President Trump uses Twitter as his choice for global and domestic communications.

Yet Twitter still struggles with its lack of control over trolls, harassment, and general abuse of users and the system. Toward the end of 2016 some new features were added to Twitter to curb instances of abuse, such as 'quality filter' and word filtering. Whether these will help is yet to be seen, as people – even famous people, such as Donald Trump – continue to post allegations and insults against others online. There are obstacles ahead but it will continue to survive despite these issues, as there are no competitors to challenge Twitter.

Google, however, which has become one of the world's most common household names, has had some competition from Yahoo and Bing for example, but not much of a challenge. So in a sense it creates its own competition: it now offers services designed for work like Google Docs, email, cloud storage with Google Drive, language translation, mapping and turn-by-turn navigation with Google Maps, video sharing through YouTube, and even photo editing. (YouTube itself is a huge business for Google with over 1.65 billion users in mid-2017.)

Google also produces hardware such as the Google Pixel smartphone, the Google Home smart speaker, and now they are even looking into driverless cars, with their project Waymo. "Waymo stands for a new way forward in mobility. We are a self-driving technology company with a mission to make it safe and easy for people and things to move around." Since the project started, Waymo has become a company in its own right owned by Google owner, Alphabet.

Google launched the project in 2009 but has not yet succeeded in commercializing these cars. Their test reports in California state: There were only 124 "disengagement" incidents in 2016, where a driver had to take control of a test vehicle on public roads, down from 341 in 2015. The cars drove nearly 636,000 miles last year, compared with just over 424,000 in 2015.

Progress is improving, particularly whilst Google partnered with Lyft, but there is a race to the finish now as Lyft has opened its own autonomous driving facility.[45] The potential in such technological advancements could threaten the likes of Uber as well as many other big brands in the auto industry.

Google's parent company Alphabet also owns Verily, whose mission is to make the world's health data useful so that people enjoy healthier lives. Verily is developing tools to collect and organize health data to create interventions and platforms for more holistic care management.

Domination in multiple sectors is clearly something that Alphabet (and Google) are trying to achieve, and it is therefore no surprise that Google as the flagship brand was the world's third most valuable brand in 2019, at US$142.755 billion. (You can see the top ten ranking in chapter 11.) Another brand, now ranked the most valuable brand in the world by Brand Finance plc, has been taking the online business world by storm: Amazon. We will discuss the online retail sector as a whole before looking at Amazon's success.

Traditional retailing versus e-commerce: on the street or online?

Marc Andreessen, co-author of Mosaic and co-founder of Netscape, commented in an interview on the demise of traditional retail, as "e-commerce becomes the place to buy."[46]

> "It is impossible to deny this, as many high street stores have an online shop now, and there are popular sites, such as asos.com, that are entirely based online. In fact, a business would struggle to survive without at least a website and an online shop. Consumers want to be able to shop wherever they are, whether that be on a train, at work, on a beach or in the comfort of their own homes. Without an online platform to sell their products, business will be losing out on a large proportion of sales. Superdry has seen sales jump significantly (25.2%) in the half year to 28 October 2017 by targeting millennials on social media, with its Varsity product range and ethically sourced down jackets proving to be best sellers. Social media has allowed the brand to reduce promotions and chief executive Euan Sutherland said, 'we have delivered another strong performance, further demonstrating the unique advantages and attractiveness of Superdry as a global digital brand."

Notonthehighstreet.com was founded in 2006 by Sophie Cornish and Holly Tucker and turned over £134,000 in its first year. The online marketplace now has more than 5,000 firms selling products from personalized gifts to wedding dresses on its site, and more than 200 employees. Its turnover was £155 million in 2015. Simon Belsham, chief executive has said the business's first pop-up shop is "an indication of where we are going", and argues that the future of retail is a mixture of online and offline. He said Open Door, a three-day pop-up shop celebrating the firm's 10th anniversary, is "absolutely not" just a marketing gimmick, and will be the first of many physical retail and workshop events. He added, "We've got about 300 different partner products on sale across eight different zones. It's a bit of an indication of where we are going in the future. My belief is that retail in the future is neither online or offline. It's going to be a combination of the two, and that's as true for our brand as it is for others. It's all about using the different channels to give customers a great experience."[47]

Asos.com, originally named AsSeenOnScreen, was founded in 2000 and changed its name to Asos in 2003. The company is a British online retailer and has tapped into the desire for easy shopping, targeting people in their teens and twenties. One can order clothes, shoes and accessories on their website or mobile app, and they will arrive as soon as the following day. Customers are able to try them on at home, and if some items are not quite to taste or fit they can return them for free. This freedom of choice and the ease with which shoppers can update their wardrobe is revolutionary and has taken sales from traditional high street retailers such as Next and Topshop.

Asos is about to extend its offerings to include products from the beauty category that will undoubtedly take away some market share from more traditional retailers such as Boots, Superdrug and regular department stores. Evidently Asos has signed a number of exclusive deals with luxury skincare and make-up brands as well as launching its own low-cost make-up range. Head of Buying for Asos Face and Body, Alex Scolding, said, "There is a big wide space in the UK beauty market between what is in the mainstream and what we offer. Our customer doesn't just shop in stores, she consults YouTube, she looks at trends, she looks at influencers to make her purchase. We aim to be that brand."[48]

The company was worth just £14 million when it listed in 2001 but is now valued at a whopping £4.7 billion as at the time of writing. Not only does Asos have 13.4 million active customers but they also have 10 million active installs of their mobile app. Furthermore, 69% of all traffic now derives from mobile devices.[49] This shows that the online industry, though new and still growing, is already rapidly moving into the mobile stream. Consumers are finding it even easier to shop on their mobile phones, rather than waiting to get to a laptop or computer; the easier it is the more popular it will be. In the digital world a company has few overheads and does not have to own outlets or even possess an inventory of its products, in order to be successful, an example being Farfetch, a British-based luxury fashion website, destined shortly for a New York stock market float worth an estimated £4 billion.

The segment of one

Some companies are going wholly for the Internet shopper and are focusing on the segment of one – individualizing their offerings to each person. The online shopping firm Net-a-Porter is currently investing £442 million to personalize its website shopping experience and is launching a tool to put together fashion outfits based on previous selections and future plans. Powered by artificial intelligence (AI), they are using a fashion-picking robot that will put together outfits for customers and give suggestions for holidays, locations and so on. Alex Alexander, CIO, says, "Personalization is key because knowing the customer helps us serve them better."

Grocery shopping has also moved into the e-commerce and mobile realms. Ocado pioneered the online grocery shopping trend with no physical stores, while Hello Fresh help busy people by planning meals and delivering fresh ingredients to their homes, and all customers need to do is follow the included recipe to make a quick and healthy home-cooked meal. Even the world of food shopping and cooking is changing rapidly.

Initially launched as a concept in 2000, Ocado partnered with Waitrose in 2002 and have been successful ever since. In 2014, Morrisons became their new business partner and Ocado delivered their online groceries.

However, the extent of Ocado's innovation does not stop there. Although other major players such as Tesco and Sainsbury's have managed to compete at the same level in terms of online shopping, Ocado are now going one step further as they trial self-driving delivery vehicles. They have jumped on the trend of driverless car technology – something in which big tech giants such as Google are heavily invested. So technology is constantly evolving to make every process smoother and easier for not only customers but for the company itself.

This does not mean as seen in the examples above, that online businesses avoid traditional means of offline promotion such as advertising and sponsorship. Just Eat has signed up with the *X Factor* television series to help accelerate its brand awareness and pull in more sales, using chefs singing to music in advertisements. The relevance is that Just Eat, an online food order and delivery service that is an intermediary between takeaway food outlets and people wanting a wide choice of meals delivered at home, allows you to have a great dinner and watch your favorite television show at the same time. So it is fair to say that multi-channel shopping is increasingly employed.

Some companies are now engaging in multi-category strategies, as a major way to make things easier for customers is by giving them all they need in one place. Amazon is one such company looking for domination across all sectors.

Case study 24: Amazon

Amazon was once known as an online retailer. Now it is so much more: it's an evolving platform with a wildly successful voice assistant, AmazonFresh is in the grocery business, Amazon Go has plans to expand its register-free shopping, and there is even some talk of a revival of the Fire phone.

Amazon, like Ocado, is also trying to revolutionize its delivery service. They have been trialing drone deliveries and have unmanned delivery boxes all over cities, where customers, can pick up their items during their lunch break at work away from home, for example. Customers key in a unique code on the keypad, which is programmed to open the box that contains the relevant items.

Amazon is even branching out to the banking world and has handed out more than US$1 billion in small loans to sellers over the last 12 months, a significant payout when compared to the US$1.5 billion it lent from 2011 through 2015, according to Peeyush Nahar, vice president for Amazon Marketplace. The money has been used to expand inventory or discount items on Amazon. The giant profits hugely from boosting sales for third-party merchants as it takes a cut of transactions. Another way it makes a profit is from payments made by sellers in order to hitch up their placement in search results, to help them catch the attention of shoppers more easily.

Amazon is steadily becoming the world leader as it successfully delivers its brand promise: to be the "Earth's biggest selection and being the Earth's most customer-centric company". Jeff Bezos, in his annual letter to stakeholders, pointed out that their "focus is on customer obsession rather than competitor obsession, eagerness to invent and pioneer, willingness to fail, the patience to think long-term, and the taking of professional pride in operational excellence."

Such focus produced Amazon Go, as it shows just how far Amazon has come from simply being an online retailer. Amazon opened a grocery store where shoppers simply scan their smartphone upon entry, and purchases are automatically charged to a credit card when they leave the store. The shop has a network of CCTV cameras and pressure sensors to detect when visitors have taken something off the shelves, at which point it is added to their virtual shopping basket. When they exit the store, their purchases are charged directly to the shopper's online Amazon account, without the need to wait at the till.

Amazon Go was created to revolutionize one's shopping experience, particularly focusing on the busy lives people lead. By shaving off valuable minutes from having to queue and pay at the till, it is no surprise that people are excited over the concept. Their 'Just Walk Out Technology' is a significant advancement in the world of the Internet of Things that is taking over society today.

Virtual assistants Alexa and Echo will be the prime influencers to drive consumer interaction and persuade them to ultimately purchase more with Amazon and Prime than ever before. The smarter Alexa becomes at understanding and remembering your needs, preferences and behaviors, the better she is at delivering a seamless experience. And the better the experience, the more indispensable she will become to the lives of customers. If Alexa manages to be as widely adopted as Apple's Siri, it could reach spectacular levels of customer loyalty. There is no doubt that we are living in a world obsessed with on-demand, led by brands like Uber, but Amazon, through Alexa and its other products and services, is redefining customer experience.

Amazon doesn't stop there with its expansion into other sectors. It has its fingers in pies like AmazonFresh groceries to compete with the likes of Ocado, Tesco and Waitrose, and has recently bought Whole Foods for US$13.7 billion. Amazon Music Unlimited competes against Apple Music and Spotify; Amazon Prime Video competes against Netflix.

The online giant has been selling fashion items since its acquisition of Shopbop in 2006 and also collects commissions from sales of other brands such as Ted Baker, but is now moving into the fashion market with its own brand called 'Find' that is a 500-piece womenswear collection. This will demand a new skill set moving from the rational world of books and electronics to a much more emotional consumer world.

Amazon has world domination in its sights and will continue to give people consistently great products and services – most likely all under the single brand name. Founder Jeff Bezos has set his sights on becoming an online powerhouse with a goal of US$200 billion in annual sales at some stage in the future. Bezos says that in order to reach this goal Amazon has to learn how to sell clothes and food. Nevertheless, Amazon is already the world's most valuable brand as shown in the Brand Finance Global 500 February 2019 ranking at US$ 187.905 billion.

The example of Amazon shows us very clearly how product-based firms can, through the Internet, move rapidly into many categories of service; and digital services are beginning to change the face of the high street, where traditional shops with high rental and staff overheads just cannot compete any more.

Digital services

There has been a significant increase in digital services recently to help make our lives easier. It is a response to a new consumer way of thinking in the digital world, based on the following principles:

- Make everything available to me.

- Help me find what I want.

- Help me get it now!

Digital services cater for the consumer segment of one – me. The digital world is built around mass individualization, where each customer has specific personalized needs and wants, to be provided for as fast as possible if not instantly, in any place, allowing 'me' to do more with my life in the way in which 'I' want to live it. Digital services are responding to these demands with alacrity.

Want to get somewhere without having to stand on the pavement to try and flag down a cab? Uber is the solution. Want to have a meal from your favorite restaurant delivered to your office? Just Eat or Deliveroo can make that happen. Want to find a place to stay where you can live with locals and avoid ludicrous hotel prices? Airbnb does just that. These and other new brands are proliferating in number but sometimes don't find it easy to gain sustainable profits.

WhatsApp, Facebook Messenger and Apple's iMessage have been around for some years now and can seem the most basic of digital services, but have been competing for first place. WhatsApp gave up the fight when it was sold to Facebook. "On February 19, 2014 Facebook announced that it has reached a definitive agreement to acquire WhatsApp, a rapidly growing cross-platform mobile messaging company, for a total of approximately US$16 billion, including US$4 billion in cash and approximately US$12 billion worth of Facebook shares. The agreement also provides for an additional US$3 billion in restricted stock units to be granted to WhatsApp's founders and employees that will vest over four years subsequent to closing."[50] WhatsApp was proven to dominate Messenger and iMessage as it is an open application for all mobile users (not just iPhone but Android users too) and there is a fair percentage of people that do not use Facebook and therefore don't use Messenger. Almost everyone has a smartphone now and there is therefore a massive global market to capture.

Let's have a look at a different kind of disruptive digital service that is changing the marketplace.

Case study 25: Uber

Five years ago, a company called UberCab made their mark in San Francisco by allowing people to hail a cab with a smartphone. Since then, the company now known as Uber has spread like wildfire across the globe. Uber, as of August 2016, operates in 58 countries and is valued at around US$70 billion at the time of writing. (Uber is just one technology company that has massive valuations given without ever making a profit! When this valuation was given Uber had lost US$3 billion. It remains to be seen how sustainable some of these companies will be.)

Unlike other cab services, Uber also provides varied fare rates for different cabs. Users are allowed to compare and get the best possible rate for their travel needs. Once an Uber cab is confirmed, the customer can check the progress and also receive estimates on the time of arrival of the cab.

There have been extensions and improvements made to the Uber app, such as UberPool. UberPool service matches riders with other customers travelling in the same direction. For those who are less concerned over time and more concerned about spending, this was a service that suited them, and furthered the reach of the app and made taxi travel even more affordable.

But the road hasn't been easy. While its valuation has continued to climb and it has attracted more and more investors, Uber has also fought rivals and regulators, facing threats from the taxi industry and even its own drivers. For example, Uber has been at war against Didi Chuxing, its biggest rival in China. After a prolonged and exorbitantly costly battle, however, Uber China surrendered to Didi in a US$35 billion mega-merger.

There have also been battles in the UK with the black cab drivers. These drivers are trained and licensed taxi drivers who feel that their jobs are being stolen from them. Uber rates are lower and the service is quicker and easier, so it is no surprise that customers are so drawn to Uber. The prestige and iconic image that one associates with the black cab isn't enough to keep customers.

This led to the invention of Gett. Not only does Gett bring black cabs to the digital age in the form of a mobile app, Gett gives customers fixed rates before they book – something that Uber does not offer except under the Uber Pool option. A bonus is that one does not have to share that black cab with someone else. This gives customers the certainty of travel prices, and brings black cabs back to the table.

Uber continues to face a considerable number of challenges that lie firmly in new CEO Dara Khosrowshahi's in tray, including what the *Guardian* newspaper refers to as its "creepy image".[51] At the time of writing, Uber is also undergoing legal proceedings to be able to continue to operate in the UK.

With the business model a little wobbly and as scandals and image issues continue to emerge and be overcome, following this story as it unfolds should be interesting. As indeed should the story about Airbnb and its future.

Case study 26: Airbnb

When Air Bed & Breakfast – as it was originally called – started out, just over eight years ago in San Francisco, Brian Chesky and Joe Gebbia could not afford the rent for their loft apartment. They then came up with the idea of putting an air mattress down in their living room and turning it into a bed and breakfast to make their rent affordable.

In February 2008, Nathan Blecharczyk, Chesky's former roommate, joined as the Chief Technology Officer and the third co-founder of the new venture. They put together a website which offered short-term living quarters, breakfast, and a unique business networking opportunity for those who were unable to book a hotel in the saturated market. The site Airbedandbreakfast.com officially launched on August 11, 2008 and the founders had their first customers in town in the summer of 2008, during the Industrial Design Conference held by Industrial Designers Society of America, where travelers had a hard time to find lodging in the city.

Airbnb has grown staggeringly quickly since then: as of June 2017, it has over 3 million listings worldwide in 191 countries.[52] Airbnb provides one of the best examples of digital services in the way it gives customers that all-important personal touch while expanding rapidly, through cultivating and engaging with a community. Indeed, spending on local communities by guests in the year to July 2017 was £3.46 billion. In the UK, where each guest spends an average of £147 per day, around half of all customers are domestic (as opposed to foreign visitors) and Airbnb boosts both local economies and communities. For example, Scotland benefited by £86 million in the year to July 2017.

The company's 'One Less Stranger' campaign – where 100,000 hosts woke up on New Year's Day in 2015, to an email from Mr Chesky saying he had paid US$10 into their bank account – was a particular instance where control was taken away from Airbnb and placed in the hands of the community.[53] The aim, according to McClure, was to encourage hosts to help someone else and meet new people with that money. Although some may have simply pocketed it, Airbnb wanted to allow their hosts to represent them and drive marketing for them through various means such as social media or word of mouth. It all builds up to the idea of a community-driven brand.

However, Airbnb haven't had challenges along the way. Its booming business has severely threatened the hotel and hospitality industry, whilst also raising tax avoidance issues. The brand has severely disrupted the hotel industry and is forcing traditional hotels, even luxury ones, to lower prices.

For example, nights booked by Airbnb in London rose from 2 million in 2015 to 4.6 million in 2016. 2.6 million extra nights equates to ten Shards. This vast network of rooms and properties is equivalent to hundreds of new hotels springing up, putting price pressure on the traditional hotels. On the tax issue, there have even been cases where Airbnb posted 'ads' in San Francisco that were passive aggressive toward the tax controversy. These ads tackled government bodies, for example some asked Parking Enforcement to use Airbnb's US$12 million in hotel taxes to feed expired parking meters, while others suggested that the tax collector should not spend the US$12 million all in one place.[54]

Apologies were issued following these ads, and the hype and criticism died down. Airbnb have since continued to grow and expand their community – but will its popularity ever stagnate? Will there be threats and further challenges in the next few years? Regulatory and other issues are inevitably going to disrupt industries as new waves of innovative services are introduced.

A further and highly interesting ongoing development in the digital world is the frequently discussed topic of the 'Internet of Things'.

The Internet of things (IoT)

The Internet of Things (IoT) is the inter-networking of physical devices, vehicles (also referred to as 'connected devices' and 'smart devices'), buildings, and other items embedded with electronics, software, sensors, actuators, and network connectivity which enable these objects to collect and exchange data.

'Things', in the IoT sense, can refer to a wide variety of devices such as heart monitoring implants, electric clams in coastal waters, or field operation devices that assist firefighters in search and rescue operations. But these 'Things' can also be Fitbits, Nest home systems, Intelligent Parking Assist Systems in cars, and a virtual assistant such as Alexa. More often than not the devices are designed to make daily life simpler, easier, faster, better, more efficient and more intelligent.

According to Gartner, Inc. (a technology research and advisory corporation), there will be nearly 20.8 billion devices on the Internet of Things by 2020.[55]

Manufacturers, enticed by the revenue potential of conquering the domestic environment, now push new ideas and technology into the digital market, in the hope that one of their connected products will become as essential to everyday life as the smartphone. The recent industry lean toward the 'smart home' is simply the latest version of this.

We have mentioned Amazon Echo and Google Home previously, and these devices can provide a simple, integrated way to access various digital controls scattered throughout the contemporary home. But there are also some brands that are dedicated to creating smart home systems such as Nest or Hive.

Nest provides home automation through thermostats, smoke detectors and cameras. Bought by Alphabet (the parent company of Google) in 2010 for US$3.2 billion, it now works together with Google Home. The company claims that, "Nest is focused on making simple, human, delightful things. That's how we're creating the thoughtful home: a home that takes care of the people inside it and the world around it."[56]

Hive, on the other hand, is a British Gas creation, which helps you control heating, sensors, lights, cameras, plugs and other add-ons. All of these things can be controlled so simply from your mobile phone wherever you are. For example, you can turn the heating on when you return home from work, so that the house is nice and warm for when you arrive.

But the issue that these smart home systems face, and the reason why they haven't been so quickly accepted, is largely to do with convincing people that this is something they need. Furthermore, people need to be convinced that the hassle of setting up these elaborate systems is worth the money and the hassle itself. But with improvements to technology, and as these systems become more readily available and therefore cheaper, it is possible that many more homes in the future will be 'smart'.

Connected cars are becoming more popular now, with functions such as parking assistance, web-connected entertainment and infotainment, real-time diagnostics and even partially or fully automated driving. Most large auto brands such as Volvo, Audi and Mercedes-Benz have connected cars on sale now, and Gartner estimates that there will be a quarter of a billion connected cars by 2020.[57]

According to McKinsey, however, despite the demand for connected cars and the race to have the best connected car, people's marginal willingness to pay and concerns over security puts the industry in an interesting position.[58] Customers will need to be reassured by a strong brand and trust in that brand before buying.

Pernod Ricard is also experimenting with IoT and connectivity, with their connected bottles. One such example is the way they promoted the Jameson brand for St Patrick's Day: their limited edition bottles had QR codes that, when scanned, gave customers information about the day and related events.[59]

What does the digital future have in store?

These days, it's difficult to predict what will happen six months ahead, never mind a few years, but we can draw some conclusions.

One would assume there would be a decline of traditional advertising and one-way communications in favor of two-way communications and greater consumer involvement. But interestingly digital services like Just Eat, Airbnb and Trivago have advertisements on TV, which suggests that traditional advertising isn't dead in the digital world. Offline campaigns are just as important in order to push for maximum awareness of the brand. This approach of having both online and offline strategies can be highly effective.

More significantly, with increased demand for connectivity and development of intelligent devices, the world will see the rise of industry 4.0 – the 'smart factory'. We can already see the beginnings with devices communicating with each other and with robots or systems doing things that are tedious or dangerous for humans.[60]

One of the first times 'Industrie 4.0' was mentioned was in 2013, in a document released by the German government outlining a high-tech strategy to computerize the manufacturing industry and free it from human involvement.[61]

The growth of industry 4.0 will include increased research into and development of artificial intelligence. Currently such technology can, for example, detect cancer more quickly than doctors. Despite the ingenuity and positivity that comes with having efficient robot systems doing our work for us, there are some very stark problems that we will encounter in the future.

These problems are already happening now, with people losing jobs to robots and security issues or risks being discovered in connected devices. Cyber attacks of great magnitude are increasing. Recently, Reckitt Benckiser was hit by the Petya ransomware virus that rendered 15,000 laptops, 2,000 servers and 500 computer systems unusable in 45 minutes at an estimate cost of £100 million. Many other companies have faced similar threats.

Regarding robotics, Nike's focus on this area is now threatening Asia's low-cost workforce as it works companies like Flex, a high-tech manufacturing company well known for Fitbit activity trackers, to make a large leap toward much greater automation that is likely to produce huge gains in profits and faster introduction of new products. Speed and cost-reductions are an irresistible partnership, and already laser cutting and other automated innovations such as automated gluing are invading Nike's supplier base, where labor costs are no longer very low. According to estimates for some products, using automation means that the cost of labor would decrease by 50% and material costs by 20%.

In some ways this militates against brands like Nike who claim to be ethical and sustainable businesses but it is unlikely to stop the production advances. Competitors Adidas and Under Armour are also pursuing automation strategies including increasing use of 3D printing. It is inevitable that big brands will use AI and robotics more and more and that is inevitably going to lead to labor displacement.

Google's parent company Alphabet has much more ambitious plans for its use of new technologies, with its involvement in sectors ranging from autonomous vehicles to smart homes to biotech life extensions. Recently Alphabet has taken another huge step into people's lives with the aim of planning, building and running part of a city. In October 2017 the city of Toronto announced a partnership with Sidewalk Labs, an Alphabet subsidiary, in order to action this project.

Sidewalk Labs will be in charge of redeveloping a waterfront district called Quayside, an area of over "3.3 million square feet of residential, office and commercial space, including a new headquarters for Google Canada, in a district that would be a test bed for the combination of technology and urbanism". This will give Alphabet its own "urban living laboratory" where it can experiment with new smart systems and planning techniques. It will be able to study how these systems and techniques work in the real world and how people are affected. The development will be one of the largest examples of a smart city project in North America: a place built around data-driven, semi-automated, networked technologies. In the following article, from where this information is taken, there is some apprehension about where the "urban living lab" could lead to in terms of a company running part of a city.[62]

Sidewalk Labs CEO Dan Doctoroff said, "We have an opportunity to fundamentally redefine what urban life can actually be." The company has defined its mission as "reimagining cities from the Internet up," and considered several U.S. cities for a high-tech makeover before applying to develop the waterfront strip in Toronto. "Sidewalk Labs will create a test bed for new technologies in Quayside," Canadian Prime Minister Justin Trudeau said. "Technologies to build smarter, greener, more inclusive cities, which we hope to see scaled across Toronto's eastern waterfront, and eventually in other parts of Canada and around the world."[63]

All in all, there is considerable debate about possible good and not so good outcomes for the future in the digital world. Eliminating the negatives, or at the very least conducting positive discoveries and developments that can help mankind, should be at the forefront of our minds, but whether this will turn out to be the case or even achievable in the future is questionable. It will be exciting to find out though!

Summary

Below are a few key points that summarize how brands have had to change, adapt and transform in order to keep up with the changes in digital technology.

- Online brands are growing very fast.

- Convergence is already here, and increasing, e.g. mobile TV.

- The 'democratization' of commerce has arrived. The power has transferred from producer to consumer.

- Multi-channel retail shopping behavior is becoming more predominant.

- Social influence marketing and social networks are game changers.

- In the world of social media, brands are not invited. To be successful brands must contribute to conversations and involve themselves in communities to promote and manage conversations.

- Word of mouth (viral) branding and marketing is increasingly important.

- Mass individualization is now the brand challenge.

- In the world of social media, brands are not invited, but successful brands contribute to conversations to create or involve themselves in communities, and try to promote/manage conversations.

- To continue to have a role in the networked society, brands have to learn how to talk to people in real time 24 x 7 x 365.

- Artificial intelligence and robotics will increasingly be the drivers for technological innovation and will provide many disruptive changes and opportunities.

- No industry/company/brand manager will be immune to this global technology shift.

- Despite the changing landscape in the digital world, those organizations that embrace new technologies will not survive without a strong brand strategy. Brand strategy allows products, services and technologies to change fast while building a sustainable identity.

The next chapter moves away from technology and back to the human aspect of brand management, which is employee engagement, or as it is sometimes known, internal branding. This is, in a different way, an equally challenging area in the pursuit of excellent customer relationship management.

CHAPTER 9

"Long Live the Brand!" Employee Engagement to Create a Brand Culture

Introduction

This chapter looks at the process of getting everyone inside the organization to 'live' the brand, an essential part of brand strategy implementation.

Brand communications, as reviewed in Chapter 7, are responsible for projecting the brand vision, personality and identity, together with its positioning in the form of key messages. Simply put, communications deliver the brand promise and it is highly important that customers see the promise fulfilled. We must not forget that it is people within an organization that are largely responsible for delivering the promise in the form of generating a consistently great brand experience for customers. This fact is often not addressed sufficiently by many businesses, but leading branded companies and organizations contend that their values, culture and people are the drivers and the foundation for their success.

Companies are judged by their behavior. Everything they say or do affects their image and reputation. In order to build a powerful corporate brand with a positive image, the company's behavior must be managed and shaped in such a way that people's perceptions of it are consistently favorable. Great customer relationships are formed via positive perceptions and these relationships will be jeopardized if the brand experience is perceived negatively.

The process of getting everyone in the organization to 'live' the brand is sometimes called employee engagement, sometimes internal branding, but it always means the same thing: the process of aligning day-to-day activities, business process, people's jobs, recognition and rewards with the brand identity in order to drive brands and results. It works by ensuring that employees understand and integrate the brand strategy into their respective roles, forming a culture based on a brand mindset that delivers a consistently great experience for the consumer. To some, it's all about moments of truth.

Moments of truth

Moments of truth determine success or failure, weakness or strength, loyalty or desertion, resolve or retreat. Moments of truth are not defined by companies or brands, but by everyday consumers whose experiences with products and services impact on their lives. Occasionally, there are defining moments of truth on a global scale, in the form of a major crisis, but smart brands recognize that they also face moments of truth every day in terms of the brand-consumer relationship.

As brands exist only in the minds of consumers, every contact with a consumer can potentially be a moment of truth. A notable example of this is when the CEO of Scandinavian Airline System (SAS), Jan Carlsson, once told his entire workforce that the airline had 12 million customers a year with an average contact rate per customer of five SAS people during a single journey, and that this translated into 60 million moments of truth – that is, 60 million opportunities to get the brand experience right or wrong. This powerful and easily understandable message indicated that *all* touchpoints with *all* consumers count, and that companies need to look closely at how they can manage these. Those touchpoints that are lacking in providing customers with a great experience are often referred to as possible 'pain points'! That's brand management thinking – the thinking and underlying philosophy that drives many of the world's top brands. I will discuss in more detail the notion of touchpoints with examples in the following chapter on brand planning and control, but unless all employees understand this concept and the brand drivers that shape the customer experience, then brand management will ultimately be less successful.

Many people with responsibility for company and brand image might respond, "If only it was that easy!" But for anyone who has studied Carlsson's strategy, we can see that it wasn't just rhetoric; he changed the airline's structure, systems, and technology, among many other things. Importantly, he empowered frontline staff to take decisions that impacted immediately on the customer brand experience. He succeeded in bringing the SAS brand to life by motivating and empowering employees so that they saw their contribution to the value of the brand and the business. In short, he created a massive organizational change project based around the brand-customer relationship, involving every function in the company. No easy task, but definitely achievable, as results of the turnaround showed.

The big challenge for CEOs and brand managers in charge of major corporate and/or product brands is to bring the brand(s) to life through strategy and change and, in particular, to motivate people to deliver on the brand promise. This is particularly important for those involved in any business that uses a corporate- or house-endorsed branding approach. This chapter examines the goals and importance of employee engagement (internal branding), how it can change the culture of an organization, and how it is brought about.

Goals of employee engagement

Some of the goals that organizations have in mind when carrying out internal branding activities for employees, besides performance achievements such as those referred to in the SAS case above, are:

- To strengthen the brand's identity.
- To serve as a catalyst for cultural change.
- To reinforce the brand strategy and deliver on corporate strategy.
- To connect employees to each other as a 'brand family'.
- To achieve 'employer of choice' status and attract the best talent.
- To instil brand values into key operations and processes.
- To deliver consistently great experiences for customers.
- To add momentum to marketing and sales channels.

As this list shows, employee brand engagement is extremely important and provides many benefits to organizations that are prepared to embark on this journey. The key to its success is to transform the culture of the organization so that it reflects the brand strategy elements of purpose, vision, personality and positioning. In other words, create a brand-driven culture.

Living the brand

Developing a strong corporate culture

To develop a powerful corporate brand image, where the company is the center of attention and customers interact frequently with employees, the corporate culture has to be built around the brand strategy to ensure that customer expectations are met. Corporate culture is a much-discussed topic these days, as companies try to accommodate modern work practices and adaptive leadership approaches. Many sophisticated training and organizational development initiatives are implemented by both internal and external specialists to suit current corporate cultures, and to help promote efficiency and effectiveness for the future. Corporate culture is often described as 'the way we do things around here'. Essentially, it is a complex blend of employee attitudes, beliefs, values, rituals, and behaviors that permeate a company and give it its unique style and feel.

An organization's culture has a profound effect on both staff and customers. For staff, it can mean the workplace is either an invigorating, stimulating, and exciting place to be, or a dismal daily grind. It can empower people or enslave them. Because culture is ubiquitous, it inevitably has an impact not just inside, but also outside the organization. Customers who come into contact with staff can sense and experience the organization's culture through the employees' morale, attitudes and comments, body language, service standards and other encounters. These impact considerably on an organization's brand image and it therefore makes sense to align culture with brand strategy. In other words, the brand becomes the source of cultural development.

A company that is trying to develop and maintain a good brand image, whether it be for a corporate brand or a service brand, must create a culture that is appropriate to, and reflects the essence of, the brand. The best way to do this is by using the brand personality (values), to provide behavioral guidelines. Branding is a very positive and well-received way to change, create and solidify a performance-enhancing culture in an organization.

Rewards for creating a values-based culture

Kotter and Heskett, in their book *Corporate Culture and Performance*, argued that "performance-enhancing cultures", such as those based on the principles I have identified in previous chapters, bring enormous bottom-line benefits to companies. Covering 200 companies in 20 countries over four years, their research revealed that companies with a strong culture based on shared values outperformed others by huge margins, as the following shows:

	Average Growth With a Performance-Enhancing Culture (%)	Average Growth Without a Performance-Enhancing Culture (%)
Revenue	682	166
Stock price	901	74
Profit	756	1

More benefits of a strong brand culture

Many of the world's most valuable brands now agree that the main benefits of a strong culture based on brand are:

- It provides something tangible for employees to believe in, keeping them motivated and energized.

- It allows each employee to see how he or she fits into the grand scheme of delivering the organization's brand vision, the promise to its customers and other stakeholders, and the effect of these efforts on business goals.

- It develops a sense of pride tied to fulfilling the brand promise.

- It provides a great recruitment and selection platform as well as a powerful retention tool.

- It confirms to everyone that the customer and the brand are the most important things to focus on.

The importance of this is underlined by people such as former CEO of BMW, Helmut Panke, who once said, "A brand isn't just a label or a marketing campaign. Creating and maintaining strong brands requires a mindset that has to permeate an organization, from the top down into everything the company does." And as Becky Saeger, former executive vice president of brand marketing at Visa said, "Our employees are our brand. Every single employee has a customer contact."

The message then is simple: define your brand values (in the form of personality traits) carefully and reinforce them with training, repetition, rewards and consistent application across all levels and functions of the organization. This is no easy task, but is essential if we are to achieve outstanding results and customer loyalty. In fact, it is widely recognized that failure to engage employees in brand implementation and management will be detrimental to success.

The internal brand challenge

Figure 9.1 illustrates that this is often the biggest challenge in brand-building. It is not too difficult to develop the brand strategy, nor build the image power via external communications campaigns and other activation programmes, but the real challenge is involving employees in linking the two. As Mark Perry, director of brand management and research for Nissan North America once put it, "Advertising puts a face and adds a voice to the brand, but it's the last thing we do. Unless we have all of our products aligned, our employees understanding where we are going, the retail experience at the point of contact worked out and aligned, we'll make a promise with advertising we can't deliver."

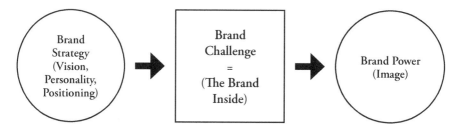

Figure 9.1: The internal brand challenge

In meeting the challenge at top levels, company business units have to apply the brand values strategically in everything they do, integrating the brand into both their business planning and employees' jobs.

In meeting the challenge at departmental levels, **all** departments (not just those that are customer-facing) have to take the brand values and come up with plans as to how they can improve their work in line with them.

In meeting this challenge at individual levels, organizations have to treat employees as internal customers. As Figure 9.2 shows, there are three main aspects to this. Firstly, they have to tell employees about the brand and why it is so important, building brand awareness throughout the organization. Secondly, they have to get employees emotionally engaged; to feel something about their brand; to establish the emotional connection with them, just as they do with customers. Thirdly, they have to get them to do something; to change how they work so that they provide a better experience for customers outside the organization. The best way to do this is by creating learning and development plans for everyone.

(Awareness)   (Emotional Engagement)   (Commitment to Change)

Figure 9.2: Getting employees engaged and committed to change

Create learning and development programs for all levels

We have seen from the discussion so far that the brand is the ideal way to bring about a customer-centric, high-performing, values-based culture, but getting employees engaged in this process is the difference between a successful brand strategy and an unsuccessful one. Given this fact, leaders must ensure they **create learning and development programs for everyone at all their respective levels** – what a brand is, what their organization's brand means, how important it is, and how they can apply the various elements of it to their work, as indicated in Figure 9.3. Basically, people need to know what brand means for:

- Business unit and corporate strategy.
- Functional or departmental change and improvement.
- Individual job performance.

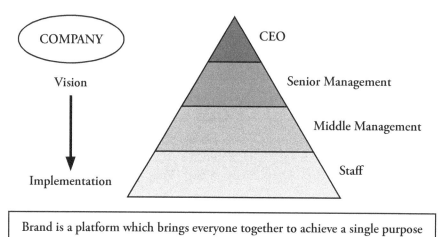

Brand is a platform which brings everyone together to achieve a single purpose

Figure 9.3: Learning, development and engagement activities must be carried out at all levels

It isn't good enough simply to select brand values or personality characteristics and then announce that they now exist. Personality characteristics must be closely defined at three distinct levels as mentioned above – corporate, departmental and individual.

First, each characteristic or value must be defined generically at a corporate-wide level, so that employees understand how they fit into the goals of the organization. If we continue with the innovative brand value example, this could be broken down into the three key behaviors of 'creative', 'resourceful', and 'proactive'. It is important that all employees are informed of the brand values and the reasons for bringing the brand to life, and why the behaviors included in the definitions are so important to the branding process. This step alone calls for a substantial awareness and briefing effort on behalf of the company, and may take the form of many short training program, a significant brand launch event or or combinations of activities.

Second, every department in the organization must examine the brand personality traits and decide which of them are most relevant, and where they can make improvements in those areas. It is important to emphasize that it is not just customer-facing departments, such as marketing and customer service, that need to do this, but back office support departments too, such as finance and human resources.

Business units, divisions, and departments within companies will find it useful to develop plans for the short and medium term with respect to how they will deliver on the brand values. It is critical to include support services in this activity, as unless they also change the way they do things it will be difficult for those departments that impact directly on consumers to implement their plans and provide a consistently great customer experience. For example, it may be difficult for a marketing or sales business unit in a telecommunications company to improve performance on the value of *friendliness* if customers continue to receive multiple bills for fixed line, mobile, Internet, and other services. Customer-friendly billing would give them just one bill covering all their transactions. Improving error rates on billing would also help. So, it is often necessary to change systems and procedures in order to provide a total impact on, and change in, consumer perceptions.

With this in mind, all divisions or departments – such as information technology, finance, research and development, human resources, production, credit control, logistics, marketing, corporate communications, and others – will need to develop strategic and tactical plans to demonstrate to top management how they intend to implement each brand value. These plans shouldn't contain vague statements of intent, but rather concrete action plans detailing timing and accomplishment criteria. (More detailed information on brand action and touch point planning is provided in Chapter 10.)

Brand strategy workshops are the best way to help departments to articulate these plans. Once managers get used to developing such plans, it becomes easier for them to establish and control the brand, and for departments to define people's jobs more clearly in terms of the brand.

As an example of brand strategy execution on a corporate scale, let's take *innovation* as a key brand value or personality characteristic. Many firms have this brand value, but they have executed it in different ways to ensure that their products and services are truly innovative. Gillette was well known for its policy of insisting that over 40% of its annual sales come from products introduced in the last five years; 3M introduced a figure of 25% to help implement the same value. Kao, the Japanese personal-care-product company, concentrated heavily on innovation and at one point in time had approximately 2,000 of its 7,000 employees dedicated to research and development – around three times the number employed in R&D at giant Procter & Gamble. Kao's aim has always been to become a global player, but it states it can only achieve this through producing a constant stream of new products to aggressively seize international opportunities. And Dupont, which has featured *innovation* among its values, once put 26,000 of its people through innovation training programs, in the belief that everyone can come up with good ideas.

Disney Corporation created a section called "Imagineering" – a think tank employing over 2,000 people devoted to developing innovations for the organization's numerous divisions. Within this section are highly paid scientists with expertise in fields such as flight simulation, artificial intelligence, cognitive psychology, neuro-anatomy, mathematics, and neural networks, among other disciplines. Their task is to create a future where, for example, there will be virtual theme parks, or where a child's wished-for toy can be conjured up on the Disney website. This is an example of a company living its brand vision of making people happy.

Thirdly, and importantly, the personality characteristics must be defined at a job-specific level. The biggest obstacle to realizing brand potential is a lack of clarity about the brand, what it stands for, and what it means to the individual. For a company to brand itself properly and meet its moments of truth successfully, everything it does must reflect the brand personality characteristics. This means that every employee, from the CEO downward, must understand and attempt to apply that personality to the job that he or she does. If they don't know how to apply the brand values to their own job, then they are unlikely to take the whole exercise seriously, which will mean the customer is unlikely to feel much impact. Thus, brand management must work closely with the human resource function to ensure not only that staff are aware of and understand all the corporate personality characteristics, but also that they know how to apply these values to their particular jobs. For example, Disney has four brand values and every Disney employee, from cleaners to the CEO, undergoes a two-day values training program on entering the company. Each value is defined in terms of each job, so that every employee knows how to apply the values to his or her job.

The message in this chapter then, is that every brand value or corporate personality characteristic has to be very carefully defined, not just at the corporate level, but also at departmental and job-specific levels. The brand has to be brought to life in every strategic way possible and by every employee in the organization. The following case study on the Virgin Group describes how the brand value of *fun and cheekiness* is brought to life in one of its businesses.

Case study 27: The Virgin Group

Let's have some fun!

Inspired by the freedom of the 1960s, Sir Richard Branson has developed his brand consistently over the last few decades. This is a prime example of how the founder of a company can create a brand in his own image. His charismatic style has influenced his various businesses and their people to "live the brand!".

The extent of the Branson empire is an interesting example of corporate, as opposed to product, branding and brand stretch from a corporate viewpoint, which I mentioned in Chapter 4 as being easier than extending product brands. From its not-so-humble beginnings as Virgin Records, the Virgin brand has now extended into many different enterprises and industries, including cola, bridal wear, cosmetics, rail travel, financial services, mobile telecommunications, Internet-related businesses, wines, and air travel. In many of its mergers and acquisitions, Virgin has brought the power and value of its brand to the negotiating table as opposed to a particular area of technical expertise.

Although not highly successful in all its business initiatives, the Virgin brand has largely been able to accomplish this amount of brand extension through single-minded commitment to its original values, namely:

- the best quality;

- innovative;

- good value for money;

- a challenge to existing alternatives; and

- a sense of fun and cheekiness.

To think about what this means commercially, consider that although Virgin management is inundated with requests for joint ventures and 90% of the projects it considers are profitable, none gets a green light unless it satisfies at least four of these five values. Virgin's values don't in themselves constitute what I would call a 'brand personality', but Branson himself adds that dimension. So the brand's personality is a reflection of his own personality, particularly with the values 'a sense of fun and cheekiness' and 'a challenge to existing alternatives' – the underdog role he plays so well. Quality, value for money, and innovation are now regarded as 'must haves', and no longer as differentiators. However, companies such as Virgin incorporate these values as reminders of what their brand stands for and what they believe in.

We can see the values applied meticulously to all consumer touchpoints, as in the case of a sense of fun and cheekiness, examples of which are given below in regards to Virgin Atlantic airline and other brands in the stable.

Brand value: sense of fun and cheekiness

- **Product:** The airline has been the first to introduce product innovations such as personal massage, live rock bands, and casino opportunities for fliers. Even the top-price seats are cheekily called 'Upper Class'.

- **Service:** In-flight staff are friendly, happy, and fun-loving; they enjoy joking with customers and generally creating a fun atmosphere. They will also go the 'extra mile' when necessary. (Once while traveling with the airline I tore my trousers as I got up from my seat. One of the cabin crew sat me 'trouser-less' in the galley while she personally repaired the embarrassing tear, much to the amusement of my fellow passengers and the other crew members!)

- **Website:** On one occasion when I accessed the Virgin Atlantic website, a plane in Virgin colors crossed the screen and a little hand waved at me through a window. Another element of fun was the reference to the "Cyber Espionage Centre", which invites visitors to "report back" on their findings. There is always something amusing to be found on Virgin's websites and in its offline communications.

- **Public relations:** Branson uses every opportunity to put across this brand value of fun. When he was about to enter a hot-air balloon capsule in an attempt to break a world record of two weeks flying around the world that nearly got him killed, Branson was asked by an observant reporter why the balloon capsule contained a British Airways (BA) seat, rather than a Virgin Atlantic one. Apparently, Branson quipped that as he had a two-week journey to beat a world record it was imperative that he stay alert and there would be less chance of him falling asleep in a BA seat.

- **Events:** At the announcement of the signing of a joint venture deal between Virgin and Singapore Telecom to form Virgin Mobile, the journalists and other media representatives were treated to a lion dance, the traditional way of celebrating in Chinese culture. After a few minutes the dance stopped, the lion removed its head, and there was Branson. He had taken the trouble to learn how to perform the dance in order to produce the unexpected and create a sense of fun. At the press conference later, a more serious Branson told the audience that Virgin and Singapore Telecom were not forming a company, but were creating a brand together. When launching the Virgin bridalwear brand, Branson dressed in drag as a bride; on another occasion, he ran naked from the sea. When a deal with Singapore Airlines (SIA) was being finalized, Branson passed a note to the CEO of SIA that read something along the lines of, "I agree to the figures, but who's paying for lunch?" These are just a few illustrations of the fun value extending into even the most serious of business discussions at Virgin. (By the way, SIA are said to have paid for the lunch.)

Brands that live their values attract not just customers, but great partners, too. A lot of Virgin's growth has been through partnering with co-investors, and it says, "Together we leverage expertise, capital and our brand to build world-class businesses. Over the years more than $5bn of capital has been invested alongside Virgin." As Virgin has grown, the brand values have evolved, but still generate the same original identity. According to the Virgin website in 2017: "The Brand's backbone is its values; providing heartfelt service, being delightfully surprising, red hot, and straight up while maintaining an insatiable curiosity and creating smart disruption." The 'delightfully surprising' element maintains the 'fun and cheekiness' originality.

What will happen when Branson goes?

This is the big issue with brands that are based around their founders. Of course, we hope that Branson stays around. He now resides at his Necker Island home and continues to run the Virgin empire, but retirement comes to everyone, and it will be interesting to see if, as with Walt Disney, the legacy and the brand values will continue to be brought to life at Virgin, enhancing the consumer's experience of the brand and carrying the company to further successes.

The best brands in the world put a huge amount of effort into developing cultures that ensure employee engagement and brand-based behaviors and leave no stone unturned.

There are no shortcuts

There are no shortcuts to internal brand building; the more time and effort taken, the more successful the brand will be. For example, in the case of a characteristic such as *caring*, the company would need to explain through employee training what this brand value means to a customer-service assistant, a receptionist, an IT manager, a production supervisor, and so on. If one of the brand characteristics is *innovative*, the company must educate all its van drivers, salespersons, accounts clerks, human resource executives, and every other individual in the company, in terms of what that characteristic means for them in carrying out their jobs. Only then will they know what specific behaviors, attitudes, and relationships to adopt in order to make that personality come alive.

The training of staff in the job-specific implications of a brand isn't optional. It has significant implications for human resource management, development, and training. It is vital to a company's performance and the achievement of brand consistency that everyone gets involved. For companies that pursue this course of action, the rewards can be spectacular. In my experience, staff take easily to personality-based values, and can understand why those values will differentiate their company from the competition. Applying their brand's personality can give them a sense of purpose that they may not get from other training and project initiatives. This is because they are used to dealing with personalities, and have a tendency to judge companies/brands they come in contact with in personality terms.

Designing internal brand programs by analyzing employee behavior

As explained above, it is very important to train staff on the company's brand strategy, and to identify how they can apply the brand values to their jobs. But, staff may need to learn new skills in order to perform well. It is important to look at each value and decide what skills are required to apply it. One way to do this is to analyze the behavior of employees who have been identified as performing to a very high standard on a particular value. Look at critical incidents where a staff member had to bring that value into action; find out what they did and how they did it. Also, interview other people who know about or were involved in the incident. This research can be very revealing in terms of identifying not just the skills associated with particular values, but also the organizational implications for helping staff to bring that value to life. As an example, the following is the result of a series of interviews with employees of a bank I worked with on the value of *caring*.

The sequence of this process was to ask managers at all levels and from all functions in the bank to nominate people whom they would consider appropriate role models based on the caring value, whether they had shown this behavioural value to either customers or colleagues. Several dozen nominations were received and the persons were interviewed about what they had done. Some wonderful stories came out and the best of these were given wide exposure in the bank's internal magazine and through briefing meetings.

The transcripts were analysed to elicit the key skills the role models had shown in demonstrating the caring characteristic and these eventually were the source of training and coaching programs for all staff. The data also pointed to certain organizational implications that needed to change if this brand value was to be enhanced throughout the bank. These are shown in the table below.

Personal Skills Required	Organizational Implications
Showing empathy	Encourage openness and honesty
Emotional resilience	Improve coaching and counseling
Suspending judgment	Train more in interpersonal skills
Listening	Develop teamwork
Giving positive and negative feedback	
Self-discipline	
Openness and honesty	
Combining formality and informality	

A general and interesting conclusion that came from this case and its real-life stories was that it wasn't easy to really care about others (including staff, subordinates, customers, suppliers, etc.). It is an attitudinal-related skill that goes much deeper than just being friendly and can be extremely stressful. An intensive coaching and training effort is required if all employees are going to be able to live the value of *caring* and bring the brand personality to life. Another learning point from this case was that a particular brand attribute may mean different things to employees in different jobs and so we must individualize the learning programs.

The brand engagement process

In order to accomplish employee brand engagement by segmenting internal audiences there are various phases to move through. These are:

1. **The strategic development phase**: This defines the scope, defines the internal audience segmentation, identifies potential change agents or role models for use in training, and develops the key messages and internal proposition. This is essential to get right in order to ensure employees buy in to, support and understand the brand strategy.

2. **The foundation building phase:** This develops materials for workshops, conducts workshops with senior managers and trains a pool of trainers if necessary, so that the training can be rolled out more effectively and quickly. I have found that in most medium to large organizations, choosing and training a pool of brand trainers is absolutely essential if rollout is to be done properly and in a timely fashion. At the same time, during this phase,

communications, events and other experiences are designed and prepared to support the implementation phase.

3. **The implementation phase:** Here all employees progress through workshops that not only tell them about brand building with world-class examples, but also tell them about their brand and how it has been developed. Such workshops usually end with some written action plans to bring the brand to life, whether it be on a departmental or individual basis. All workshops adopt the Think-Feel-Do approach explained earlier in this chapter. The results of the training interventions are monitored and measured for effectiveness, and modified for adjustment and improvement.

The larger, global companies use various methods such as this, but all go to extreme lengths to ensure that their employees understand and apply their brand values, as the following case study on Intel illustrates.

Case study 28: Intel Corporation

Training for maximum brand performance

From the 1990s, Intel made serious inroads into training all its employees in how to apply its values in their jobs. For each of Intel's six brand values, the company defined the associated behaviors, trained staff in those behaviors, and specified how performance on that value would be judged. The following summarizes how Intel trained its people to apply one of its values: risk taking.

Intel used internal communications to link all its values to the company's mission, objectives, and strategy. In addition, everyone in the company undertook a one-week training program, where senior managers explained how the values were linked to Intel's success. They also stressed the importance of people becoming role models on the values.

Risk taking was found to be a difficult value for people to understand and apply. Employees found themselves being punished for taking risks that failed, despite the good intentions of their managers. Problems also occurred in the practical application of some of the company's other values. As a result, an Intel Values Task Force was formed, which identified five key behaviors for each value. For the value of risk taking, these were:

1. embrace change;

2. challenge the status quo;

3. listen to all ideas and viewpoints;

4. encourage and reward informed risk taking; and

5. learn from our successes and mistakes.

Intel found that employees were still unsure about some aspects of risk taking, such as, "How can I take a risk when it might be detrimental to quality?" Intel provided additional tools to help its employees judge when risk taking was appropriate behavior. For example, a self-assessment survey evolved into a 360-degree core management survey that was used around the world. Under each key behavior for each value, employees had to rate themselves and have others rate them. For instance, for the key risk-taking behavior of "encourage and reward informed risk taking", employees were rated on how often they acted in the following ways:

- failed to clearly define expectations and limits;

- rewarded only successful activities;

- communicated that failure is not tolerated;

- provided insufficient time for implementation;

- criticized employees for pre-approved risks that failed; and

- insisted on clear ownership and accountability.

The use of role models and training kits

Intel searched for role models – people who demonstrated success in the values. Their behaviors and skills were analyzed in a similar fashion to that used in the bank example earlier in the book. Risk taking was the top priority for Intel, and was the first value to have its own training kit featuring ten items that included team and individual exercises, written and video interviews with role models, advice on specific issues of concern, and a list of further resources to use.

Values 'owners'

Intel appointed an 'owner' of the role model strategy, and the 'owners' of a value or value process had to prove they could implement it and recruit others who wanted to be co-owners. Laurie Price was the owner – or values champion – and she produced courses for employees that were based around the following two questions:

1. Do you know what the values mean?

2. How does your behavior match them?

Pre- and post-testing of results was used, and the results showed not just greater awareness of the values, but also significant improvements in performance. Eventually, the whole program was offered to all employees via Intel University.

The role model advocate award

All nominations for this annual award are accepted, but the selection process is rigorous, with only three or four awards a year being given out. Winners must demonstrate not only that they are role models for all values, but also that they are outspoken advocates of them.

Intel is itself a role model. It serves to remind us that there are no shortcuts in getting people to "live the brand"; it requires well-planned hard work. Companies must use whatever means necessary to help their employees create a brand culture. They must also be prepared to undertake the difficult task of assessing what constitutes good and bad performance on the brand values.

Rewarding and recognizing brand performers

However loyal and enthusiastic a company's employees are, whenever it introduces a new process they will want to know what is in it for them. Employees will always perform better if they gain some kind of recognition and reward for changing their work practices. Therefore, to accelerate the acceptance of personality characteristics into corporate culture, it is a good idea to think of ways by which employees can gain recognition and rewards.

Rewards

It is not unusual for companies to allocate a certain percentage of their employees' remuneration packages based on values performance. General Electric, for example, has been known to link 50% of its incentive compensation to performance on values, while Toro linked 25% and Levi Strauss one-third. Poor performance on brand values has been a career killer at Levi's, leading to loss of promotions and increments. Putting brand values into performance management and appraisal schemes ensures that the values are translated into corporate behavior, so that the consumer sees and experiences consistency. This influences their perceptions and has a major impact on the brand image of the company. Further, it increases profitability. Harvard Business School research reveals that companies implementing "performance-enhancing cultures" achieve profit growth of several hundred percent more than those that don't.

Recognition

It is not only financial rewards that can motivate employees to perform well on brand values. Here is a list of some ideas that have been applied successfully by client companies with which I have been involved:

- *Role models* – seek out people who perform outstandingly well on all values, as well as those whose performance is outstanding on individual values.

- *CEO awards* – reward outstanding brand values performance with special certificates or memorabilia.

- *Competition awards* – reward teams, departments, business units, and so on, for performing well on brand values.

- *Public acknowledgment* – use company newsletters and magazines to publicly acknowledge people whose outstanding performance you want to expose to everyone in your own company, as well as to companies you deal with.

- *Customer recognition awards* – highlight people in your company who have helped delight customers by giving them outstanding brand experiences.

- *Peer group awards* – involve peers at different hierarchy levels in nominating and choosing winners of best-in-class awards related to brand values.

- *Outstanding team awards* – reward innovative contributions to the development and practice of brand values.

- *Brand ambassadors* – select people who are really committed to the brand, and who enjoy the respect of others in the organization, and give them opportunities to talk about the brand, and to share their thoughts on best practice and success stories. Wherever possible, ask senior managers in every market in which the company operates to make recommendations to top management for improving brand execution.

The company has an obligation to help people understand the brand and bring it to life. In addition to the strategy facilitation and training described so far, corporate literature can help in the creation of a brand culture.

Brand handbooks

Some companies have handbooks or manuals that set out clear guidelines on what can and cannot be done with the company's brands. They usually refer to the visual aspects of the brand, and are often referred to as corporate identity or visual identity manuals. Such manuals are essential for day-to-day brand management, and as a reference for advertising, promotion, and other agencies.

In employee engagement programs, brand handbooks are often developed as learning and training tools, providing guidance for staff. Employee brand handbooks are different to the visual identity brand handbooks used by marketing departments and agencies for guidance on how to communicate the brand externally.

Brand handbooks are intended for all employees, with the purpose of explaining what the brand means for all jobs within the organization. They are often distributed at a brand launch initiative or a brand-related training event, where employees are given the opportunity to ask, "What does the brand mean in terms of my job?" and "How can I incorporate the brand values into my everyday work?"

Brand handbooks typically include:

- a message from the CEO about the central importance of the brand to the future of the business;

- a definition of brand used by the company;

- examples of powerful brands and the benefits they bring to companies and employees;

- an explanation of the brand vision and personality/values (and sometimes positioning) chosen by the company;

- examples of how employees can bring the brand to life in their work;

- questions for people to answer relating to what actions they will take to "live the brand".

Brand handbooks that invite employee interaction, by including quizzes and other interactive methods, are generally more effective than purely descriptive text. If well-designed, with good use of color, they will stay in sight and in mind, and employees will tend to refer to them more often. Brand handbooks are best supported by training at the departmental/section level, so that every employee knows what each brand value means in relation to his or her job and understands how to implement them in his or her everyday work. Many companies now deliver brand handbooks via their intranet facilities, but having a hard copy to refer to can still be effective.

Repetition of internal brand communications

Internal brand communication needs to be frequent and repetitious, but in a variety of forms to keep messages consistent and relevant. Some companies use posters, some intranet messaging, screensavers, and other internal brand activities. Whatever the mix, the point is that if only carried out sporadically, employees may not see these messages as important and momentum may reduce. It is no good launching the brand internally with a spectacular event revealing why the brand is so important and why the personality characteristics or values need to be lived by everyone, and then not follow up. Sadly, I have seen this happen. Everyone gets excited, then momentum slowly dies away and it becomes just another management-led event that fades into obscurity.

The most effective way to keep employees focused on the brand is to incorporate it somehow into a rewards and recognition system such as performance appraisal or as part of a scorecard that includes mutually-defined key result areas based on the brand values. This, combined with continuous, consistent – but refreshed – internal brand communications, will ensure the culture of the organization is built around brand performance.

A note on customer service

The role of customer service in brand delivery is absolutely critical, whatever business you are working in. If we look for consequences of delivering inadequate or poor customer service, we don't have to look far. For example, the Technical Assistance Research Programs Institute in Washington, DC once published some alarming statistics showing just how significant customer service problems had become:

- Complaints about service had increased 400% over the years of the study.

- Ninety-six percent of customers will never tell you they have a problem. They will simply take their business elsewhere.

- For every customer with a problem a company knows about, there are 26 others that it doesn't know about.

- The average customer with a problem talks to nine or ten other people about it.

- Thirteen percent of the customers with problems will tell as many as 20 other people.

- For every customer with a problem, there are 250 people who have directly or indirectly heard negative comments about the supplier.

- One of the primary reasons customers switch loyalties is because of perceived neglect or indifference – 68%, in fact! If your customers don't feel valued or respected, your business may well be in trouble.

On the positive side, the Strategic Planning Institute in Cambridge, Massachusetts, found that companies noted for outstanding quality and service:

- charge on average 9% higher prices;

- grow twice as fast as the average company;

- experience yearly market share increases of 6%, while the average company loses 2% a year; and

- receive an average annual return of 12%. (The average during the research period was 1–2%.)

Customer service is all about staff attitude and values performance, as opposed to public behavior and 'customer first' scripts. Customer service training should therefore rely not on generic interpersonal skills courses, but on dedicated values performance courses. The brand values should be layered on top of the generic behavioral skills. Some companies I have been involved in have trained their service staff not just in how to deal with customers, but also in how to enhance the perception of trust through the use of certain words and phrases and appropriate body language, depending on whether the conversations are in person, online, or by phone.

Also essential for outstanding customer service is empowering employees so that they can deal with problems. What use is there in training people to understand and appreciate customers' problems, if they then have to refer the problems to higher levels to be resolved? Many companies are now allowing frontline service people to take direct action, including spending up to specified amounts, to solve problems on the spot.

But customer service isn't confined to the interaction between frontline staff and customers. Many other things make up the total 'service value package' in the minds of consumers. They include:

- warranties, guarantees, reclaim and returns procedures and policies;

- speed of response following a breakdown or product failure;

- employees' dress and personal presentation;

- employees' tone of voice and verbal style;

- written response times and style in letters and emails;

- employees' product and service knowledge;

- retail layout and window presentation;

- customer-friendly telephone response system (with a minimum of menu options before speaking to a customer representative!); and

- call center expertise.

Companies therefore need to communicate and live out their brand values in both words and actions. All such factors that affect the brand-customer service experience should be benchmarked against best practice. For instance, AT&T Universal Card has been well known in the past for:

- collecting and analyzing daily more than 100 measurements of customer delight;

- using these to produce company-wide and departmental indices;

- giving all employees a bonus on days when global numbers exceed targets;

- giving the bonus based on total company indices, so that all departments co-operate with one other; and

- making 5,000 customer calls per month for follow-up interviews to make sure all is well.

For companies that get employee engagement right, there is further good news in that success can be quantified. For example:

- *Fortune* magazine's "Most Admired Companies" stock prices appreciated 50% over peers after instituting employee motivation and brand alignment efforts.

- Satisfied employees are on average 30% less likely to leave, saving 1 to 1.5 times annual salary per employee turnover.

- Employees with a high level of engagement are 38% more likely to have above-average productivity.

- A UK bank study found that retail branches with highly engaged employees were associated with greater revenue growth (+6%) and profit margin growth (+100%).

- A significant improvement in communications effectiveness is associated with a 29.5% increase in market value.

Summary

I would like to conclude by summarizing some of the main points from this chapter.

There are various issues to keep in mind when establishing and building a brand-based culture through employee engagement, the main ones being:

- The brand strategy must be clear and well explained at all levels.

- A high level of commitment is needed. No internal branding process will succeed without leadership role modeling. This means there must be no visible contradictions from top executives.

- Messaging inside and outside the organization must be consistent.

- The challenge of getting everyone to align around common ideas when different groups serve different masters. Training programs must cater for departmental relevance, but be clearly linked to the brand strategy.

- Responsibility for employee engagement in branding is often caught in no-man's land, between brand, marketing, corporate communications, human resources, etc. Responsibility should be clear, and the best way to do this is to make it a part of the brand action planning process via the brand management structure. More will be explained about this in the next chapter on brand planning and control.

- To achieve the benefits and overcome the challenges, employee engagement is best viewed as an ongoing process, involving training and other organizational change activities, designed to ensure that all employees understand and embrace an organization's brand and are able to bring it to life inside and outside the organization. Its main aim is to ensure that employees are able to relate to and share the brand strategy, its purpose and goals.

- The best way to deliver success with an employee engagement program is to build a brand-based culture. This has been proven to enhance performance in businesses and create organizations that are able to live up to and exceed the expectations of their customers and other stakeholders.

- Employee motivation is an additional major benefit of internal branding, as a strong internal and external brand serves to attract and retain talent.

In the next chapter we will focus on the third main area of brand management, which is brand planning and control, and discuss how organizations can meticulously maintain the implementation of brand strategy. Following this, the final chapter discusses tracking brand success, which includes details of the methodology involved in calculating the monetary value of brands.

CHAPTER 10

Brand Planning and Control

T he big challenge for CEOs and managers in charge of major corporate and/or product brands, is to bring the brand(s) to life through strategy and change, and to motivate people to deliver on the brand promise. This is particularly important for those involved in any business that uses a corporate- or house-endorsed brand architecture approach. While the previous chapter focused on bringing about alignment behind the brand strategy through employee engagement, this chapter examines how strategy implementation can be achieved through careful planning and control of the brand and its activities. There are many aspects to consider in brand management but if it is not carried out well the strategy could fail.

The basic aim of brand planning and control is to manage all touchpoints that customers have with the brand to maximise their experience in a consistent way, and to do that better than competitors. This can be a monumental task as touchpoints are numerous and not always under the control of brand managers. Touchpoint analysis can be looked at from both macro and micro aspects, and both will be outlined in this chapter. I will also discuss the need for brand action planning and the structure(s) neccesary to carry out all brand management activities efficiently.

Macro aspects of brand touchpoint control

There are various methods and models that are used to view the more macro aspects that can influence the brand strategy and affect the identity and image of the brand. One method that I use is called the brand management wheel, as shown in Figure 10.1.

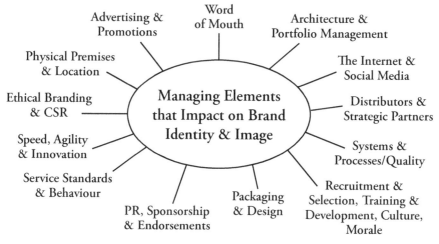

Figure 10.1: The brand management wheel

The brand management wheel

The brand management wheel shows the larger kinds of touchpoints impacting on the consumer experience that must be carefully managed. Few companies do this well but the top brands in the world are meticulous in their approach. It is the brand strategy that drives brand management from the center out to the 'spokes' of the wheel. The inner part of the wheel guides everyone in the organization as to what needs managing in each area of responsibility. If a company has a clear brand strategy, then it is much easier to manage the outer areas.

Without clear guidelines on brand vision, brand personality and positioning, there is little hope for brand consistency among the different areas (the 'spokes' of the wheel), as these will be managed on an ad hoc basis. This usually results in a confused, mixed, and relatively poor brand image. For example, the absence of a clearly defined brand strategy means that advertising agencies commissioned by a company to promote its brand will have little idea of what it stands for, what its brand platform is, and what the key messages should be when addressing the different target audiences. One of my clients asked me to find out why its advertising agency wasn't portraying its brand messages the way the client expected. When I asked the client company if it had given the agency a proper brand brief, they answered "yes". But when I asked to see the brief, the client said it had been verbal, not written. The client hadn't clearly defined its brand positioning or personality for the agency, and so the advertising creative team's interpretation of the brief was very different from the client's expectations, leading to a history of continuous misunderstandings between the agency and the client.

Below I describe each of the 'spokes' of the brand management wheel as they relate to the brand manager's task.

Advertising and promotions

It is difficult not to use advertising in some form, but companies are often lured into using tactical advertising, instead of image advertising. It is advisable to use a combination: tactical advertising to deal with changing competitor moves and brand features, attributes, and innovations; and image advertising to build a consistent brand message. Promotions can similarly be held to accomplish both purposes. However, use promotions sparingly so as not to dilute the image of your brand. Frequent 'special offers' and other promotions can make the brand appear cheap. Ensure that any co-branded promotions are relevant to your customer base and appropriate in terms of brand fit. In Chapters 7 and 8 I explained online and offline communications in detail.

Above all, when using the services of outside agencies, the briefing documents should contain all aspects of the brand strategy in addition to the creative and campaign objectives if relevant. Major brands now also ensure that agencies are employed on a results basis instead of the traditional way of charging fees.

Physical premises and location

Even your buildings and offices represent your brand, so ensure that they are appropriate and in line with your desired consumer perceptions. If your company is linking its brand to innovation for example, is your reception area and are your outlets innovative in design and function?

Ethical branding and corporate social responsibility (CSR)

Consumers now demand that businesses and brands are more ethical, genuine and transparent in the way they act. People are now quick to blame organizations for a variety of causes including the damage to the environment, cruelty to animals, poverty and many others. Millennials especially are concerned about the power and behaviour of big brands, and this has forced many large corporations to adopt CSR programs that give back to communities instead of just taking from them.

Such is the impact of this force for change demanded by consumers that some companies, such as Unilever, have now completely changed their organizations to focus on sustainability, so much so, that they do not refer to this as a CSR program and have been reported as having removed the CSR department as part of implementing the philosophy of 'Sustainable Living' at the heart of every aspect of the business. As the company says, "The Unilever Sustainable Living Plan (USLP) is our blueprint for achieving our vision to grow our business, whilst decoupling our environmental footprint from our growth and increasing our positive social impact. The Plan sets stretching targets, including how we source raw materials and how consumers use our brands."[64]

This trend toward sustainability and brands giving back to communities will inevitably continue as consumer power grows.

Speed, agility and innovation

The pace of change is rapidly increasing and those organizations that do not embrace the attributes of speed, agility and innovation will not survive in the long term. A good example of this is the clothing brand Zara.

Case study 29: Zara – instant fashion

Zara is a prime example of speed, agility, and innovation in retailing and it has become a global fashion giant through demonstrating its prowess in these three areas. Owned by the Inditex Group from Spain, Zara opened its first store in 1975, and now has over 2,100 stores in 88 countries.

The Zara business model, founded by Amancio Ortega has been described by him as "instant fashion". And it has totally disrupted the traditional way of design, production and distribution favored for so long by mainline fashion companies. The time limitation for fashion clothes is the speed of design, with traditional fashion houses tending to have few designers who can take up to six months to produce new designs, enabling them to only have two or three collections per year. Zara has a large team of designers, which enables the company to react quickly to new trends and consumer demands.

Incredibly, Zara produces more than 12,000 clothing product designs each year and 450 million items annually, far more than most fashion retailers. To accomplish this it has developed the capability to drastically shorten the product life cycle. Indeed, from the design stage to arriving in store can take as little as two to three weeks. If the design is just a modification, it may take less, and no one design stays in the stores for more than four weeks. Should an item prove to not sell the numbers as planned then it is withdrawn and production stopped.

Each Zara designer can create up to five products a day, and the onward speed required to get to store is augmented by a computerized inventory system that links the factories producing Zara's large number of products to the retail outlets. This just in time (JIT) system is not especially new (it was originally developed by Toyota), but Zara has learnt from other industries and used this to significantly reduce the need to hold large inventories.

This combination of speed, flexibility and innovation has led Zara to be a very powerful brand, giving it a sustainable competitive advantage. This, naturally, brings several benefits to customers and the company.

What's in it for customers? There is an interesting and positive impact on the consumer. First, it means that Zara shoppers have a constant source of new, fresh products to choose from. Second, customers know that any item they buy will be more 'exclusive' than those from other stores, as their items will only be on sale for the maximum time of a month.

What's in it for Zara? The benefit for the company is that Zara customers tend to visit stores, on average, 17 times a year, as opposed to the fashion retailing average of three or four times. And the frequent turnover encourages them to buy every time they visit the store as they know the products will only be available for a short time.

There is no need for a big marketing spend either. In fact, Zara has an almost zero marketing budget preferring to spend that money on store expansion. Getting the pull factor with customers is the key as opposed to the push factor of advertising and promotion. Zara gains consumer insight by merchandisers talking to customers in-store and sending back their comments to headquarters for new and preferred designs at the touch of a button on their hand-held devices.

All in all, it's a win-win situation for Zara, its customers, suppliers, and logistics partners.

As technology continues to add to the disruption by enabling players to move into markets they have not been traditionally in, innovations will increase and change will get faster.

Service standards and behavior

Service quality is one of the most difficult elements of brand management to get right, but also one of the most essential. Poor-quality service can permanently damage a brand. It is essential to monitor closely all aspects of customer service on a continuous basis. Regard it as a never-ending process and not just a one-off training course. Touchpoint analysis and customer journey mapping are increasingly used to improve the brand experience and are discussed in detail later in this chapter.

Public relations, sponsorships and endorsements

Public relations (PR) is a good source of brand building and it is a good idea to use PR as a part of the communications mix to positively promote your brand name in the market and to respond to a crisis. This has also been explained in detail in Chapter 7.

Packaging and design

Design is increasingly becoming an important differentiator in the brand proposition, as really attractive design generates emotional power. Design can also be used as a strategic competitive advantage, when defining first-mover product features and benefits, as with the case of Apple's iPod and iPhone. Packaging follows design, and attracts customers, helping a company's products stand out from the crowd, especially in outlets where the shelves are filled with competing brands.

HR, employee morale, and brand culture

As discussed in the previous chapter, the whole brand has to be brought to life. An organization's culture needs to be appealing to its employees if they are to have good morale that encourages them to go the extra mile to support your brand initiatives. All aspects of human resource development and management must be involved and the best way to build a powerful culture is to focus on the brand – this will inspire both customers and employees. In addition, having a great brand culture will attract and retain talent. The previous chapter on employee engagement outlines how this works in detail.

Systems and processes/quality

To build a strong brand, the product or service must be of the highest quality. Only a strong brand such as Toyota will be able to recover from a major quality issue as it did with its massive car recalls, law suits and heavy fines. In order to sustain the highest quality, it is imperative that systems and processes are extremely efficient and have the latest technology and testing methods.

Distributors and strategic partners

In order to gain scale and market coverage, many brands use agents, distributors and strategic partners. This is especially true in B2B businesses. In B2C businesses one popular way of doing this is to issue franchises and licenses. Whatever road is taken it is essential that all partners understand your brand thoroughly and, importantly, know how to represent your brand properly. This can be difficult if, say, distributors represent competing brands as well. All aspects of the brand values need to be given attention and it really is a case of 'your life in their hands'. When putting your brand in the hands of other parties, ensure that they represent your brand properly, and focus on fighting other brands in the market, rather than fighting other distributors who are also offering your brand on the basis of price. Poor representation by channels has led some companies, such as Gucci, to buy back all their franchises.

Training for strategic partners and frequent monitoring of these businesses should be part of a consistent, ongoing brand management process.

The internet and social media

I have discussed the Internet and social media at some length in Chapter 8 and emphasized that it is critical for all brands to have both online and offline communications and e-commerce strategies.

Architecture and portfolio management

As explained in Chapter 4, the trend is now definitely toward linking the corporate brand name to product and sub-brands for many reasons.

Word of mouth

One of the most powerful ways of building brands is through word-of-mouth recommendations by happy customers. Google, Amazon and many of the social networking brands testify to this. Customer advocacy can only come from a consistently great brand experience, and so we come full circle. Do all the other things right, and word of mouth will become your biggest brand-building weapon.

I once had a great customer experience at the Pan Pacific Hotel in Vancouver, and have since told thousands of people in training, consultancy and conference situations about this experience. I have become a brand ambassador, so to speak, and if there are many more like me then it becomes clear how word of mouth can be a powerful brand-building tool. This case, in detail below, is also a great example of how engaging employees in brand building and management can achieve amazing results.

Case study 30:
The Pan Pacific Hotel, Vancouver

While on an assignment to speak to the Canadian government about branding, I stayed at the Pan Pacific Hotel in Vancouver, an experience I have never forgotten. On the first evening of my stay I had dinner in a restaurant. The following morning I was walking in the lobby when a member of staff said hello to me by name and said he hoped I had enjoyed my meal in that restaurant the previous evening. I did not know him or recollect seeing him before and he certainly did not serve me in the restaurant, so it was quite a surprise.

But the level of attention from staff and attention to detail continued throughout my stay. Before I left I asked to see the general manager as I was intrigued as to how the service levels were so consistently outstanding. He arranged to see me at breakfast before I left.

When I asked him about this, he said that if you empower staff they will do a great job, but he explained to me that if you want to work in his hotel, whatever job it was, an applicant may have to have up to 12 or 14 interviews! There would be one with him, others with department and section/unit heads and finally interviews with each member of the team that the applicant would be working with. All of these interviews were arranged so that everyone could feel comfortable that the applicant had the right attitude toward service quality and would fit in with the existing staff, whom incidentally were not called staff but 'Associates'.

He explained that his philosophy was to "hire on attitude, train on skills". In other words, it was not difficult to teach new employees work skills but it was very difficult to teach them to have the right attitude to customer service.

In addition to this, Associates were empowered to fix any problem encountered with a customer on the spot, whatever the cost. I came across an example of this very recently when speaking at a conference in Malaysia. I was telling my Pan Pacific story and asked the audience if anyone had stayed in this hotel. One lady put her hand up to say she had. I asked if it was a good experience and she said it was fantastic. Evidently, she arrived at the hotel with no baggage as the airline had lost it and so she had practically nothing. She went on to explain to the several hundred people in the conference room that the hotel immediately assigned an Associate to sit with her, make a list of everything she needed, and then physically go with her to different shops to buy all that was on her list. This was a wonderful experience for her and she was glad to share that experience.

So here is the result. In every program I run and at many of the conferences I speak at I tell this story. Over the past few years I have told it to thousands of people. Now that lady in the audience has also told hundreds of people. We have become brand ambassadors for the Pan Pacific, Vancouver. There is no better way to build your business and your brand then have customers become your brand advocates.

Build on consistency

Great brands are built on consistency, including consistent and appropriate behavior in all areas of operation; however, consistency can only come from a clearly defined brand strategy. This is where brand managers need to be especially skillful. Take a hard, analytical look at the 'spokes' of the wheel, and ask yourself and your colleagues:

• Is our brand vision and platform clearly articulated in written statements?

• What is currently happening in each area that is affecting our ability to manage the brand consistently?

• What needs to be done to improve our management of the brand in each area?

Every 'spoke' of the wheel is vitally important, although some might be more relevant to your brand than others. Once you have carried out the analysis and answered these questions, then develop action plans to incorporate any necessary or relevant improvements, and review all spokes of the wheel frequently with all people responsible for managing these activities and guarding the brand. Brand action planning will be discussed toward the end of this chapter.

Micro aspects of brand touchpoint control

While the brand management wheel assists in the assessment of touchpoint effectiveness from a broader standpoint, there is also a need to dive further into the interactions between customers and brands. This can be done by looking at each single interaction before, during and after customers buy products and services and by mapping out customer journeys along that route.

There are three main areas for individual brand-customer engagement in the purchase process.

1. **Pre-purchase touchpoints**: A collection of brand touchpoints that significantly influences whether a prospective customer will place your brand

into his or her final consideration set on the way to making a purchase. These can include advertising and promotions, brochures, visiting outlets, talking with sales staff, digital searches including the brand's website, email etiquette, press conferences, and trade shows (e.g. booth design). For example, at tradeshows, if your brand represents quality and warm service, then you must demonstrate this. You will have to show that in how you present yourself, your promotional materials (must be of high quality), your brochures must be of high quality, and when you talk, you need to show that you listen and are concerned about your customers' needs. You can also show your track record that manifests this and even references of what your past and present customers say. This will also have an impact on the word of mouth that gets around about your brand.

We can also include in this category what we call influencer touchpoints such as blogs, magazine reviews, expert opinions, annual reports, recruiting materials, press releases, sponsorships and endorsements.

Outside of the brand manager's control in this area would be other activities such as customers talking with their friends and family. However, if this is carried out on social media the metrics available now can tell brand owners what people are saying about their brand but more on an aggregate and not an individual basis.

2. **Purchase touchpoints**: These are all the brand touchpoints that move a customer from consideration of your brand to purchasing it at the point of sale, which may depend on the sales staff (if in a retail outlet), demonstrations, dealer sales incentives, or even click-through Internet comparison websites. For example, in a retail outlet how the design of the outlet presents itself and how the sales person presents him/herself are important. How sales people speak, their tone of voice, product knowledge, etc. has to be consistent with the brand personality. If the purchase is made electronically this has to be made easy and convenient for customers.

In a B2B scenario, the purchase touchpoint could be a sales presentation to the prospects. So, the quality and content of your brochures, presentation slides and the way the sales persons projects themselves must reflect what the brand stands for. If your brand positioning is based on solving solutions quickly and efficiently, your solutions should demonstrate that. Your service should also do that, so if a potential client requests you to go back and work on some sample cases that they provide, your turnaround time should reflect this efficiency. And you should show flexibility in your specifications. Further, when the client has accepted your proposal, you will need to process the order speedily. Now it may be the turn of your IT programmers and consultants to project the brand values of quality and efficiency. The entire life cycle of the sales process is a part of the purchase touchpoint.

3. **Post-purchase touchpoints**: This category can include warranties, guarantees and after-sales service including service hotlines and the speed and friendliness of solutions offered and implemented to rectify customer problems including returns. In fact, anything that can leverage and reinforce the purchase decision and lead to the customer becoming a brand ambassador for you.

One way in which touchpoints can be analysed with some clarity and certainty is through the use of customer journey mapping techniques.

Mapping customer journeys

Brand managers can get to grips with this wide range of touchpoints by mapping the customer journey through the purchase-related sequence, by employing market research techniques, and measuring their competencies on each touchpoint against those of competitors.

Philips created a touchpoint tool that does exactly this. For example, when a young person buys a consumer electronics product such as a music player, Philips' research found that the sequence of touchpoints encountered was chronologically as follows:

- Decision to buy a product in the category.

- Looking at relevant advertising.

- Talking with friends.

- Searching on the Internet.

- Discussing with family.

- Visiting retailers.

- Acquiring promotional literature.

- Listening to or reading expert opinions.

- Comparing brands.

- Visiting retailers again.

- Talking to sales persons.

- Comparing branded product features.

- Comparing prices.

- Talking to friends again.

- Buying the chosen brand.

- Testing product and understanding features and functions.

- Showing their purchase to family and friends.

- Justifying their brand choice.

- Explaining and recommending the brand they have bought to friends.

For all the touchpoints that can be controlled, measurement of how Philips compares to competitors is undertaken and improvements made where necessary.

Once this has been completed, brand managers can start to prepare action plans. Even if objective research has not been undertaken, it is possible to compare your touchpoint capabilities against others. The following is a suggested way of doing this.

Touchpoint action planning

Here is a simple but effective way of ensuring that customers get a good brand experience. The purpose of this exercise is to list all the touchpoints that your brand has with customers, and generate a priority list for action and improvement. This can be carried out at an overall organizational level, as is often the case with smaller businesses, or at a departmental level in larger organizations.

1. To facilitate your thought process, plot all the customer-journey touchpoints from 'pre-purchase' through 'during-purchase' to 'post-purchase'. Include any 'influencing' touchpoints.

2. Then from the list select ALL touchpoints that you can manage and control. (There is little point in wasting resources on areas over which you have no control.)

3. From this list, rate how well each touchpoint is currently performing compared to your competitors. Rate 1–5, where 1 represents very poor, 3 is fair and 5 very good. If you don't have any external-specific research then you can use your own judgment plus feedback from customers and staff. When in doubt, be critical on scoring.

4. Lastly, indicate the priority of improving each touchpoint to your customer. Rank Low, Medium or High. Rank **Low**, when a brand touchpoint is already performing well (i.e. scoring 5). Here there will be little need to plan for urgent improvement but still there is a need to monitor the consistency of this over time. Indicate **Medium**, when a brand touchpoint is performing fairly (i.e. scoring 3 or 4). For these items plans must be developed to improve competitive performance and to maintain a minimum level of brand delivery. Finally indicate **High** when a brand touchpoint

is underperforming by scoring 1 or 2. It is critically urgent that plans be developed to address any shortfalls here.

The next task is to transform the above details into an action plan by:

- Listing the brand touchpoints according to priority, in an action planning worksheet.

- Using the action planning worksheet write down the objectives, strategy, detailed plans, start and end dates, main person responsible, cost and resources needed to improve each touchpoint and how the improvement will be measured.

Plans such as these can then be approved and monitored. It is likely that timeframes may differ and normally brand plans fall into the following categories.

- High Priority, Short Term (1–18 months)

- High Priority, Medium Term (18–36 months)

- Medium Priority, Short Term (1–18 months)

- Medium Priority, Medium Term (18–36 months)

This way of assessing areas for improvement is not particularly difficult and it emphasizes the need to constantly ensure that customers enjoy the best possible brand experience, especially one that is better than your competitors. Without understanding the customer journey this is difficult to accomplish.

Touchpoints are not the only source of brand action planning. The whole organization needs to be involved in the process and this needs a structured approach. Brand management is not effective without some form of structured guardianship.

The need for brand management structure

Who is responsible for brand management?

Many people ask me, "Who is responsible for brand management?" The answer is "everyone" because, as I hope I have made clear, everyone in an organization can make an impact on brand image. Similarly, every department and every employee can, and should, help to manage and guard the brand. Nevertheless, the CEO must drive the efforts and be seen to be doing so, and is largely accountable for its success.

The role of the CEO

Although CEOs cannot be made solely responsible for brand management, they must drive branding from the top and help create the conditions necessary for strong brand management to take place. Without forceful leadership at this level, brand managers will find life very difficult, as they generally lack the power to influence the other functions upon which their success often rests, such as human resources. One of the best ways to ensure that the brand culture is built properly is for the CEO to be involved in the brand process by way of boards of management and other brand planning and control entities. Brand discipline can only be ensured by structured governance, and although brand has to be inclusive it is always top-down driven.

Establish a brand management structure

Brand management activities are so important that they have to be structured and supported, particularly at a senior level. One way in which this is done is illustrated in Figure 10.2 on page 273, which shows two main bodies that are responsible for implementing, monitoring and improving the strategy of the brand and the resultant image. These are a Brand Management Council (BMC) and Brand Working Committees or task forces (BWC). The main roles of these entities are as follows:

BMC roles

A BMC is very strategic and can often be an extension of a management committee or executive committee that makes decisions on the business and operational aspects of the organization. Its roles in the management of the brand are usually:

1. To determine the architecture of the brands under their control and to ensure that brand discipline and consistency is adhered to across the organization. Brand discipline will include the prevention of new logos and brands that do not fit with the master brand from being introduced. It will also ensure that new brands, which are approved, adhere to the rules of the brand architecture.

2. To establish and confirm all aspects of brand strategy and set the strategic direction for brand communication initiatives. This includes both internal communications involving staff, and external communications involving the various stakeholders.

3. Exercise the final veto on major initiatives affecting brand image, for example, major advertising campaigns. The BMC must have the authority

to stop any major initiatives that may have a detrimental effect on the overall brand image. This will ascertain that a consistent brand image is being communicated to various stakeholders and markets.

4. To review and monitor all internal and external brand communications performance. This will include internal brand communications (e.g. newsletter, intranet, email, poster campaigns, competitions, and so on), as well as external communications (e.g. corporate visual identity, public relations, sponsorships, event management, corporate website, use of websites and so on).

5. To provide advice to the various subcommittees on branding issues. That is, it will ensure all decisions put forward by the various subcommittees are in line with the brand strategy of the organization.

6. To approve co-branding, strategic alliances, and major partnerships initiatives. This will ensure that partner brands selected to work with the organization will not transfer any negative elements to the brand. Concurrently, the organization should benefit from leveraging on some of the positive associations linked to its branded partners.

7. To be responsible for selecting and briefing future brand partners on relevant aspects of the brand. This will ascertain that future brand partners comprehend the values and identity of the brand, and help prevent them from misrepresenting the brand in any negative way.

8. To evaluate and approve all brand plans put forward by the BWC. With this, the BMC will prioritize and filter various brand-related initiatives put forward. This will help to optimize use of resources and utilization of budgets, and maximize impact on corporate image.

9. To allocate financial resources for brand development. That is, BMC will evaluate initiatives and budgets put forward by the BWC. For initiatives that are approved by BMC, the BMC will put up the respective budget to the Management Committee or Board for approval. Annual brand-related spending would normally be put up in one budget.

10. To be accountable and responsible for the organization's competitive identity and the positioning of the brand in all markets. This will include approving all business and market development activities that will have an impact on how the brand is being portrayed and positioned. For new markets to be developed, the BMC will have to consider new sub-positioning issues.

11. To ensure clear reporting and tracking mechanisms for all brand initiatives are in place. It has to ensure that it receives consistent updates on all initiatives that have an impact on the brand. In addition, it has to track how the

perception of the brand is changing with the entry of new competitors and initiatives taken. With this, the BMC will be able to monitor the effectiveness of the various brand-related initiatives that have been introduced.

12. To be responsible for ensuring that all branding activities are related and linked to any performance management or scorecard systems.

BWC roles

The main aim of a Brand Working Committee (BWC) is to provide operational information and comprehensive brand action plans for the brand to the BMC. A BWC provides information and responds to requests on subjects such as market research, customer relationship management, brand tracking, design and packaging, all brand communications and new product development.

A BWC is also responsible for ensuring that everyone in the organization is trained in what the brand stands for and how they can play their part, and this ranges from individuals at lower levels in the organization to all departments, functions and levels. It is the idea generation team that gathers lots of plans and ideas and feeds these to the BMC in prioritized fashion, with timescales and measurement criteria to allow the BMC to make informed decisions on all major brand activities. As an example, in one particular public sector organization (a maritime industry regulator) after a newly set up BWC held a half-day ideas session with all departmental heads, over 130 possibilities for improving the brand image of the organization were identified. These then were separated into short-, medium- and long-term time frames and more detail obtained on what the outcomes from these ideas should be, how they would be measured for success, who would lead the process and how much financial and human resources would be required. It does not take much to involve and motivate people and sessions of a consultative and creative nature like this can be extremely rewarding, the end result also ensuring that commitment and buy-in is there.

Whereas the BMC might meet on a quarterly basis, the BWC should tend to meet on a monthly basis as there is a lot of work to do. This kind of detailed work needs a team of people to be involved, but it works well. The BMC has the final say on which plans go ahead and gives the sign off. The more important and impactful ideas may need policy changes and the BMC may need to take these to a higher approving authority, such as an executive- or board-level entity. When I have set up these arrangements and structures in the past I have found it best to tie the BMC into that policy decision-making body to facilitate progress. This can be achieved by having the BMC agenda backed on to that of the executive committee or board. This sometimes works well as the top-level people are often similar in position.

In larger organizations, or industries, it may be that there are several BWCs focusing on different areas for change and brand improvement such as communications, CSR, internal employee engagement and others.

One final point to mention is that a senior representative from each BWC should be a member of the BMC or at least attend BMC meetings in order to ensure good communication and understanding of the items to be discussed. Quite often a few members of a BWC are invited to attend relevant parts of the BMC meetings for discussion and explanation of proposed plans.

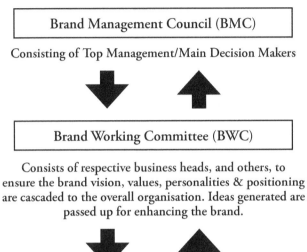

Figure 10.2: An example of a commonly used brand management structure

One of the most important tasks for both committees is to create, implement and review brand action plans; activities to ensure priorities are given due attention and everything duly reinforces the brand strategy.

The next case study describes a company that understands the need for a good, strong brand guardianship and management structure, and has ensured its implementation.

Case study 31: Philips

Brand philosophy: making brand guardianship happen

Gerard Kleisterlee, former president and CEO of Philips, clearly stated his commitment to value creation through a strong Philips brand. He didn't believe that building business value and brand value are different processes. He believed that the way to create value is to understand consumers better than the competition can, and argued that this skill is at the heart of the marketing function.

A big part of the current effort in building brand value at Philips has been in strengthening overall marketing competence right through the company. This is done structurally, as well as individually. Philips believes that the brand is important because it can deliver a potent promise with the power to make people choose its products, its jobs, and its stock, in preference to those of other players on the market.

The Philips brand values were summarized at that time by the promise of "sense and simplicity". As explained on the company's website when Kleisterlee was in post:

> Technology exists to help make our lives easier and more productive. So why is it so often such a hassle, full of complexity and frustration? At Philips, we believe that technology should be as simple as the box it comes in. It's this very simplicity that transforms a task into an opportunity, a burden into a pleasure. Which is why we are committed to delivering products and solutions that are easy to experience, designed around you, and advanced. Simplicity can be a goal of technology. It certainly is the goal at Philips. It just makes sense.

This represents the company's ability to enhance people's quality of life with its wide range of products, as well as by the jobs it creates, and the way Philips tries to become part of the societies in which it operates. In this way, Philips feels it clearly differentiates itself from other brands in the market.

Brand management structure

The Brand Equity Board (BEB) was set up as the highest marketing body within the company. The BEB has the task of clearly setting out the company's fundamental values, and then creating the means for them to be applied consistently right across the company. The BEB's "agreed" definition of brand equity was "positive associations that drive the net present worth of a brand's sustainable or potential contribution to profits and market valuation."

Philips chartered a course to fully leverage the power of its brand and improve its equity. This process started with the founding of the Brand Equity Board and Global Brand Management (GBM), and has been invigorated with the introduction of management by brand as a corporate core process.

The key driver of this process was the president and CEO himself, who announced:

> "The Philips brand is a significant company asset and its proper care and development is critical for the company to achieve its goal. Its addition as a corporate core process represents the clear intent of the board of management to re-emphasize the brand and its values in the company's approach to the market and to its stakeholders."

The Brand Equity Board was founded in mid-1999 when Philips determined there was a need for a cross-divisional entity to help enhance its brand equity and share best practices. It started with 11 members, representing each consumer product division, regional organizations, and corporate staff functions. The president and CEO was the chairman of the BEB.

The purpose of the BEB was to ensure that brand management strategy and policies are developed in concert with the organization and, consequently, have the full support of, and full deployment into, the organization and the businesses of the company.

The mission of the BEB was "to build premium brand equity for Philips" by:

- developing the ways and means to create a balanced, cohesive, and relevant face to the market, and a deeper and more significant relationship with our stakeholders;

- creating networks, forging specific processes, and fostering discipline and synergies to leverage the power of the brand across Philips; and

- building and strengthening the Philips company culture through a stronger customer and market orientation.

GBM supports the board of management in developing brand strategy and managing issues around the Philips group portfolio of brands. It develops and monitors global brand standards and guidelines and challenges the businesses and the regions to set appropriate brand goals, contributing to raising the standard of marketing competence in the company.

GBM's mission was to, "Increase the value of the Philips brand by ensuring its development and protection, and encourage a stronger consumer/customer focus within the company."

GBM's objectives were:

1. *Brand strategy*: Through the creation of a brand platform, to set standards and goals for the development of the brand through corporate and product division initiatives.

2. *Setting global standards and targets*: GBM consults with the product divisions and regions on developing appropriate marketing efforts to achieve brand objectives, advises the board of management when discrepancies exist, and develops plans to counteract them, if necessary.

3. *Competence building*: To build the company's overall marketing communication competence through training, sharing best practice, advising on key relevant personnel hires, and agency relationship management.

4. *Brand health reporting*: To hold quarterly brand health "barrel" reviews with the board of management. These are scheduled meetings between the brand and Philips' business groups/core corporate functions, with the purpose of reviewing progress on core strategic competencies.[65]

Summary

It is clear that the world's best brands take brand management extremely seriously, involving everything the business does. While existing and well-established brands such as Philips continue to work hard on their brand management, companies that are just starting to do branding will find that it often involves total organizational change, but the objective of brand management is clear – to strive hard toward giving every customer a consistently great brand experience.

Touchpoint analysis at macro- and micro- levels is required in order to maximise the customer experience, and touchpoints can be many and varied, virtual or physical. It is the job of brand managers to try and outperform the competition on all of the touchpoints that are under their control. It is an ongoing and never-ending process!

As the world's leading chemical company BASF states, "Through different brand touchpoints, the BASF brand proves every day that it stands for connectedness, innovative solutions, value-adding partnerships and sustainability. To maintain and strengthen our position as the world's leading chemical company, ongoing professional brand management is required." The company goes on to say, "This contributes to our customers' confidence in their buying decisions and to our company value."[66]

The final step in the brand management process is to measure results, and the most effective way to do this is by tracking brand value. Brand valuation is now a significant business around the world and the next chapter looks at best practice in this important area of brand management activity.

Measuring Brand Success: Market Research and Brand Valuation

I n the previous chapter, we looked at the complexity that surrounds the role of the brand manager and how important it is to focus on the big picture regarding the strategy for the brand while focusing every day on meticulous control of a host of variables that influence brand impact.

In addition to the activities so far mentioned, we must not forget that the whole purpose of building and managing brands is to increase brand value. It is vital to continuously track the effectiveness of your brand against the competition, especially when the stimuli to which consumers are exposed are constantly changing. I won't discuss here the many well-known ways in which brand effectiveness can be measured, as most readers will be aware of these. Instead, I will devote most of this chapter to discussing brand valuation as this methodology has more potential for use in effectively measuring brand impact and helping brand managers to track brand success accurately and make better decisions about the future.

Continuous tracking of brand performance

There are many items that can be tracked to help brand managers assess how their brands are doing in the marketplace, and what effect certain market interventions are having on their brand equity. For instance, purchasing, consumption, brand, and advertising awareness can be tracked against advertising spend, pricing policy, product launches, and in-store promotions.

Also, tracking by demographic segments can enable brand managers to assess whether marketing campaigns are influencing the target consumer groups.

Some companies also track their brand values or personality characteristics against the competition, to see whether they are gaining or losing ground. There are many available research methodologies that cover such areas of interest, and my advice to any company that wants to track brand success is to look at measuring several variables. In Chapter 5 I described the Emotional Brand Ladder of Success and it is possible to measure each of the steps on the ladder. Of particular interest are measures of trust and loyalty as these give a good indication of the strength of a brand, and in addition, many companies now measure the lifetime value of customers as the basis of initiatives with respect to customer relationship management.

The Emotional Brand Ladder of Success is particularly apt for the measurement of brand equity. Based on this concept, market research tools have been developed to measure the total impact of the brand on consumers, partners, or whoever else is important to the success of the brand. One such methodology is called BrandSPACE™, which takes into account the fact that the human brain has both left and right hemispheres that function differently in terms of rational and emotional activity. It is important for a brand to capture the hearts and minds of consumers and this means combining the rational dimension with the emotional dimension in the brand proposition and measuring its effectiveness.

The BrandSPACE™ research tool (shown diagrammatically below) measures this and:

- Helps find out whether or not the brand strategy is working – by tracking where a brand is in consumers' minds.

- Evaluates the level of emotional connection a brand has with the target audience.

- Provides insights to help sharpen brand positioning under circumstances of intense competition.

- Provides guidelines to fine-tune brand image to stay competitive and achieve brand objectives.

- Tracks the effectiveness of brand expression and communication.

- Monitors share of heart and share of mind in addition to market share.

One of the interesting outputs of this brand management tool is the Passion Scorecard™, an easy-to-digest output that identifies key areas to focus on in order to strengthen the brand-customer relationship such as brand expression and communication, competitive advantage, customer's satisfaction and brand values/personality.

Figure 11.1: The BrandSPACE™ Hearts and Minds Model*

(*Developed by Temporal Brand Consulting Ltd on license to Intage (Thailand) Co.Ltd.)[67]

There are many other ways of researching brand equity that look at the rational and emotional impact of brand, but increasingly both public and private sector brands have become interested in assessing not just brand equity but also the financial value of brands and the place they occupy in brand value rankings or indices.

Other studies used to assess brand health and strength include annual surveys such as that conducted by the Havas Group on Meaningful Brands® mentioned earlier in Chapter 5. Havas says, "Meaningful Brands® is the first global study to show how quality of life and wellbeing connects with brands at a business level and measures the benefits brands bring to our lives. It is unique in both scale and scope; covering 1,000 brands, 300,000 people, 34 markets across 12 industries, with the UK study covering 168 brands and 19,429 consumers." It goes on to say, "The research covers all aspects of people's lives, including the roles brands play in society (contributing to the economy or employment), in our personal wellbeing (healthy lifestyles, connectivity with friends and family, making our lives easier, fitness and happiness) and product performance (price, quality and other marketplace drivers) … A meaningful brand is defined by its impact on our personal and collective wellbeing, plus its functional benefits."[68] Some interesting findings are contained in the Havas report, including the fact that, "Meaningfulness in brand marketing can increase share of wallet by up to 9 x." Meaning and purpose demonstrated by brands are vital to their health, with 75% of people expecting brands to make a greater contribution to wellbeing and quality of life and only 40% of them believing that brands actually do this.

Many other market research companies offer measures to assess various aspects of brand health and success with brand managers often using more than one way of tracking progress as an ongoing part of their work. However, I would like to focus this chapter on how to track brand value, which is of the utmost importance. This is ultimately where the real value lies in monetary terms.

The background to brand valuation

In the late 1980s, many investment analysts and fund managers were still basing their investment decisions on traditional measures of financial health, principally earnings per share, dividend yield, and balance sheet asset values. Such measures can fundamentally misstate corporate value.

The main impetus for acknowledging the value of brands, and other intangible assets, came from the corporate raiders and asset strippers of the 1980s who targeted brand-rich companies and paid significantly more than their net asset value. This resulted in huge 'goodwill' values that had to be accounted for. Alarm bells rang in the boardrooms of many underperforming branded goods companies, as directors realized there was a clear need for a method of accounting for brands that would recognize their true value on the balance sheet and avoid arbitrary write-offs that damaged investor perceptions.

A realization that the full value of brand-owning companies was neither explicitly shown in the accounts nor always reflected in stock market values led to a reappraisal of the importance of intangible assets in general, and of brands in particular. This in turn raised the question of how such assets should be valued and disclosed. Although the accounting profession has only partially adapted to a world in which intangible assets are the main drivers of value, business leaders and investors have been quicker off the mark.

Despite volatile economic times, mergers and acquisitions continue, and brands continue to play a significant role in this activity. In 2000, French Telecom paid around US$30 billion for a mobile phone brand that had only been in existence for six years. Within its home market, Orange boasted higher customer acquisition, retention, and usage rates than its rivals – all key factors of a successful brand. Orange had achieved the magic ingredient that positioned it as a lifestyle brand. Instances such as this bring the value of specific brands into the public domain, but the bulk of intangible asset value remains "off balance sheet", and brands and other intangible assets contribute the bulk of shareholder value in many sectors.

In most stock markets around the world, as much as 72% of the value of companies may not be reflected in published balance sheets. This percentage varies by sector, but it highlights the importance of intangible assets, of whose "unexplained value" brands form a significant part. Other intangibles such as patents, customer lists, licenses, know-how, and major contracts also play a role. Patents, for instance, are a major component of value in the pharmaceuticals sector.

Investors and business leaders have recognized that brands are major drivers of corporate value. Marketers are increasingly using brand valuation models to facilitate marketing planning; however, they should go one step further. Investors need and want greater disclosure of brand values and marketing performance. Brand managers and marketers should play a lead role in ensuring that such information is adequately communicated to investors, rather than waiting for statutory disclosure requirements to catch up with reality.

Recent developments

Over the last ten years, brand valuation has become a mainstream business tool used for the following purposes:

- merger and acquisition planning;
- tax planning;
- securitized borrowing;
- licensing and franchising;
- investor relations;
- brand portfolio reviews;
- marketing budget determination;
- resource allocation;
- strategic marketing planning; and
- internal communications.

A particular trend has been the increasing use of brand valuation methodology as a tool to aid brand and marketing management. The focus here is to increase the effectiveness of the marketing effort and aid brand management. A prime benefit in this regard is the fact that a brand valuation model is linked to the company's business model and provides a financial measure that is understood throughout the organization and by investors.

A well-constructed brand valuation pulls together market research, competitive data, and forecasts of future performance. This increases the understanding of the brand's value and its contribution to demand in each segment and identifies opportunities for leveraging the brand. A dynamic brand valuation model can be used for scenario-planning purposes.

The ability to place a financial value on a brand within each key market segment isn't the only output of a valuation study. Other outputs include the following:

- Research into the drivers of demand yields information that aids a range of decisions, including portfolio planning and product positioning. It can help define the focus of the advertising message.

- An identification of causal relationships within the business model facilitates an increase in advertising effectiveness.

- The competitive benchmarking study that forms part of an assessment of the risk attached to future earnings provides a gauge of the brand's strength, in relation to competitors, from segment to segment.

Brand economics

How do brands add value? In economic terms, the answer is simple: they impact on both the demand and supply curves.

On the demand side, brands enable a product to achieve a higher price at a given sales volume. Strong brands can also increase sales volumes and decrease churn rates. In some instances, price and volume impacts are achieved at the same time. An example, taken from *The Economist* some years ago, was the GM Prizm and Toyota Corolla in the US. These vehicles were virtually identical, coming off the same production line and having similar levels of distribution and service levels. However, the Corolla traded at an 8% premium and sold over double the volume.

Brands also establish more stable demand through their relationships with consumers, and this helps to establish barriers to entry. The relationship with consumers is due to both functional and emotional attributes. On the functional side, brands ensure recognition and further aid the purchase decision through a guarantee of quality. From an emotional perspective, they satisfy aspirational and self-expression requirements. This is most evident in the luxury and fashion sectors.

A further benefit of branding that has increased in importance in recent years is the ability to transfer the equity or values associated with a brand into new product categories. In order for brand stretching to be effective, it is necessary that the core values of the brand are image-based, rather than product-based.

While there are numerous examples of successful brands that have achieved significant price premiums or higher volumes, the impact of branding on the supply curve is often ignored. Brands tend to shift the supply curve downward, for the following reasons:

- greater trade and consumer recognition and loyalty, which results in lower sales conversion costs and more favorable supplier terms;

- lower staff acquisition and retention costs;

- lower cost of capital; and

- economies of scale achieved through higher volumes.

The challenge is to identify how your brand – or your client's brand – impacts on the business model, and to monitor whether strategies are successful in adding value to the brand. I will now move on to look at best practice in brand valuation and explain the methodology in greater detail.

Best practice in brand valuation

A number of methods can be used to value brands. Cost-based brand valuations are rarely used, as the cost of creating a brand tends to have little relationship to its current value. An exception to this is in the case of newly formed brands where market-based and income approaches are speculative in nature. Market-based comparisons are unsatisfactory as a primary method of valuing a brand, because of the scarcity of comparative data and the uniqueness of brands. However, where available, market comparisons are useful for testing, or corroborating, primary valuations. Income-based methods of brand valuation tend to be those favored by financial and legal communities, in particular the royalty-relief methodology.

This approach is based on the assumption that if a brand has to be licensed from a third-party brand owner, a royalty rate on net sales will be charged for the privilege of using the brand. By owning the brand, such royalties are avoided, hence providing an economic benefit. The royalty relief methodology involves estimating future sales, attributable to the brand, and then applying an appropriate royalty rate to arrive at the income attributable to brand royalties in future years. The stream of notional brand royalty is discounted back to a net present value – the brand value.

Although the royalty relief method is technically sound, it provides little understanding of how and where the brand is creating value. It might, therefore, be an appropriate method of valuing a brand for balance sheet or tax purposes, but it will be of limited use to a marketing director wishing to leverage the value of a brand for strategic purposes.

Brand contribution, sometimes called a strategic brand valuation, integrates consumer research and competitive analysis with the brand's forecast earnings. As such, it provides a foundation for brand management in addition to determining the value of the brand by market segment. As this method is of most interest to marketers, it is discussed in more detail in this chapter.

In order to place a commercial value upon brand equity, it is necessary to link it to commercial impact. To do this, a brand contribution analysis is undertaken to identify the total contribution of the brand to the overall economic value generated by the branded product or service. The key question addressed with brand contribution analysis is: *What was the incremental economic benefit (brand contribution) derived from the brand equity during the time frame in question?*

To address the question above, market research methods are employed to identify how strongly a brand influences choice relative to a conceptual unbranded equivalent (sometimes referred to as a generic or floor brand within the category).

In order to estimate this influence, or impact, of a brand on business performance (brand contribution), it is necessary to isolate the revenues and profits attributable to the incremental effect of a brand versus the effect that would be achieved if there were no brand i.e. versus a generic alternative with no inherent brand equity.

There are two basic market research analytical methods to address this: conjoint research and equity drivers analysis. Both methods involve the use of statistical techniques in order to determine a price (or volume) premium attributable to the brand being analysed. Deviations, or incremental brand effects, are linked to financial business value drivers and allow the valuer to arrive at a monetary value of the financial contribution the brand makes to the business.

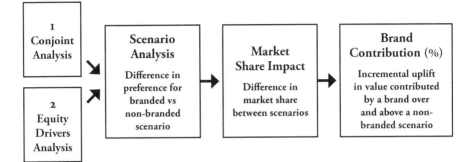

Figure: 11.2: A snapshot of the conceptual framework

Placing these techniques in context

Cutting through these price/volume premium explanations, we arrive at a relatively simple concept – assessing, in value terms, the impact owning a brand has on a business. This provides a rather important distinction against other methods of valuing brands, the contribution the brand makes to the business is what marketers are usually interested in, not a technical asset valuation for balance sheet or tax purposes.

The focus is on the return earned as a result of owning the brand – the brand's contribution to the business, both now and in the future. This framework is based on a discounted cash-flow (DCF) analysis of forecast financial performance, segmented into relevant components of value. The DCF approach is consistent with the approach to valuation used by financial analysts to value equities and by accountants to test for impairment of fixed assets (both tangible and intangible) as required by international accounting standards. It is worthy to note that the royalty relief methodology is also based on a DCF technique, the cash flow in this case being a notional future royalty stream as opposed to incremental contribution the brand gives to a business versus a generic alternative.

Important valuation considerations

While brand valuations can be based on a multiple of historical earnings, it is clear that past performance is no guarantee of future performance and that investors base value judgments on expected future returns, rather than actual historical returns. However, historical results are crucial for an accurate valuation, mainly because they provide information and data relationships that help to forecast the future more accurately.

Valuations based on projected earnings are therefore the preferred approach by Brand Finance, with the caveat that forecasts must be credible. Where forecasts are credible, the valuation results are both robust and actionable. The rest of this chapter examines key structural considerations when undertaking a brand valuation.

Financial forecasts

Typically, explicit forecasts for periods of three to five years are used for such valuations and should be identical to internal management planning forecasts. An important part of a brand valuation, as with any income-based valuation method, involves ensuring that forecasts are credible.

Forecast revenues

Macroeconomic review

It is necessary to conduct extensive due diligence on each of the markets in which the brand operates to ensure the valuation takes into account all the macroeconomic factors likely to affect the level of demand for the brand. These could be technological, structural, legislative, cultural, or competitive. The brand valuation exercise needs to consider the likely trends for both volume and value for the market as a whole and for the brand being valued. This often involves detailed discussion between the brand valuation team and the internal competitor analysis, corporate strategy, market research, and marketing departments.

Microeconomic review

It is necessary to consider the factors that have historically affected the performance of the brand in each of its markets. This can involve econometric modeling or some other form of statistical analysis of past performance to show how certain causal variables have affected revenues.

One of the key issues in terms of branding is to understand the causal relationship between total marketing spend, pricing, and sales results. It is equally important to understand the relative effect of different media on the overall level of sales. The task of the brand valuation team is therefore to ensure that brand and marketing factors are being accounted for properly in the modeling and analysis taking place, and that results are used to obtain the most appropriate forecast sales values.

In the same way that it may be desirable to use econometric analysis of past influences on sales, it may also be appropriate to use projective price elasticity research to predict the effect of price on sales. Price elasticity modeling of this type is typically based on large-sample quantitative research and is used to improve the accuracy of future sales forecasts. To the extent that this isn't already being done, Brand Finance recommends that it should be considered as an input to the brand valuation process to help refine forecast earnings.

Forecast costs

It is also necessary to understand fully the basis on which forecast costs have been determined. The brand valuer will need to confirm that the basis of cost allocation is sensible between each of the geographic, product, or customer segments on a current and forecast basis.

Segmentation

In applying the valuation framework, one of the first and most critical tasks is to determine the nature of the segmentation for valuation purposes. It is then important to identify how internal financial and marketing data, and external market and competitor data, can be obtained in a way that fits with the chosen segmentation. The principles behind effective segmentation for brand valuation purposes are as follows:

- homogeneous geographic, product, and customer groupings to ensure that the valuations are relevant to defined target markets;

- clearly definable set of discrete competitors in each segment to ensure that we are comparing apples with apples; and

- availability of market research data to match the chosen segmentation.

There is little point in choosing a valuation segmentation based on an aggregation of product or customer groupings that obscures important underlying differences. Equally, there is little point in choosing a particular detailed segmentation against which it is impossible to obtain volumetric or value data to the appropriate level of detail. Without these it may be difficult, if not impossible, to estimate relative market shares and to compare performance and forecasts against competitors.

Much of the success of a brand valuation lies in the selection and planning of the relevant segmentation and the sourcing of suitable data. A dilemma in relation to customer segmentation is that below the broad categories lie many more specifically defined demographic, socioeconomic, or psychographic sub-segments. The marketing and market research teams may well want to 'drill' down to a more detailed level for new product development or communications planning purposes, while for practical reasons the valuation may need to be cut at a higher, more aggregated level. It is often impossible to sub-segment the financial valuation to the same level of granularity that may be desirable for a market-mapping segmentation. The brand valuation team therefore needs to ensure that the segmentation for the valuation cascades up from a more detailed underlying segmentation if one is used.

Another difficulty in relation to product segmentation is that volumetric or value measures for each product group may be difficult or impossible to obtain, particularly in less well-developed or well-defined product and service areas or countries. It is also common to find that, in some client segments, it is difficult to obtain reliable data for total market size, as competitor data may be unavailable. A pragmatic approach and a medium-term strategy to populate data gaps may be required, allowing subsequent years' valuations to have an increasing level of detailed comparative analysis.

The difficulties of selecting and populating the chosen segmentation with data have been noted to highlight the need for care and experience in planning and constructing the brand valuation.

Assessing brand-specific risk

The final step in the brand valuation is to determine the appropriate discount rate to use in the DCF analysis. Brand Finance has developed an approach to discount rate determination that is a transparent adaptation of the capital asset pricing model. The appropriate discount rate is built up from first principles, as follows:

- Discount rate = [BrandBeta˚ adjusted cost of equity × (proportion of equity funding)] + [cost of debt ×(proportion of debt funding)]

- BrandBeta˚ adjusted cost of equity = risk-free rate + (equity risk premium × sector beta × BrandBeta˚)

- Brand-specific risk premium

The ten years' risk-free borrowing rate in the geographic market under review is the starting point. The equity risk premium is the medium-term excess return of the equity market over the risk-free rate. This can be obtained from investment data providers and a number of risk evaluation services. So, too, can the sector beta, which is used to determine an average implied discount rate for all brands in the sector under review.

This sector-specific discount rate is finessed to take account of the relative strength of different brands in the given market. Brand Finance calls this 'BrandBeta˚ analysis' and bases it on key brand-related criteria for which data is usually publically available, or the brand in question would have available – these represent the best indicators of brand strength from Brand Finance's perspective. A basic list of the types of brand measures Brand Finance's

BrandBeta® uses is shown in Figure 11.3. It must be stressed that these attributes are evaluated in each instance to ensure that the most appropriate grouping of risk measures for a specific sector is identified.

Measure		Attribute*	Score	Importance
Inputs (25%)		Product/CX investment	XX	5.0%
		Distribution	XX	5.0%
		Online Presence	XX	5.0%
		Marketing & Ad Spend	XX	5.0%
Brand Equity (50%)	**Consumers** (35%)	Familiarity	XX	5.0%
		Consideration	XX	7.5%
		Preference	XX	7.5%
		Satisfaction	XX	7.5%
		Recommendation/NPS	XX	7.5%
	Staff (5%)	Employee Score	XX	5.0%
	Finance (5%)	Credit Rating	XX	2.5%
		Analyst Recommendation	XX	2.5%
	External (5%)	Sentiment Index	XX	1.25%
		Community	XX	1.25%
		Governance	XX	1.25%
		Environment	XX	1.25%
Outputs (25%)		Acquisition/Net Additions	XX	5.0%
		Retention/Loyalty	XX	5.0%
		Price Premium	XX	5.0%
		Revenue	XX	2.5%
		Revenue Growth	XX	2.5%
		Market Share	XX	2.5%
		Brand Strength Score:	**XX / 100**	**100%**

Figure 11.3: A basic example of a BrandBeta® scoring framework

Careful planning will be required to define which competitors need to be monitored and evaluated, and in which sectors. There may also be a need to change the competitor set over time if the focus of the business shifts into new areas.

A score of 50 implies that the brand offers average investment risk in the sector under review and therefore attracts a BrandBeta® of 1. This means that the discount rate used in the valuation will be the average composite rate for the sector. A score of 100 implies a theoretically risk-free brand, which would be discounted at the risk-free rate. A score of 0 implies a particularly weak brand that doubles the equity risk premium.

The review of data for the BrandBeta® analysis provides invaluable insights into the competitive position of the brand in its market and acts as a useful focus for a balanced scorecard for the brand. Where available, perceived quality of brands is a strong alternative to simple 'brand awareness' in the BrandBeta® scorecard. The scorecard is data-driven, transparent, and produces supportable discount rates.

Brand in the context of the wider business

Best practice dictates that a brand should be viewed in the context of the wider business. Importantly, the term Branded Business is used. This is identified as the group of assets, and associated liabilities, directly related to the brand in question – this concept differs to enterprise value which may represent an ensemble of branded businesses. In the case of an entity operating under one brand only the Enterprise value equates to the Branded Business value. To illustrate with an automotive example, Volkswagen Group would represent the enterprise, while Audi, Bentley and Porsche would be examples of individual branded businesses within the Volkswagen Group.

The importance of brands within businesses should not be understated. In 2015 Brand Finance performed an analysis on stock prices, comparing average performance versus performance of strongly branded companies. Between 2007 and 2015, the average return across the S&P was 49%. However, by using Brand Finance's brand value data, investors could have generated returns of up to 96%. Investing in companies with a brand value to enterprise value (BV/EV) ratio of greater than 30% would have generated returns of 94%. Investing exclusively in the ten companies with the highest BV/EV ratios would have resulted in a 96% return. These findings demonstrate the powerful effect brands can have on the long-term financial performance and enterprise value of businesses.

Static versus dynamic brand evaluation

The result of the foregoing analysis is a branded business value for each segment identified. In addition, the valuation team produces a detailed competitive review with risk scoring and a robust estimate of the contribution the brand makes in each segment. This is used to derive a value for the brand alone within the total value of the branded business. Also produced is a sensitivity analysis indicating the impact on value of altering certain key assumptions.

The static valuation methodologies discussed thus far provide a robust point-in-time brand valuation model drawing directly on financial, analytical, and marketing research activities that either are, or should be, in place already. In a sense, it merely brings together existing measures and processes in a coherent way. It is therefore a suitable way of producing valuations on a periodic basis by and for internal management. It is often preferable to create a static valuation model, and then increase the sophistication of the model and introduce a scenario planning capacity.

This is the purpose of a dynamic brand valuation model: to incorporate causal relationships into a brand valuation model; to use the model to carry out scenario planning in order to select the most appropriate strategy; and then to track the impact of the selected strategy. Such a model can be used for considering and comparing the level of marketing investment behind the brand in different segments. It can be used for flexing key assumptions on the basis of hypotheses and testing the value impact of changes to brand activities. It can show where brand and corporate value is being created and destroyed, together with the intermediate measures that cause the growth or decline.

Such a tool sounds like the marketing Holy Grail; however, it must be remembered that the predictive ability of the model will only be as good as the research that has been used to determine the causal relationships. Even in the absence of ideal research, we have found that the process of estimating cause-and-effect relationships and assessing the sensitivity of the business model to changes in these assumptions can be extremely useful.

While the benefits of a contribution valuation have been discussed in detail, there is the obvious requirement of extensive information which in many cases is not publically available. Reasonable estimates for static valuations are, however, possible using publically available data.

Brand Finance produces an annual study of brand valuations based on the royalty relief methodology using information only available in the public domain. These static valuations relate strictly to the 'Trademark asset and associate marketing related IP', while still of interest to marketers for measurement, comparative comparison and value tracking the strategic use of these valuations is limited. Brand Finance identified the world's most valuable brands, in 2019, to be:

2019 Rank	Brand	Brand Value ($m)
1	Amazon	187,905
2	Apple	153,634
3	Google	142,755
4	Microsoft	119,595
5	Samsung	91,282
6	AT&T	87,005
7	Facebook	83,202
8	ICBC	79,823
9	Verizon	71,154
10	China Construction Bank	69,742

Source: Brand Finance plc

While strategic contribution valuations are arguably more important to marketers, static valuations also have important business uses, including; internal licensing, financing, M&A discussions, investor relations, balance sheet recognition, tax/transfer pricing, litigation and joint ventures. Some brief related examples are mentioned below.

The first example illustrates the use of a brand valuation to help resolve a specific issue. The impetus for the project had been the acquisition by a global financial services company of a number of new brands. This had resulted in a cluttered portfolio that required rationalization. The brand valuation was segmented by product and customer for all of the group's brands in the UK, Europe, Australia, Hong Kong, and the US. The project formed the framework to inform brand rationalization and brand architecture decisions.

In the case of a retail bank, a brand evaluation project was carried out in order to assess the contribution of the brand in the corporate, as opposed to the consumer, market segment. The study was also segmented by major product groups. Consumer research was commissioned to quantify the drivers of demand. The study impacted on the allocation of marketing resources between market segments and was applied to measure the effectiveness of marketing investment.

A global insurance company provides an example of a valuation initially carried out for a specific purpose, but that has now been repeated. In this instance, brand valuation and competitor benchmarking techniques were combined to determine the optimal global advertising investment behind the client's corporate brand. The results were used by senior management to set corporate advertising levels. The exercise has been repeated periodically by management in order to understand and monitor the effect of brand investment decisions on corporate brand value.

In the case of a listed food manufacturer, brand valuation was conducted in order to communicate the value of the company's main brand to analysts and investors. Management commissioned the study, as they believed the shares were undervalued and the company was vulnerable to takeover.

A major tobacco company illustrates the use of a brand valuation model on an ongoing basis. The corporate marketing finance team commissioned the construction of a brand evaluation model to monitor the performance of key client and competitor brands in local markets and at a global level. The brand valuation has been placed on the company's intranet and is supported by a manual that clarifies what information is required to be entered into the model and how the results can be used. The model is kept up to date by operating companies in approximately 60 countries. The data produced by the model informs local decision making as well as group planning.

Summary

In this final chapter we have looked at the importance of tracking the success of brand creation, development and management. While there are myriad ways in which various aspects of brand success can be measured and assessed, in the final analysis the true worth of the brand needs to be measured in monetary terms and its contribution to the value of the business.

Brand valuation is without doubt the best way in which brand managers and boards of directors can link brand to revenue and profitability, and the key steps in the valuation process have been outlined in detail. Perhaps one of the most important lessons we can learn from this approach to tracking brand success is that the intangible asset of a brand can be worth multiples more than the net tangible assets of the business itself, and that brand valuation gives the boardroom and brand managers clear indications of the sources of this intangible wealth that can provide them with strategic direction for the future.

Endnotes

1   www.pressreader.com/uk/daily-mail/20161028/282024736808466

2   www.americangreetings.com

3   www.unilever.co.uk/about/who-we-are/our-vision/, accessed 14/2/2017

4   micro.magnet.fsu.edu/optics/intelplay/

5   Sources: www.forbes.com (16/09/2016) and www.cnbc.com (18/08/2015).

6   group.hugoboss.com/en/investor-relations/investment-case/strategy

7   www.basf.com/en/company/about-us/strategy-and-organization/
    our-brand.html

8   www.carrefour.com, www.ahold.com, www.annualreport2008.ahold.
    com/documents/pdf/ar_summary_2008.pdf, www.gerbertechnology.
    com/case_study/Carrefour.pdf, www.progressivegrocer.com/
    progressivegrocer/content_display/supermar-ket-industry-news/
    e3ia50cdcb373435f1baf0909c9fa243f79

9   www.lvmh.com/group/about-lvmh/the-lvmh-spirit/

10 References: Reuters, October 2008; shop.cat.com, accessed May 20, 2009;
    www.usatoday.com/money/advertising/2008-04-15-licensing-chart_N.
    htm; www.caterpillar.com/en/company.html accessed 14 June, 2017;
    bullitt-group.com/brand-partners/ accessed 14 June, 2017.

11 Reference: www.confectionerynews.com/The-Big-Picture/Wrigley-s-no-
    longer-a-family-affair

12 www.mazda.co.uk/aboutmazda/design/

13 Source: http://careers.gm.com/gm-brands.html

14 References: corporate.hallmark.com/OurCulture/Beliefs-And-Values

15 www.meaningful-brands.com/en

16 www.nestle.com/stories#/category/featured-stories/1

17 References:
    www.absolutad.com/absolut_about/history/story/
    www.intelligentnaivety.com/2009/06/05/visions-in-an-absolut-world/
    www.marketwatch.com/story/pernod-ricard-execs-tout-defend-
    absolut-acquisition
    www.nytimes.com/2008/04/01/business/worldbusiness/01iht-
    vodka.4.11588217.html
    www.roadtovr.com/deadmau5-absolut-vodka-release-vr-experience/

18 Reference: www.innocentdrinks.co.uk/us/sustainability

19 References: www.cnet.com/news/super-light-nike-flywire-shoes-to-make-
    olympic-debut, news.nike.com/responsibility, news.nike.com/news/nike-
    human-race-the-world%E2%80%99s-largest-one-day-running-event.

20 www.telegraph.co.uk, March 28, 2008

21 www.haier.net/en/about_haier/

22 Source: www.haier.net/en/about_haier/haier_strategy/

23 www.telegraph.co.uk/news/2017/07/17/adverts-depicting-gender-stereotypes-banned-2018/

24 www.dailymail.co.uk/money/investing/article-4900400/Can-profit-investing-sport.html

25 www.tagheuer.co.uk/int-en/1860-the-first-time-changing-pioneer-in-tag-heuer, www.tagheuer.com/en-gb/ambassadors/sport, www.tagheuer.co.uk/int-en/don-t-crack-under-pressure

26 uk.reuters.com/article/uk-athletics-bolt-puma/bolt-signs-10-million-deal-to-stay-with-puma-idUKBRE98N0AH20130924

27 www.sportspromedia.com/news/usain_bolt_signs_on_with_xm_group

28 www.forbes.com/sites/kurtbadenhausen/2017/08/14/the-highest-paid-female-athletes-2017/#42c3be1d3d0b

29 tennis.life/2017/05/09/mother-serena-perfect-sponsor/

30 www.skysports.com/tennis/news/12110/10990894/serena-williams-targets-more-grand-slam-success-in-2018

31 www.forbes.com/sites/kurtbadenhausen/2017/08/29/the-highest-paid-tennis-players-2017/#57aef9ad435d

32 fortune.com/2014/09/20/ray-rice-adrian-peterson-tiger-woods-athletes-dropped-endorsements/

33 www.dailymail.co.uk/sport/cricket/article-4971678/New-Balance-end-200k-deal-England-s-Ben-Stokes.html

34 http://www.youtube.com/watch?v=SI-rsong4xs

35 http://strongerhead.com/wp-content/uploads/2012/10/DSMM-IMC-project-Best-job-in-the-world-ref-2.pdf

36 www.dailymail.co.uk/sciencetech/article-3835282/Yahoo-patents-smart-billboard-spy-passers-passing-cars-listen-conversations-target-ads.html uk.businessinsider.com/yahoo-patents-smart-billboard-with-camera-and-microphone-2016-10

37 www.usatoday.com/story/money/business/2016/09/30/pampers-now-makes-diapers-1-pound-infants/91310624/

38 www.toms.com/improving-lives

39 www.dailymail.co.uk/sciencetech/article-4644592/Facebook-2-BILLION-monthly-ctive-users.html#ixzz4nvaAJfCc

40 www.slate.com/articles/technology/technology/2017/11/facebook_was_designed_to_be_addictive_does_that_make_it_evil.html

41 uk.businessinsider.com/how-many-people-use-snapchat-user-numbers-2017-2

42 www.newyorker.com/business/currency/why-is-snap-calling-itself-a-camera-company

43 www.cnbc.com/2017/06/20/instagram-crushes-snapchats-daily-active-users-rate.html

44 twittercounter.com/pages/100

45 www.cnbc.com/2017/07/21/lyft-is-following-uber-into-self-driving-cars.html

46 http://www.ecommercelift.com/the-rise-of-ecommerce-and-the-risk-to-retail.html

47 www.thisismoney.co.uk/money/smallbusiness/article-3578703/Boss-online-retailer-Notonthehighstreet-turns-shops-taste-future.html#ixzz48AYBILpu

48 www.thisismoney.co.uk/money/markets/article-4866450/Asos-targets-High-Street-beauty-giants.html

49 www.asosplc.com/asos-story

50 newsroom.fb.com/news/2014/02/facebook-to-acquire-whatsapp

51 www.theguardian.com/business/2017/aug/30/dara-khosrowshahi-uber-20-issues-new-chief-executive-must-address

52 www.airbnb.co.uk/about/about-us

53 www.campaignlive.com/article/airbnb-lets-users-pay-forward-onelessstranger/1327693

54 https://www.theguardian.com/technology/2015/oct/22/airbnb-apologises-dear-san-francisco-tax-adverts

55 www.gartner.com/newsroom/id/3165317

56 nest.com/uk/about/

57 www.gartner.com/newsroom/id/2970017

58 www.mckinsey.com/industries/automotive-and-assembly/our-insights/whats-driving-the-connected-car

59 digiday.com/marketing/pernod-ricard-using-internet-things-get-closer-customers/

60 www.forbes.com/sites/bernardmarr/2016/06/20/what-everyone-must-know-about-industry-4-0/#53f36dbe795f

61 www.techradar.com/news/world-of-tech/future-tech/5-things-you-should-know-about-industry-4-0-1289534

62 www.theguardian.com/commentisfree/2017/oct/24/google-alphabet-sidewalk-labs-toronto

63 www.citylab.com/life/2017/10/sidewalk-labs-living-laboratory/543165

64 www.unilever.co.uk/sustainable-living/

65 Source: Philips

66 https://www.basf.com/en/company/about-us/strategy-and-organization/our-brand.html

67 http://www.intage-thailand.com

68 Sources: www.havasmedia.co.uk/meaningful-brands/ and www.meaningful-brands.com/en

Index

3M 137, 241

Absolut Vodka 129–30
Accenture 24, 147
Adidas 45, 76, 142, 189, 231
advertising 101–2, 182–7, 259. See
also marketing
Ahold NV 74–5
Airbnb 225–8, 230
Alphabet 65, 219, 229, 231
Amazon 147, 214, 219, 222–4, 229, 263, 293
Apple 28, 38, 72–3, 112, 218, 223, 225,
262, 289, 293
Asos 220–1
AT&T 193, 255, 293
Athleisure 45–6
Audi 229, 292

balance sheet reporting 17
Barclays Premier League 189–90
BASF 24, 52, 114–15, 131, 210, 276–7
Bebo 214
big brands 16
BMW 48–50, 60, 66, 86, 145, 153, 156, 237
Body Shop 123, 143
Bolt, Usain 191–2
brand ambassadors 251
brand architecture 59–81
    brand collectors 76–81
    co-branding opportunities 68–70
    levels of 60–4
    merger and acquisition issues 73–5
    portfolio management and
    sub-brands 65–7
    trend toward corporate branding 64–5
brand awareness and recognition 18
brand communications 181–2
    attracting customers with brand
    stories 209–10
    communications copy 201–9
    importance of consistency 210–11
    traditional communication
    channels 182–201
brand culture 174–5, 233–5, 262
    brand engagement process 247–50

brand handbooks 252–3
    customer sophistication 253–5
    designing internal brand programs 246–7
    internal brand challenge 238–9
    lack of shortcuts 245–6
    learning and development
    programs 239–45
    living the brand 236–8
    rewarding and recognizing brand
    performers 250–1
brand deletion 105–8
brand elasticity 87–8, 90
brand equity 18–19, 28
brand extensions 83–7
    advantages and disadvantages 92–3
    possibilities and difficulties 84–5
    reasons for 83–4
    symbolic and functional 85–7
brand handbooks 252–3
brand management
    brand management wheel 258–65
    changing roles of 15–30
    and internal communications 102–3
    need for structure 269–76
    owners and builders of brands 30–1
    and strategy 12–13
brand performance 28, 279–82
brand personality 18, 99, 118–20, 163–4
    creating 127–33
    and not brand values 125–6
    psychology behind 118–20
    and symbolic meanings 121–4
brand planning and control 257, 2767
    brand management structure 269–76
    macro aspects of brand touchpoint
    control 257–65
    micro aspects of brand touchpoint
    control 265–9
brand platform 120
brand positioning 47, 135–7
    for equality 159–60
    multi-positioning 148–52
    positioning statements 160–9
    power-positioning strategies 137–52
    repositioning 153–9

for superiority 160
tag lines 169–76
brand revitalization 93–104
brand strategy 52–5
    alignment of corporate and 52–3
    four keys steps in building 54–5
    importance of 97
    and management 12–13. see also
    brand management
    rational and emotional sides of 109–10
brand strategy and management 39–44
brand stretch 82–105
brand success, measuring 279–95
brand touchpoint control 257–69
brand value 16–18, 28, 132, 157, 282–91
    versus brand equity 18–19
    versus brand personality 125–6
brand vision 113–18
brand working committees 270–3
brand-consumer relationship 20
branding
    myths about 36–8
    power and rewards of 8–10
    what can be branded? 35–6
brands
    big 16
    caring 21
    in the context of the wide business 292–5
    day in the life of a brand 10–12
    definition of 38–44
    driving business strategy 20
    fascists or friends? 20–1
    global. see global brands
    meaningful and purposeful 117–18
    owners and builders of brands 30–1
    power 110–18
BrandSPACE 280–1
brand-specific risk 290–1
business evolution and the consumer 15–21
business strategy 20
business-to-business 23–4

Carrefour SA 74–5
category management 22–3
Caterpillar Inc. 88–90
celebrity endorsements 188–93
CEO awards 251
co-branding opportunities 68–70
Coca-Cola 7, 69, 87, 90, 94–5, 114, 144, 154, 156, 189, 197
Colgate 206

communications copy 201–9
competition 156
competition awards 251
consistency 210–11
consumer insight 41–2
corporate branding 60–1
    with product descriptors 61–2
    and product shared branding 62
    trend toward 64–5
corporate building 23–4
corporate social responsibility 259–60
country-of-origin issues 172
crisis management 193–8
cross-branding 76–7
cult of belonging 123
customer recognition awards 251
customer service 253–5
customer sophistication 3, 5

day in the life of a brand 10–12
development programs 239–45
digital world 3, 5, 213–14, 232
    dark side of social media 216
    digital services 224–8
    fundamental change 215
    future of 230–1
    Internet of Things 228–9
    rise of social media 215–16
    speed factor 214–15
    traditional retailing vs. e-commerce 220–1
direct marketing 187
Disney 17, 35, 241–2, 245
distribution coverage 19
dream sellers 77
dream team 124
Dupont 241
Durex 140
dynamic brand evaluation 292–5

e-commerce 220–4
economic instability 3, 6
emotional brand ladder of success 111–13, 280
emotional capital 110–18
employee engagement 233–5, 256, 262
    brand engagement process 247–50
    brand handbooks 252–3
    customer service 253–5
    designing internal brand programs 246–7
    goals of 235
    internal brand challenge 238–9
    lack of shortcuts 245–6

learning and development
  programs 239–45
  living the brand 236–8
  rewarding and recognizing brand
  performers 250–1
endorsed branding 62–3
endorsements 188–93, 262
Equifax 197–8
ethical branding 259–60
external investor relations 17

Facebook 27, 40, 130, 213–18, 225, 293
fair trading 18
Federer, Roger 192
feel-good factor 123–4
financial accountability 29–30
financial forecasts 288
financial revenues 288–9
Fonterra 197
foundation building phase 247–8
franchising 17

General Motors 106–7
Gillette 193, 241
global brands 3–4
globalization 3–4, 22
Google 5, 8, 27, 65, 214–15, 219, 222, 229, 231, 263, 293

Häagen-Dazs 145
Haier 171–3
Hallmark 116–17
heritage link 123
Hewlett-Packard 24
Hugo Boss 51, 76
hybrid branding 70

IBM 24, 60, 140–1, 155
ICBC 293
Ikea 148–9
implementation phase 248
industry focus 22
Innocent Drinks 143–5
Innovation UK 167–9
Instagram 215–18
integrated brand communications 198–200
Intel 44, 68, 83, 210, 248–50
interactive, integrated
  communications 200–1
internal brand challenge 238–9
internal communications 17

internal marketing management 17
Internet of Things 228–9

Johnson & Johnson 62, 85, 185, 198
just in time system 261

Kao 241

Land Rover 128–9
leadership 18
learning and development programs 239–45
Levi Strauss 17, 87, 127, 203–4, 250–1
LG 72, 155
licensing 17
life cycles 3–5
line branding 64
litigation support 18
living the brand 236–8
local market focus 22
loyal friend 122
loyalty 18. See also satisfaction
luxury brands 76
Lycra 35
Lyft 216, 219

Manchester United 189–90
mapping customer journeys 267–8
market boundaries 3–4
market focus 22
market fragmentation 3–4
market orientation 16
market price 19
market research 279–95
market segmentation 46–55
  benefits of 47
market share 19
market volatility 3, 6
marketing 38, 47–8, 187, 200
marketing budget allocation 17
Mattel 44, 196
Mazda 95–104
meaningful and purposeful brands 117–18
mental associations 18
Mercedes-Benz 49, 73, 202, 229
mergers and acquisitions 17, 73–5
Microsoft 35, 60, 62, 214, 293
Möet Hennessy Louis Vuitton Group 78–81
multi-positioning 148–52
MySpace 214

Nestlé 22, 46, 66, 118, 141, 145

new product development 18
niche markets 47
Nike 149–52, 193
Nokia 70, 72

Ocado 221–2, 224
Oldsmobile 106–7
Olympic Games 35, 189, 193
Orange 114, 282
ostrich syndrome 198
outstanding team awards 251
owners and builders of brands 30–1

Pampers 52, 60, 205–6
Pan Pacific Hotel 264–5
peer group awards 251
perceived quality 18
perceived value 18
perception gap 136
Philips 83, 267–8, 274–6
portfolio management 65–7, 263
positioning statements 160–9
power and rewards of branding 8–10
power brands 110–18
price premium 18
Procter & Gamble 23–4, 41, 52, 60, 63–4,
205–6, 209, 241
product branding 23–4, 63–4
product diversity 3–5
product focus 15–16
product management 22–3
public acknowledgment 251
public relations 193–8, 262

Raffles International 67
real me 124
recognition 251
relevance 204
repositioning 153–9
  and change 157–8
responsibility 27
role models 249–51
Rolex 69, 85–6, 142, 192–3, 196
Rolls-Royce 142, 156

Sainsbury's 222
sales promotion 188
Samsung 72, 83, 293
Sanlu 197
satisfaction 18. See also loyalty
securitized borrowing 17

Sidewalk Labs 231
Snapchat 216–18
social media 263
  dark side of 216
  rise of 215–16
social responsibility 29–30
Sony Ericsson 65, 70–3, 83, 88, 141
sponsorships 188–93, 262
static brand evaluation 292–5
strategic development phase 247
strategic issues for the 21st century 7
strategic thinking 22
sub-brands 65–7
symbolic meanings 121–4

Tab Diet Soda 94–5
tactical thinking 22
TAG Heuer 78, 155, 190–3
tag lines 169–76
target markets 47, 154–5
Tata 115
tax planning 18
Tesco 222, 224
Thung Kula Farm case study 24–6
Tide 7, 64
touchpoint control 257–69
traditional communication channels 182–201
trusted partner 122
Twitter 215–16, 218
Tylenol 198

Uber 219, 224–6
Unilever Malaysia 42–3

Verizon 293
Virgin 8, 60, 62, 70, 83–4, 88, 145,
191–2, 242–5
virtual brand worlds 27
visual identity 68
Volvo 137, 185, 229

Waitrose 222, 224
Walmart 173, 293
Williams, Serena 192
word of mouth 263
world market trends 3–6
Wrigley 91–2

YouTube 12, 27, 65, 213–14, 219, 221

Zara 260–1

CPSIA information can be obtained
at www.ICGtesting.com
Printed in the USA
LVHW081621021221
705093LV00002B/314